CW00969218

SOUTHAMPTON CITY RECORDS OFFICE

Britain's Convicts to the Colonies

Wilfrid Oldham

Edited by
W. Hugh Oldham
Commentary by
Dan Byrnes

LIBRARY OF AUSTRALIAN HISTORY
SYDNEY
1990

LIBRARY OF AUSTRALIAN HISTORY
17 Mitchell Street, North Sydney NSW 2060

© Text — Wilfrid Oldham
© Commentary by Dan Byrnes
© Index — W. Hugh Oldham

First Published 1990
ISBN 0 908120 77 X

This book arises from a Ph.D. Thesis submitted to London University under the title *The Administration of the System of Transportation of British Convicts, 1763-1793* in December 1932. The present version was substantially revised and rewritten by the author.

All rights reserved. No part of this publication may be copied or reproduced, stored in a retrieval system, or transmitted in any form or by any means, electronic, mechanical, optical, photocopying, recording or otherwise, without written permission from the publishers.

Book design by Philip G. Graham
Typeset by Photoset Computer Service Pty Limited, Sydney, NSW 2000

Printed in Australia by Star Printery, Erskineville, NSW 2043

Contents

Wilfrid Oldham 1890-1959
The Author

Foreword

Wilfrid Oldham 1890-1959

MY FATHER Wilfrid Oldham was born in the village of Kabakada on the island of New Britain, now part of Papua New Guinea but then a German colony; his father, Frederic Bignell Oldham, had travelled there from Melbourne to be a Methodist missionary. When Wilfrid was four, the family moved to New Zealand and then back to Australia, where Frederic became a Minister of the Methodist Church. It was customary for Ministers to move from one "circuit" to another every three years, so Wilfrid's schooling began in New Zealand and continued in episodes at several South Australian country schools. When it was time for high school he had to board in Adelaide and attend Adelaide High, where he matriculated. He then went on to the University of Adelaide as a student of the Teachers College. He gained a B.A. in 1914 and began teaching at high school level.

His teaching career was interrupted from 1917 to 1919 by military service; in early childhood an injury had almost destroyed the sight of one eye and made him ineligible for fighting service, but he was accepted for the Army Medical Corps and served in Australia and England. After the war he resumed teaching and university study, and gained his M.A. at Adelaide University in 1920. In 1921 he changed from teaching to lecturing at his old university, first as Assistant Lecturer and ultimately as Senior Lecturer in Modern History and Political Science. At his retirement in 1956 he had the longest period of service of anyone on the Adelaide University staff.

During the early part of his career, lecturing was more precarious than it is today: in 1930 Oldham's position was not tenured, there was no regular system of paid sabbatical leave, and salaries reflected the shakiness of the world's economy. His study at London University was made possible only by a scholarship from the Rockefeller Foundation of New York. In 1920 he had married Marjory Anderson, and they had two children: Brenda Helen in 1921 and Wilfrid Hugh in 1924. Funds would not permit the whole family to go to London, so Wilfrid had to go alone. Throughout his absence the University of Adelaide generously paid two-thirds his ordinary salary, but his diary records a very frugal existence, anxiety when Rockefeller's monthly cheque did no arrive on time, and little opportunity to enjoy many of the things that Britain could offer an historian.

I doubt whether he had any particular subject in mind before he enrolled at London University, and Convict Transportation was not his first field of investigation. For several months he studied Spanish influence in the Pacific, but this was hampered by inability to find any evidence of a British policy towards the Spanish. Then came a disagreement between him and Professor Newton about the period to be covered in his study, and the fact that he had been learning French language instead of Spanish — "Exactly my own protest when he set the subject . . .", as Oldham's diary remarks. The revised topic soon proved to be fruitless, and within a few days he began researching Convict Transportation — his own choice this time, readily accepted by Newton. The change of tack ruled out any chance of gaining his doctorate within the year, but the Rockefeller Foundation agreed to continue his scholarship for a second year and Adelaide University generously extended his leave.

A convict subject, though of interest to historians, would have found little sympathy with the Australian people. The feeling then was that such morbid matters should be forgotten. Times have changed, and many Australians are now eager to discover a convict ancestor. I think the attitudes of the 1930s may have helped to rule out commercial publication of the thesis then, and Oldham judged private publication as being beyond his means. His modest and self-effacing disposition probably played a part, too. N.F. Hall's offer to help with publication, mentioned in the Preface, was evidently a casualty of the Depression.

Certainly Oldham himself had no transported convict among his ancestors. His grandfather George Oldham, a school teacher, migrated to Victoria with three brothers in the heady goldrush days of the 1850s. They came from Newark-on-Trent, Nottinghamshire, children of James Oldham, from a flour milling family, and his wife Elizabeth Eggleston. Both families can claim distinguished descendants in Australia.

★ ★ ★

The signed typescript that my mother handed to me was a condensed version of the thesis my father had presented to London University. Its 1933 date shows that he had prepared it after his return to

Australia, obviously with the idea of having it published. Many parts remained unchanged, but minor detail had been left out and the writing shows much evidence of careful revision. My contribution has been to remove inconsistencies of presentation, split some long sentences and paragraphs, recast many of the tables, and rewrite some passages that would now seem dated or ponderous; in short, I have tried to make it more readable without reshaping the author's style. In a few instances also I reinserted material that my father had omitted from his condensed version. Finally I prepared it for typesetting by typing it on a word processor.

I must acknowledge the part played by several people in bringing this work to publication. First, my mother preserved the revised typescript and passed it on to me. Then Mr Patrick Connelly and Mr Bert Rice of Melbourne stiffened my resolve to try to have it published. Dr Don Baker of the Australian National University kindly read the typescript and was generous in his support and advice. And finally the Library of Australian History agreed to publish it. Mr Dan Byrnes's praise of the thesis and enthusiasm during his writing of the Commentary have reinforced my own admiration for my father's achievement. My father and mother would have delighted in the knowledge that this thesis, which had so greatly affected their lives, should be accepted in Australia's Bicentenary year for publication.

Canberra, 1989   W. HUGH OLDHAM

★ ★ ★

Bound in with the author's revised version of the thesis was a handwritten letter from the head of the History Department in which he worked — Professor W.K. (later Sir Keith) Hancock. The following is a transcription.

The University of Adelaide
Adelaide

October 20, 1933.

My dear Oldham,

       I return your thesis which I have read with great appreciation of the scrupulously honest work which has gone to the making of it. I am certain that you have made absolutely a clean job of it: the bit of work which you chose is done for all time. It will be useful, not only to students of colonial history, but to students of eighteenth century society and the penal system.

Thanks for letting me see it,
Yours sincerely,
W.K. Hancock.

Illustrations

Preface

THE TRANSPORTATION of English[1] convicts[2] during the period 1763-1793 naturally falls into three divisions, viz. 1763-1776, a period of successful transportation to North America; 1776-1786, the interval of experimentation after the stoppage of the American system; and 1787-1793, a period of successful transportation to New South Wales.

The greater histories of America hardly touch upon the subject of convict transportation. All the references to it in the more than twenty volumes of "The American Nation, a History" could easily be compressed into a single page. Channing and Doyle each assign to it little more than a few lines. Some serious attempts to discuss the subject in its relation to certain colonies have been made. J.C. Ballagh's "White Servitude in Virginia" and E.I. MacCormac's "White Servitude in Maryland" are careful studies based upon available local sources. Basil Sollers's "Convict Labourers in Maryland" in the second volume of the *Maryland Historical Magazine* is a brief but very instructive article. All these writers, however, laboured under a common limitation; they were forced to rely upon the Calendars of State Papers which every worker in the London Public Record Office knows are far from complete. The most recent exposition of the early American system is Abbot E. Smith's "Transportation in the 17th Century". It is founded upon the material stored in the Public Record Office, but at the time of the preparation of this introduction it remained unpublished.

English writers have paid even less attention to the treatment of felons during the period 1776-86. So great a work as Lecky's "History of England in the 18th Century" contains a single paragraph on the Hulks which formed a substitute for transportation during those years. In neither the catalogue of the British Museum Library nor in the *Encyclopaedia Britannica* does the word "Hulks" appear as a heading of any article. Writers on the Gold Coast and Honduras, each of which was a proposed asylum for English felons, have directed their studies in ways which barely touch upon transportation; thus the experimentation of that decade is very imperfectly revealed by little more than passing references.

The voyage to Sydney Cove and the first few years of the Colony of New South Wales have been treated at considerable length by officers who were engaged in founding that settlement, but their descriptions include little more than what they could see and necessarily are not adequate sources of information for the transportation itself. This can be explained only by a study of the departmental papers preserved in the Public Record Office. For this reason the various histories of Australia fall within the same limitation as do those of America.

As discussed in the following thesis transportation is directly associated with, and gains its inspiration from, contemporary gaol difficulties due to overcrowding. The American system is introduced to illustrate the time honoured method of avoiding those difficulties. Chapters 3 to 6 discuss unsuccessful attempts to solve the problem which the cessation of the American transportation forced upon the British Government. Unofficial suggestions to remedy the evil are described in Chapter 7. The complete failure of all these experiments and suggestions necessitated the establishment of a new colony in an unsettled area. The last four chapters demonstrate the success of that experiment and the modifications which experience suggested. The whole is concluded by certain appendices which elaborate facts contained in the text.

I take this opportunity to thank those who helped me to complete this thesis. The generous aid of the Rockefeller Foundation enabled me to remain in England during the period of its preparation. To that Foundation's adviser, Mr N.F. Hall, of University College, London, I tender sincere thanks both for his advice during my stay in that city and for his unsolicited offer to assist in the publication of this thesis after my return to Australia. The work itself was performed under the guidance and inspiration of Professor A.P. Newton of King's College, London, whose help I gratefully acknowledge. The difficulty of the undertaking was reduced by the willing assistance of the officials in the places in which I worked, viz. the London Guildhall Department of Archives and Library, the Bristol Archives Department, the Oxford County Hall, the Royal Empire Society's and the British Museum Libraries, and the Public Record Office. To Mr. J.R. Crompton, of the last)named institution, I am particularly indebted for assistance in the discovery of numerous documents. The kindness of Mr Abbot E. Smith, in allowing me to read his manuscript on 17th Century transportation, of Louis H. Dielman of the Peabody Institute, Baltimore, Maryland, U.S.A., in forwarding to me on several occasions transcripts of local sources of information, of Professors Basil Williams and

Oswald Dykes, of Edinburgh, in helping to elucidate certain difficulties associated with Scottish transportation, of Professor H.H. Bellot of
University College, London, in referring me to matter connected with
transportation to America, and of Mr. A. Milne, M.A., in bringing before my notice the Bentham Reports on the Hulk system and other information, materially added to my stock of knowledge.

In conclusion I thank Professors Sir William Mitchell and W.K.
Hancock, both of the Adelaide University, and also Rev. F.B. Oldham,
Mr G.H. Pitt, B.A., and Mr James Anderson for the trouble they took
in reading and estimating the value of my manuscript and for the improvements that they suggested.

Adelaide, 1933   W.O.

Courtesy National Maritime Museum, London

Convicts working — the Thames River, Woolwich, London circa 1790

Courtesy National Maritime Museum, London

London — Customs House from the River Thames, with part of the Tower, 1753

Artist: T. Laurence   Engraver: W. Sharpe 1812   Courtesy National Maritime Museum, London

Sir William Curtis, Lord Mayor of London 1795-96
Curtis' ship Lady Penrhyn *carried convicts to Sydney in the First Fleet*

1

Introduction

I N THE YEAR 1584 Richard Hakluyt, deploring the "multitude of idle
and mutinous persons within the realm — whereby all the prisons
are stuffed full" suggested that "the pety theves might be employed for
certain years in the western parts in sawing and felling of timber and in
planting of sugar canes".[3]

About the year 1784 William Eden, moved by the great number of
convicted felons within the gaols of England, wrote, "The more enormous offenders might be sent to Tunis, Algiers, and other Mahometan
parts for the redemption of Christian slaves; others might be sent to establish new colonies, factories or settlements".[4]

Neither was a thoughtless scribbler; a common aim inspired them
both, and each, in pointing the way towards colonial expansion along
the path of convict transportation, was expressing the view of the great
bulk of the thinking and law-abiding Englishmen of his day. Though
Hakluyt's words were in nature prophetic, Eden's were the result of
two centuries of experience; for the interval between their writing had
witnessed the rise of a great English empire whose trans-Atlantic colonies had been founded and developed in some measure by the labour
of thousands of transported felons. That empire had waned; many an
old belief had been cast aside, but for two hundred years the conviction
that criminals could play a useful part in the building of empire persisted.

Nor was that belief confined to the British Isles. In 1725 the
Governor of Maryland complained, "I could heartily wish they [i.e.
convicts] were sent to any other of His Majesty's Plantations but while
we purchase them they will send them".[5] Nine years later the
Governor of New York emphasised the disadvantages of a "too great
importation of negroes and convicts";[6] and in the decade that preceded
the American Revolution, when Maryland passed a Quarantine Act, its
Governor deprecated the desire for gain which impelled certain
planters to take the risk of purchasing convicts from infected ships.[7]

That desire, due to the agricultural economy of the central and
southern continental colonies, created a demand for labour which the

1

inmates of British gaols alone could not have met, and Home Governments might have disposed of their convicts with considerable profit had not the need been supplied in large measure by the introduction of the African negro.[8] But the demand for convict labour continued in some parts of America beyond the period of this introduction until, in fact, the political disputes of the Revolution ended the system of transportation to the American continent.

That system, as might be expected, has found little favour among American historians and it is not surprising that their works are often tinged with sarcasm,[9] for, while in actual fact the English Government was ridding the Mother Country of a serious nuisance, it claimed that its action was benevolent. Thus James I, in his commission which inaugurated the colonial transportation system, declared that his intention was to temper justice with mercy and permit petty offenders to perform profitable service for the Commonwealth.[10] In 1618 he commuted a sentence of death to transportation because the convicted person was a carpenter and carpenters were needed in Virginia.[11] And just a century later the preamble to the great transportation Act, 4 Geo. I, c.11, included the words, "Whereas in His Majesty's Colonies and Plantations in America there is great want of servants".

The practice of banishing criminals had begun long before the discovery of America, but the acuteness of the economic distress of the latter half of the Tudor period and its attendant crime led in 1597 to a restatement of the penalty, in the Act 39 Eliz., c.4. This provided two forms of punishment for vagabonds and disorderly folk, namely, employment in the royal galleys[12] and banishment from the realm; but as the galley found scant favour among English naval experts and as no oversea English settlement then existed, little relief was derived from the measure. Thus we can realise the satisfaction of harassed officials when the establishment of a permanent colony opened the way for the removal of convicted felons in the following reign.

James I, by his commission of 21 January 1614-15, gave to a Committee of the Privy Council authority to reprieve and stay execution in cases of felony (save rape, murder, witchcraft and burglaries) where the bodily fitness of the condemned permitted his employment in foreign service or discovery.[13] This method was renewed from time to time until the year 1633, when reprieve by Royal Warrant was introduced. The reprieved were handed to merchants or colonising companies who disposed of their services. The strict legality of these measures may be questioned as Blackstone plainly states that no power on earth, except the authority of Parliament, could lawfully send a criminal out of England against his will.[14]

Pardons conditional upon transportation appeared during the Pro-

2

tectorate in 1655 and were continued by succeeding rulers. They were granted by the Crown on the recommendation of presiding Justices and remained a part of the transportation system long after the loss of the American colonies.

Charles II's reign witnessed the passing of a few Acts of a temporary or limited character which authorised the transportation to America of Northumberland and Cumberland moss troopers[15] and those who stole cloth, embezzled His Majesty's stores[16] and burnt ricks,[17] but it was not until the reign of the first Hanoverian ruler that Parliament prescribed transportation as the regular punishment for all the lesser felonies by the Act 4 Geo. I, c.11. This Act empowered courts to transport convicted felons for either seven years or fourteen years and also to convey such felons to the use of any person or persons who might contract for their transportation. These contractors then acquired a property in the service of those whom they removed, a service they could legally sell within the area to which the condemned had been transported.

This was the legal foundation for all subsequent transportation to America. Later laws provided for a more speedy removal of felons, created new felonies, and defined more clearly the offences that rendered evil-doers liable to transportation; [18] but the measure of 1717-18 which provided for felonies within, or without, the benefit of clergy was comprehensive enough to prevent an accumulation of malefactors within British gaols before the American Revolution and, in the words of Ballagh, to make "the colonies a reformatory and dumping ground for the felons of England".[19]

The method of executing the sentence of transportation varied with the circumstances. While the Virginia Company retained a charter it assumed the responsibility. Thus at a Company Court, held in London on 28 April 1619, "Mr Treasurer" announced that His Majesty had sent a man suspected of deer-stealing to be transported to Virginia.[20] Later in the same year also James ordered the immediate removal of 50 other criminals.[21] But the ease and the efficiency of the contract system were soon recognised and the Act of 1717-18 only perpetuated a system that had been in operation for many years. As early as February 1638-39, the Sheriff of Surrey received a warrant to deliver to "William Flemmen of London, Gent" certain convicts who were to be transported to Virginia.[22] In 1677 the Sheriffs of London and Middlesex were directed to deliver malefactors to William Freeman, merchant of London, to complete the number for St Christophers.[23] Jonathan Forward was a most active contractor in the period that followed the Act 4 Geo. I, c.11. The Archives of the Guildhall of the City of London prove that he was regularly employed in carrying overseas the convicts of London and its surrounding counties.[24] On 5 April 1742 Andrew Reid, another merchant of London, entered into a contract with the Treasury to convey "transports" from Newgate and the County Gaols of Hertford, Bucks, Essex, Kent, Sussex, and Surrey to America for a period of 21 years.[25] In addition to the profit derived from the sale of these convicts Forward and Reid were paid a bounty of five pounds a head for those shipped on board their vessels, and the Calendar of Treasury Papers shows that more than 1400 pounds was paid annually by the Treasury for this service during the period 1729-45.[26] But Reid was transporting long after that date; on 17 April 1750 he contracted and gave security for the removal of 48 convicts.[27]

Forward's and Reid's agreements with the Treasury gave to them what was virtually a monopoly of the carriage of felons from the gaols of London and the Counties of the Home Circuit. But criminals were not restricted to those areas; their removal from other gaols was equally imperative. In the year 1730 the Justices of Warwickshire had petitioned for an extension of the Treasury contract to the other counties of England. The Treasury, however, definitely refused to "enlarge" what was then Forward's contract.[28] The Act 6 Geo. I, c.23 had in fact provided for their transportation some years earlier, by giving to county courts authority to appoint two or more Justices of the Peace to contract with any person or persons for the removal of those whom they had sentenced to be transported.

The numbers carried by the various ships naturally varied from voyage to voyage. During the period 1742-45 Reid made at least seven voyages which averaged 92 convicts per vessel, but the extremes for those same voyages were as far apart as 61 and 167.[29]

Death reduced the number on the way. The *Virginia Gazette* of 22 July 1737, after announcing the decease of Captain Hugh French who had sailed from London on a convict ship, gave as the supposed cause of his death, "the gaol distemper which he got on board". Gaol fever (typhus) and smallpox were not unknown within English prisons and it would be reasonable to suppose that those who left them were sometimes infected by these diseases.[30] The certificates of arrival in America, signed by Governors or Customs officials, are an index of the mortality on some of the vessels. Thus on 23 April 1720 in the Port of Annapolis, John Lux, mate of the ship *Susannah and Sarah*, deposed on the Holy Evangel that out of 79 felons shipped, James Kettle, John Newton, and eight others died at sea. On some vessels of this period the death rate was appalling as the figures in the next table show:

But these figures alone give an exaggerated account of the terrors of the passage. *The Prince Royale* which arrived on 23 November 1721

SHIP	ARRIVAL IN AMERICA	LANDED ALIVE	DIED AT SEA
Goodwill	28 July 1722	31	19
Rappahanock	31 August 1726	57	38
Forward	14 May 1728	69	27

lost only 12 out of 114 convicts, and the *Forward* landed 124 out of 134 at Annapolis in December 1725.[31]

That convicts were not entirely free from the effects of brutal cruelty may be inferred from charges brought by Reid against two masters in his employ, Sargent and Bond. Sargent was accused of robbery and murder on the high seas;[32] Bond, of murder and robbery of several convicts.[33] But before we charge the contractors with inhumanity we must be sure of the facts. They certainly had good economic reasons for landing convicts in a condition fit for sale. It is noticeable also that some of them at least employed the same masters on different ships for different voyages, and ordinary business practice opposes the belief that they were chosen because of their superior destructiveness.[34]

Records prove that some of the voyages were eventful. A certificate signed at Port York, Virginia, on 20 January 1721 states that 16 of the convicts mutinied, overcame the crew, and forced the master into the port of Vigo where they escaped.[35]

The masters delivered their convicts to colonial agents or factors who sold them.[36] The disposal of the felons carried by the *Margaret* in September 1719 makes it clear that the sale of one ship load occupied, on occasion, several days and that some of the purchasers bought more than a single convict.[37]

Those who were transported laboured in many different areas. According to English law, convicted felons could be sent to any of His Majesty's colonies, but it would seem that few social convicts were ever carried to New England[38] although early Maine, according to a contemporary, was "stocked out of all the gaols of England".[39] The Guildhall Archives prove that they were carried to South Carolina, Maryland, Nevis, Barbados, and Virginia.[40] In 1734 the Governor of New York deplored the too great importation of negroes and convicts into his colony.[41] General Oglethorpe of Georgia is said to have purchased 40 Irish convicts after they had previously been refused in Jamaica.[42] An order of the Lords Justices dated 2 July 1697 directed the sending of 50 women convicts to the Leeward Islands.[43] In 1664 the King granted a licence to Sir James Modyford to take all felons convicted in the circuits and Old Bailey and afterwards reprieved in order to transport them to Jamaica.[44] St Christophers, in 1680, lamented the non-arrival of 300 convicts. [45] In the opinion of MacCormac, convict immigration into Pennsylvania was insignificant because its German population met the demand for labour. [46] The conclusion would seem to be that, with the possible exceptions of New England and Nova Scotia, all the English American colonies received convicts. [47]

To state even approximately the number of felons introduced into the New World before the year 1763 is clearly difficult. Some records of the Treasury contractors remain, and certain American Port Entry Books exist, but those historians who have essayed the task for Virginia and Maryland alone describe the hopelessness of the attempt. Forward and Reid during the period 1729-45 carried on an average at least 280 a year. From evidence which will appear in a later chapter[48] we may assume that this was half the total sent from England and Wales, which therefore amounted to 560 per annum. A Mr Ringold who was an agent for the sale of convicts in Maryland declared, in 1767, that 600 had been introduced annually for the preceding 30 years into that colony alone. [49] He was in a position to speak with authority, but at that time he was engaged in a controversy concerning the ill-effects of the importation and may have exaggerated. It is significant, however, that his opponents did not dispute his figures. But the contract system, permitting as it did, carriage by private individuals, left even the Secretaries of State ignorant of the numbers transported. [50]

Resistance to the importation began early. In 1665 John Styles of Jamaica complained of the sending of gaol birds "rotten before they are sent forth". [51] A little more than 50 years later another Jamaican heartily wished the same colony "might be troubled with no more of them". [52] Maryland, in 1676, forbade their importation, and nearly half a century later passed a similar prohibition. [53] In 1700 Massachusetts ordered all masters of vessels carrying passengers to produce certificates stating the character of each, under a penalty of 5 pounds a head. [54] Virginia was granted exemption from further importation in 1670 but the favour was cancelled eight years later. [55] In 1723 the same colony passed what was virtually a prohibitory Act by requiring sellers of convicts to give security of 100 pounds a head for the good character of those they sold. [56] Pennsylvania, in May 1722, imposed a duty on convicted felons and required importers to give security for their good behaviour during a period of one year. [57] In 1742 the duty was fixed at 5 pounds a head. [58]

But measures of this kind were met by Royal or Proprietary vetoes. Where, on occasion, they failed to arouse the opposition of some contracting merchant, they remained in force for some years. Thus the Pennsylvania measure of 1722 was not deemed objectionable until 1739. [59] As late as 1755, when a contractor named Stewart complained that Maryland had imposed an import duty of 20 shillings a head on convicts, the Attorney General "expressed himself with much warmth against the Assembly" and declared that if the Proprietor "did not dissent to the Maryland Act" he would severely proceed against it.[60] Consequently, in the following year, Lord Baltimore forbade the collection of any fine or duty on any bona fide convict.[61]

The resistance just cited was the result of easily discoverable causes. The pride of many of the colonists naturally revolted against the English assumption that colonies were penal settlements. The behaviour of the convicts frequently provoked hostile comment. The epithets "gaolbirds" and "Newgates" were commonly applied to them.[62] In colonial papers of the period appeared such notices as: "Friday last arrived the Thames frigate with 130 of His Majesty's passengers who were at home so expert and knowing in some arts that they were obliged to travel for the better peopling of His Majesty's American Plantations, at least for the term of seven years".[63] In 1718 Sir N. Lawes wrote, "These people have been so far from altering their evil courses ... that the greatest part of them are gone and have induced others to go with them a pyrating ... The few that remains proves a wicked, lazy, and indolent people".[64] Beverley, of Virginia, in 1722 attributed many murders to them,[65] and the Virginian Attorney General's salary was increased because of the additional work imposed upon him "since the importation of the number of convicts brought annually".[66] In 1751 Maryland passed an Act making legal the testimony of convicts against convicts because murders and robberies were so frequent,[67] and Sir William Johnson in 1756 imputed the uneasiness among some of the Indian tribes to the machinations of convict deserters.[68]

But no amount of argument can explain away the fact that convicts were in demand in some parts of the American colonies until the close of the colonial period. The superiority of the negro as a field labourer had diverted the greater portion of the convict stream from the West Indian Islands and Virginia, but the following table for convicts arriving at the port of Annapolis shows that not even the operations of the Seven Years' War prevented a considerable flow into Maryland during the period 1756-59, and it is a well known fact that merchants continue selling only so long as buyers can be found.[69]

Thus when our period opens, Government, merchants, and ship masters had been actively engaged in transporting convicts from England for more than a century. Contractors, both government and private, through years of experience were well acquainted with the system; after entering into bonds and agreements with appointed officials they conveyed the condemned to New World agents who disposed of

DATE	SHIP (tons)	OWNERS FOR VOYAGE	CONVICTS	PORT FROM
1756 29 Apr	Greyhound (120)	Stewart & Armour	75	London
25 Jun	Lux (100)	Sydenham & Hodgson	47	London
1757 15 Jul	Thomas & Sarah (150)	R. Dingley & Co.	46	London
5 Dec	Betsey (130)	Sedgeley & Co.	67	Bristol
12 Dec	Thetis (200)	J. Stewart	118	London
1758 19 Jun	Peace (80)	Wm & John Buck	16	Bideford
20 Jun	Eugene (130)	Sedgeley & Co.	70	Bristol
4 Nov	Betsey (130)	Sedgeley & Co.	39	Bristol
1759 17 Jan	Tryal (120)	Stewart & Armour	91	London
18 Jun	Maryland Merchant (70)	Wm & Geo. Buck	12	Bideford

their labour for stated numbers of years by the normal business method of advertisement and sale. The practice had aroused spirited opposition in several colonies. This had been overridden by Royal or Proprietary orders, but when the Seven Years' War came to an end English merchants still confidently anticipated a continuance of the system. Events were to prove that their optimisim was justified.

2

Transportation to the American Colonies, 1763-1776

THE PEACE OF PARIS, signed in February 1763, introduced an interval in which the British Government was free to assert its authority over evil-doers without a fear of foreign interruption. To the administrators of the 18th Century, wars were recurring evils; they came and went. Crime remained; its intensity varied from time to time, and in the early months of the year 1763 different signs pointed to an increasing activity. Unemployment, the normal aftermath of war due to the discharge of thousands of soldiers and sailors, was to be expected. Unemployment implied distress, and distress was associated with crime. To those who reasoned in this way the following figures,[70] taken from the Session Papers of the Old Bailey, would have brought at least the melancholy satisfaction of a sense of accuracy:

NUMBERS OF TRIALS IN THE OLD BAILEY

Year 1762	312 trials
Year 1763	508 trials
Year 1764	590 trials

But these figures were not known in February 1763. The immediate aim of the Government was to preserve order, and the weapons it adopted were those which had been in use before the war. Most important among these was transportation. Other forms of punishment were less often inflicted. Hangings were advertised and drew large crowds of onlookers; dissection, after hanging, was the fate reserved for many of those who had been found guilty of the more atrocious crimes. Women convicted of murdering their husbands were publicly burned. Other offenders were branded, whipped, fined, or imprisoned. The relative importance of these forms of punishment is revealed by a comparison of the sentences taken from the Proceedings of the Old Bailey:[71]

All those who had been transported for social offences had been convicted of felony. In other words, and according to legal definition,

9

YEAR	DEATH	TRANS- PORTATION	BURNING IN THE HAND	WHIPPING	IMPRISON- MENT
1763	47	168	13	5	0
1764	48	264	14	22	4
1765	39	229	10	11	11
1766	33	205	10	20	2
1767	40	236	18	19	1

they had been found guilty of capital crimes.[72] Blackstone, writing within the period, estimated that 160 offences were punishable by death.[73] Some of these offences did bring to the gallows those who committed them; executions followed one another with the same regularity as did the sessions of the Old Bailey, but many who were sentenced to death were not hanged. John Howard gives the following figures for that court:[74]

YEAR	CONDEMNED	EXECUTED	PARDONED
1763	61	32	29
1764	52	31	21
1765	41	26	15
1766	39	20	19
1767	49	22	27
	242	131	111

These statistics show that nearly one-half of the capitally con-demned were pardoned.[75] According to strict legal definition those who were transported also deserved to die. If their number be added to that of the pardoned the total will demonstrate that the great majority of the convicted felons who passed through the Old Bailey were not executed. The same was true of the other courts of England.[76] In fact, the penal code, by administration, lost much of its sanguinary character and this was possible because the law-makers who had dispensed death lavishly with one hand had distributed life freely with the other.

The Crown's right to pardon or commute a sentence removed much of the terror which the gallows might otherwise have inspired. Petitions, praying that the lives of the condemned might be spared, poured in upon the Secretaries of State from all classes and parts of England.[77] They referred these petitions to the judges who had tried the convicted and in return received reports and recommendations. Thus Lord Rochford, on 25 August 1774, wrote to Charles Morgan Esq.: "In consequence of your letter to me on behalf of Wm. James ... I did not fail to write to Mr. Justice Ashurst for his report".[78] The results of this practice were as follows:[79]

YEAR	NO. PETIT-IONED FOR	FREE PARDON	FINAL SENTENCE		
			DEATH	TRANSPOR-TATION	REPRIEVE ETC.
1763	112	14	1	80	17
1765	216	13	3	168	32
1767	279	15	4	218	42
1769	183	13	5	145	20
1771	160	9	1	137	13

These figures, which apply only to those cases in which reports were written, demonstrate that justice was prepared in many instances to set aside the written law and renounce its right to shed human blood. They show also the attitude of the judges towards the law, for their recommendations were, as a rule, accepted without comment. In reality, however, the judges were spared the unpleasant duty of sentencing large numbers to death because of the humanitarian attitude of juries towards the accused. The Old Bailey Session Papers show that juries repeatedly found offenders guilty of stealing 39 shillings when it was evident to everybody that the prisoner had stolen money or goods of greater value. The reason is clear: to steal 40 shillings was a capital offence demanding a death sentence; transportation was the sentence assigned to those guilty of stealing smaller sums.[80] Those who secretly removed goods from shops were found guilty of stealing "but not privily", while many who entered houses were convicted of stealing "but not of burglary" for the same reason.[81] The injured occasionally complained of the lenity of judges and juries[82] but serious critics praised their humanity and deplored a system which, by rendering punishment uncertain, encouraged serious crimes.[83]

Benefit of clergy also reduced the severity of the existing law. This privilege, designed originally to secure for clerical offenders a right of trial within church courts, had in the course of the ages become attached to certain offences.[84] In practice, at the close of Anne's reign, it enabled lay men and women who had been found guilty of these offences to avoid execution.[85] The privilege, however, could be enjoyed once only. To prevent repetition the guilty were burned in the hand. In spite of this limitation its influence on the administration of the law was very considerable.

The importance of 4 Geo. I, c.11 lay in its substituting transportation for burning in the hand as the punishment for clergyable offences.[86] Transportation to an American colony became the normal sentence for offenders found guilty of the less serious felonies. It provided that persons who before 20 January 1717 had been convicted of offences within the benefit of clergy and also those who after that date were convicted of the same, except receivers and buyers of stolen goods (known to be stolen), were to be transported to the Plantations for seven years, and it gave to the courts before whom they had been convicted power to contract for their transportation.

Persons convicted of offences which excluded them from the benefit of clergy, but who had been granted a Royal pardon, and receivers[87] and buyers of stolen goods were to be transported for fourteen years in the same way.

Persons contracting for the transportation of offenders were to have a property in their service; that service they might legally sell within the area to which the condemned were to be transported.

Any convict who returned before the expiration of his period of servitude was to become liable to a sentence of death without benefit of clergy.

Contractors were to give security for the effective transportation of the convicted and procure certificates of landing from the Governors or Chief Custom House Officers of the place to which they were conveyed.

The Act was to extend to all His Majesty's dominions, provided always that nothing in it was to "be construed to extend to that part of Great Britain called Scotland".[88]

Thus, from the year 1718 the Government had in its hand a very useful weapon with which to oppose the forces of evil. Later Acts made it more effective: 6 Geo. I, c.23 gave to any subsequent court sitting in the same county, though at a different place, the right to exercise a sentence of transportation imposed by any court of the county. It granted to courts authority to appoint two or more Justices of the Peace to contract with any person or persons for the transportation of the convicted, and the right to cause the delivery of such offenders to those who contracted. Securities for effective transportation were to be in the names of the Clerks of the Peace, and all charges incurred were to be borne by the county concerned. Succeeding measures, designed to meet special circumstances, declared transportation to be the punishment for practising as an attorney after conviction for perjury or forgery,[89] for assaulting others with intent to rob or injure clothing,[90] for assisting escape from any gaol, constable or vessel,[91] for stealing linen,[92] entering lead mines or hiring others to enter with intent to steal,[93] receiving watches, jewels, plate etc.,[94] for practising fraud on stamped vellum[95] and for counterfeiting coins.[96]

To provide for the more speedy removal of convicts, 8 Geo. III, c.15 declared that where the King's mercy was extended to them on condition of transportation they were to be delivered to the contractor forthwith, instead of lying in prison until the next session of the court to plead their pardons.[97] The ostensible reason for this measure was the desire to supply the colonies with healthy labourers but it is possible that its inspiration came from contractors, who complained of the physical unfitness of prisoners after long imprisonment, or from those who had to provide their maintenance while in gaol.

The Act 4 Geo. I, c.11, as we have seen, distinguished between clergyable and non-clergyable offences. The noticeable tendency in following years was the desire of the law-makers to reduce the number of clergyable felonies. The effect of this was to restore capital punishment for a first offence where clergy had withheld it.[98] Two results followed: a more frequent use of the discretionary power of pardon by the Crown and a great increase in the number of non-clergyable offences. Colquhoun, a contemporary but writing a few years later than the year 1763, gives the following list of crimes which in his words were "punishable by death and where upon conviction the offenders must be sentenced to death":[99]

> treason, petty treason, counterfeiting gold and silver coins, murder, arson, rape, stealing an heiress, sodomy, piracy, forgery, destroying ships, burglary, highway robbery, house-breaking in daytime, private stealing or picking a pocket above one shilling, shoplifting above five shillings, stealing above forty shillings, maiming or stealing a cow, horse, or sheep, breaking a house, church, or fishpond, cutting down fruit trees in avenues, cutting hop binds, returning from transportation, sending threatening letters, challenging jurors above twenty, standing mute, uttering counterfeit coin (third offence), breaking prison, robbing the mail, and several more.

Thus during the closing years of the American colonial period severe statutory restrictions had been placed upon the privilege of clergy. That its benefit was still felt by many may, however, be inferred from Colquhoun's statement that about five-sixths of the 2000-2500 offenders tried in the metropolis each year were for larcenies, acts of vagrancy, and smaller offences where the benefit of clergy either attached or did not apply.[100] Moreover, when crimes caused accused persons to be tried for non-clergyable offences, juries, as we have seen, often designedly reduced the seriousness of the offence to enable a transportation sentence. In country areas, where sheep stealing and similar crimes were more common, this could not easily be done. The accused had then to trust to a Royal pardon to retain his life. As a result the proportion of pardoned "transports" was fairly high in those areas.[101] This of course is no proof that the country dwellers of England were morally worse than their city brethren. When they entered upon a course of crime they became the victims of less favourable circumstances.

13

The conclusions drawn from this discussion and from the figures of the Old Bailey Session Papers for the four years of peace 1764-1767 are that, on an average, 274 persons were convicted of felony annually in that court,[102] that 40 of those were sentenced to death, that a greater number would have received a capital sentence had juries interpreted facts literally, that of the 40 condemned to die nearly one-half were pardoned,[103] that of the total number found guilty of felony approximately 7.5 percent were executed while the remainder with very few exceptions were transported. Further, the records show that those who were transported were not atrocious villains. Such, after conviction, were hanged. Those whom the courts sent to the colonies were petty thieves, shoplifters, pickpockets, and petty burglars together with a smaller number of receivers, sheep stealers, forgers, and the like. There was little, if anything, admirable about the great majority of them but the comparative youthfulness of large numbers of them made reform for some, at least, not impossible.[104]

The figures compiled from the Proceedings of the Old Bailey demonstrate how infrequently the sentence of imprisonment[105] was imposed. To the men of the time, that was natural enough: their object was not to fill gaols but to empty them. The transportation system had hindered or rendered unnecessary an improvement in English prisons, and any dislocation in that system put demands upon them which they could hardly meet. The practice of imprisoning debtors strained the resources of many a gaol.[106] As there was no centralised system of prison control, much of the expense fell upon local authorities who naturally complained of additional expenditure. The Government itself set them the example of transporting rather than retaining the sentenced.

Gaol difficulties increased with the coming of peace in 1763. Transportation had continued during the war, which had absorbed many whom the country regarded as undesirable. The Calendar of Home Office Papers shows that in the year 1761 at least 120 of those condemned to death were pardoned on condition of serving by land or sea.[107] In 1762 the number fell to 63, and in the following year no case of pardon on this condition appears. One means of relief therefore vanished with the signing of the Peace of Paris; the effect of its absence was soon felt. Transportation was, however, the traditional means of relief. Consequently it is not surprising that the Government should turn to it to overcome the trouble. Within a few weeks of the declaration of peace it concluded two contracts for the removal of convicts from London, Middlesex, and the counties Hertford, Bucks, Essex, Kent, Sussex, and Surrey.[108] To understand the system a knowledge of these contracts is essential. The following excerpts explain their more important conditions:

Articles of Agreement[109] . . . agreed upon this seventh day of April, 1763, between the Right Honorable the Lords Commissioners of His Majesty's Treasury . . . and John Stewart, Esq. of London, Merchant.

Imprimis. The said John Stewart doth covenant and agree with the said Commissioners . . . to convey or cause to be conveyed on board some ships . . . bound for America all and every malefactors . . . lying under sentence of transportation in Newgate in the City of London[110] without excepting or refusing any by reason of age, lameness, or any other infirmities whatsoever within fourteen days after the end of every 2nd. session . . . at his own proper costs and charges.

Item. The said Commissioners do hereby promise that the said John Stewart shall receive £5 by the head for each malefactor taken out of the said gaol of Newgate upon producing a certificate signed by the commander of the ship . . . whereon shall be expressed the number and names of the malefactors received. *Item.* The said John Stewart doth further covenant that he will as soon as conveniently may be procure an authentic certificate from the Governor or Chief Custom House Officer of the place whereinto the said malefactors shall be so transported of their being landed there (the danger and casualties of the seas and mortality excepted).

Item. The said John Stewart doth further covenant that none of the said malefactors shall be suffered to return before the end of the term for which they are . . . transported by the wilful default of the said John Stewart or his assigns.

Item. The said John Stewart doth further covenant that before the delivery to him of such malefactors he will enter into bond with two sufficient sureties to the proper officers of the Court at the Old Bailey in such penalties as the court shall think reasonable . . . that they shall be shipped and transported accordingly and that they shall not return contrary to the true intent and meaning of these presents.

By the second contract, signed on the same day, Stewart guaranteed for the same period, viz. seven years, to remove from the county gaols of Hertford, Bucks, Essex, Kent, Sussex, and Surrey all convicts sentenced to transportation, on the same conditions as those set forth in the first contract, with one important difference. In this contract the amount of the penalty to be exacted in case of failure was definitely stated to be £40 for every convict not effectually transported.[111] Seven years later, on 6 April 1770, Stewart renewed both these contracts.

Elsewhere local authorities were responsible for the system. By 6 Geo. I, c.23, as already stated, courts were authorised to appoint two or more Justices to contract for the conveyance of convicted felons, the charge falling upon the authority concerned. Its effect is seen in the Assize Books of the period. Thus that of the Western Circuit records, after enumerating the names and sentences of offenders tried at Taunton on 31 March 1764, that the court appointed Edward Phelps, John Collins, James Marwood, Henry Robord, John Hellier, Esquires,

15

and the Rev. Wm. Fewtrelleth,[112] six of His Majesty's Justices of the Peace of and for the county of Somerset, or any two of them, to contract with any person or persons for the performance of the transportation. As required by the Act, security was to be taken by a bond in the name of the Clerk of the Peace to ensure an effectual removal of the felons concerned. The contract and security were to be "rectify'd by the said Justices to the next general court of gaol delivery" to he held in the county.

Crime nevertheless flourished; executions became more numerous. The Government, troubled by their frequency, and inspired by humanitarian motives, then considered the practicability of employing those who would otherwise be executed on public works in the colonies. On 5 November 1763 Lord Halifax informed the Lords of Trade that it was His Majesty's pleasure that they should consider and report on the possibility of employing convicts of both sexes in America.[113] Nine days later the Lords of Trade replied that they had given the matter their most serious consideration but it was with the utmost concern that they had to report that there "were no such public works carrying on" in that part of the empire as would furnish an opportunity for effecting so desirable and humane purposes unless they were under the direction of the military department, which did not come within the cognizance of the Board.[114] Thus this proposed method came to naught and transportation remained the only effective remedy for overcrowding in English gaols.

After conviction, transportable felons remained in prison until the means of their removal had been decided. Within London and its surrounding counties a uniform method was possible. The contractor, together with two sureties, entered into a bond to remove the convicted. Unfortunately those bonds have disappeared but it is probable that they differed little, if at all, from those of Jonathan Forward who was the government contractor less than 30 years before the opening of this period. His bond, dated 19 December 1737, reads as follows:

> "Know all men by these presents that we Jonathan Forward of London Merchant, James Forward of London Merchant, and John Whiting of the Parish of St Paul's . . . Mariner, are held and firmly bound to Miles Man, Esquire, Common Clerk of the City of London in one thousand and forty pounds[115] . . . to be paid to the said Miles Man or his successors which payment well and truly to be made we bind ourselves . . . our Heirs, Executors etc.".

In the contract which follows, Jonathan Forward engaged to transport to some of His Majesty's Colonies or Plantations in America for the space of seven years Joseph Gilham, Richard Hill, John Street, and 23 others convicted at the sessions of Gaol Delivery of Newgate in the

Old Bailey on 7 December and at several preceding sessions. The conditions of the contract were as follows. Forward or his assigns was within one month to transport the several felons to Maryland or Virginia, to secure an authentic certificate of their landing from the resident Governor or Chief Custom House Officer, and not suffer them to return by any wilful default to any part of Great Britain or Ireland during the space of seven years. For every convict not transported within a month and for every convict whom the contractor should wilfully permit to return within the space of seven years Forward was to forfeit to Miles Man, his successors etc. the sum of 40 pounds. Under similar or identical conditions convicted felons were carried to the American colonies during the period that followed the Seven Years' War.[116]

Having arranged for the removal of the convicts there followed the task of conveying them from the gaol to the transporting vessel. The responsibility for this seems usually to have fallen upon the gaoler. In the records of the Western Circuit recur again and again the words "the said Justices are to cause the said felons to be delivered by the Gaoler, in whose custody they shall be, to the persons contracting for them". In London the task was frequently undertaken by Mr Akerman, the Keeper of Newgate.[117] Thus Howard in his descriptions of the Poultry Compter and Wood St. Compter states that the transportable felons were taken by Mr Akerman.[118] From the cost of this land transportation the contractor was normally free. The Act 6 Geo. I, c.23 directed that the charges connected with this removal were to be borne by the county concerned. The procedure, however, varied from place to place. Often the gaoler was paid a fixed amount which varied with the distance that had to be traversed. Thus the Huntingdon Gaoler's fee was 12 pounds if only one convict were carried, 9 pounds each if a greater number were to be taken, but he had to pay the Clerk of Assize a guinea for each of them. The Lancaster County gaoler was paid four pence a mile per head while the Oxford County gaoler presented a bill of expenses. The Treasury paid Mr Akerman 14s 10d per convict. The Worcester Castle gaoler on the other hand gained nothing by the transaction as the Clerk of the Peace "contracted with the merchant".[119] The lack of uniformity needs no further demonstration.

From Newgate the convicted were usually conveyed to Blackfriars whence they were carried in lighters to the waiting ships. Thus the *London Magazine* of 2 June 1764 records that 69 transports (56 men and 13 women) were taken from Newgate and put on board a lighter at Blackfriars which carried them to the transport ship at Blackwall. Thirteen of them, who were indisposed, were carried in two carts to the waterside. None were allowed to travel in coaches. The males alone

17

were chained. The inference here is that the healthy marched, a practice very common at the time,[120] but this was not always the case. Influence and money played their parts in the 18th Century. The *Annual Register* of 23 November 1771 reported that Mr Eyre was carried in a coach from Newgate to Blackwall, and the wealthy if they were prepared to pay for their own transportation were frequently granted that privilege by the courts which convicted them,[121] and in this way secured private cabins for their own use.

Time has drawn a veil over the land transportation of country convicts. There are references to turnkeys who accompanied prisoners, but the fact that those awaiting their trial were compelled on occasion to walk in irons distances of ten to fifteen miles[122] discourages the belief that officials erred in the direction of over kindness when conducting those who had been convicted. We may safely assume that they went in irons; as a deterrent to assisted escape, irons were a useful precaution.[123]

The convicted went to different ports. More were shipped from the Thames than from any other part of the Kingdom. Bristol probably occupied second place in the scale of importance. The Maryland Shipping Returns show that Bideford was the port of departure for many during the Seven Years' War.[124] Westmoreland convicts were conveyed to Whitehaven.[125] The system, in fact, permitted shipment from any port and it would be reasonable to suppose that cost sometimes determined the port from which the convicted sailed, although the repetition of the same place names in the shipping records suggests the use of a limited number only.

The ship-masters employed by the Treasury contractors were required to certify the receipt of the convicts on board their vessels and it is probable that county Justices demanded a like return for the satisfaction of the sentencing courts. Without a certificate of this kind the Treasury refused to pay the five pounds a head which Stewart's contract allowed. In practice the master merely added a statement to the list of convicts drawn up by the clerk of the court involved in the agreement. The following is a typical certificate:[126]

> List of convicts ordered to be transported from the Town and Port of Dover . . . and from the last Michaelmas Sessions held . . . for the County of Kent, viz.:
>
> Town and Port of Dover
> 1. John Gibbs for 7 years.
> Michaelmas Quarter Sessions,
> 1. Jonathan Bowler } for 7 years
> 2. Richard Ellis
>
> These are to certify that John Stewart of London, Merchant, hath con-

tracted and given security for the effectual transportation of the above named felons and that the securities are in my custody. Witness my hand this 18th day of January; 1769.

Jerome Knapp. Clerk of the Assizes of the said County of Kent

I do humbly certify that the within list of names of the convicts . . . have been shipped on board the Thornton of which ship I am master in order to their being effectually transported to some of His Majesty's colonies or Plantations in America.

London. 20th. January. 1769 Christopher Reed.

The names of some of the contractors have been preserved. Edward Sedgeley was actively engaged in conveying felons from Bristol.[127] Howard describes Messrs Stephenson and Randolph as contractors for the same city in 1774.[128] Jonathan Forward Sydenham described himself in 1768 as "the contractor with the greatest part of the counties of England".[129] William Temple was both owner and master of the ship *Little Nancy* which transported 20 convicts into York River on 8 June 1764.[130] John Stewart (or Stuart) was the government contractor from the year 1763 until his death in 1772. His successor and former partner was Duncan Campbell who in 1778 declared he had been in the business for many years.[131] Any captain, however, who could provide the necessary securities had a right to contract for the removal of county convicts at least, and there is nothing in Stewart's Agreement to prove that he had an absolute monopoly of Newgate and Home Circuit transportation. But Sydenham's statement and the fact that Forward was conveying felons from Oxford[132] while he was government contractor suggest that the work was undertaken mainly by a few men who operated over large areas.

The contractor assumed responsibility for the safe keeping of the convicts as soon as they were on board. This is demonstrated by Sydenham's difficulties of the year 1768. On 23 August his ship, the *Middleton*, while lying at anchor off the Limehouse was approached by about 600 riotous sailors who threatened to set free the convicts already on board unless the master complied with their demands concerning certain payments of money. They were paid nine pence and left declaring their intention to return. Sydenham hastily wrote to the Earl of Shelburne pointing out that he was liable to forfeit 40 pounds for every convict found at large after delivery on board his ship. He consequently asked for armed protection, which was forthwith despatched.[133] Not all the contractors were as fortunate as was Sydenham on that occasion. Both before and after the period of this chapter convicts took possession of their transporting vessels, but throughout the period itself the precautionary methods adopted by ship-masters seem to have been successful. That these were not always gentle is instanced by a report in the *Maryland Gazette* of 23 August 1764, that a captain preserved discipline by firing among his convicts and "bleeding a few". Shipwreck increased the contractors' difficulty for it apparently did not rid them of the responsibility of landing the survivors in the appointed colony.[134]

That the agreements were not interpreted lightly is proved by the following case. In 1746 the ship *Plain Dealer* carrying convicts was captured by the enemy. The convicts were sent to England in exchange for certain prisoners and the question of their disposal followed. This was referred to the appropriate authorities who gave the following ruling: "We are of opinion the contractor for transporting the convicts is obliged to transport them notwithstanding the capture. Therefore they ought to be delivered to the contractor for that purpose".[135]

The law itself occasionally permitted the return of some who were already on board a transporting ship. Thus in May 1767 the Mayor of Cork was directed to demand from a vessel carrying felons consigned by Messrs. Sedgeley, Wilhouse & Randolph of Bristol, Thomas Sawyer, one of the convicts given a free pardon.[136] These pardons were normally the result of judges' reports consequent upon petitions forwarded to the Secretary of State. Numerically they were not negligible, for a large proportion of the comparatively few petitions secured the desired object. Over a period of several years it averaged 60 percent as the following figures show:[137]

YEARS	PETITIONS FOR PARDON FROM TRANSPORTATION	FREE PARDON
1763	10	8
1765	21	16
1767	33	17
1769	32	22
1771	52	26

Death was probably the most potent agent in reducing the contractors' profits. The tragedy of transportation lay in the contrast between the ideals that were associated with it and the results that were obtained. The law plainly declared that the aim of the system was to provide labour needed by the colonists. Cynics probably viewed it as a means to rid English gaols of superfluous prisoners; practical men possibly championed it because it freed the nation of those who were not a productive asset at home. But the beliefs that idleness was a most fruitful cause of crime and that systematic labour was a powerful corrective of evil were generally accepted by those who discussed the subject in print. Howard saw in the lack of work and wicked associations of English gaols the true causes of the more expert villainy of those who left them;[138] Sir John Fielding described transportation as the most humane and effectual corrective because it answered the great ends of punishment, viz. example, humanity, and reformation.[139] The early leaders of Methodism abhorred idleness. Thus within England there must have been many who regarded with favour a system which provided a means of steady employment for those who had fallen into sin.[140] From many of these unfortunates, however, the opportunity was taken by death while on their way to America.

Publication of the mortality might have secured better results. In an age when public leaders themselves were ignorant of much that went on about them[141] the populace could hardly be expected to know the facts. Contemporary journals and newspapers announced the departure of convicts but they were singularly silent regarding the events of their passage. This cannot be attributed to a conspiracy of silence for in April 1768 the *Gentleman's Magazine* reported the sufferings of certain felons who set out in the *Rodney* for Maryland. Storms drove them to Antigua where, upon arrival, the "poor wretches" were in "a most deplorable condition", full of sores and vermin; eleven had died and many had been forced to eat their shoes. This is an isolated account; the journalists were evidently ignorant of the facts. Business men are not prone to publish their affairs. We can hardly, therefore, blame the contractors for not divulging the misfortunes of their livelihood, and the certificates of arrival were certainly not made for all who had eyes to see. To assume that the Secretaries of State or Treasury officials considered them seriously is to assume a diligence which official ignorance denied. Within the period a Secretary of State addressed to Maryland a demand for a copy of a contentious Act only to be informed that it was already in his possession.[142]

To state the exact number of deaths in the closing years of the American period is impossible as the certificates of arrival have been lost. Duncan Campbell, in evidence given to a Committee of the House of Commons, declared that rather more than one-seventh of the felons died during the interval between their sentences and their arrival in America.[143] Ten percent during the voyage alone was considered a moderate loss; the number of women who died was "only half in proportion of the men".[144] Campbell attributed this lower rate of mortality to their less impaired constitutions but it is probable that it was a result of a lack of chains and less strict confinement. Nevertheless his figures demonstrate that some improvement had taken place since the days of Jonathan Forward, when the certificates show that between August 1726 and September 1736 more than 21 percent died at sea,[145] yet the fact remains that out of every hundred assigned to be carried by the government contractor, fifteen at least perished between the passing of sentences and the arrival of the ships in America. Before, however, we condemn the contractors we must consider the conditions of the transportation.

The ships employed were, according to modern standards, almost absurdly small. Among them Stewart's *Justitia* of about 300 tons was a large vessel.[146] Within ships of this size accommodation must have been limited even if the convicts and their requirements alone were conveyed. But there is reason to believe that the criminals were only part of the outward cargo that was carried, for the *Justitia*, which left the Thames with convicts about the middle of the year 1767, is entered as arriving at Rappahannock, Virginia, with European goods on 7 November of the same year. This leaves little doubt that she had discharged her convicts in Maryland and proceeded to Virginia with other cargo that she carried.

The numbers transported in the vessels that cleared Newgate and the Home Circuit gaols were considerable. Campbell in the evidence already referred to stated that he carried on an average between 100 and 200 on a ship. A few examples taken from the masters' certificates support this assertion:[147]

YEAR	SHIP	TONS	CONVICTS
1764	*Tryal*	160	166
1764	*Justitia*	305	206
1768	*Tryal*	160	102
1771	*Justitia*	305	238

The ordinary passage, according to Campbell, occupied about two months. Its duration, being dependent upon wind, weather, and the sailing qualities of the ships, must have varied considerably, a variation which doubtless had a material effect upon the convicts' health.

What food the convicts received is not recorded, but it is almost certain that many of them were not worse off than those in English gaols. Howard discovered that in about half the county prisons debtors had no bread. They lived on charity. Felons had "in some gaols two pennyworth a day, in some three halfpenny worth, in some a pennyworth, in some none".[148] The greed of turnkeys and the farming of bread by gaolers often reduced the amounts prescribed by prison rules. As a result many prisoners, when freed, were "almost famished, scarce able to move and for weeks incapable of labour". But philanthropy, uncertain even on land, could not assist those on the sea. To keep his wares alive the contractor was forced to feed his convicts, and it is not improbable that they were fed with some regularity.

Little is recorded about the conditions under which they travelled. A writer who boarded one of Stewart's ships to see a prisoner declared,

22

"all the states of horror I had ever had an idea of are much short of what I saw this poor man in; chained to a board in a hole about 16 ft. long, more than 50 with him, a collar and padlock about his neck and chained to five of the most dreadful creatures I ever looked on".[149] The little evidence available points to their being lodged between decks. Thus Governor Sharpe wrote that one effect of the Maryland Quarantine Laws was to cause Messrs Stewart & Campbell to open portholes on each side between decks.[150] It is possible that the condition of the convicts mentioned above was worse at the time because of their proximity to land. Discipline could be relaxed a little at sea. It is possible also that the conditions were exaggerated by one accustomed to the comforts of a good home, but the facts concerning the chains, size of the room, and number of convicts can be accepted as not far from the truth. Many convicts wore iron while in English prisons and as the shipping returns show that the ratio between convicts and crew[151] was often higher than 6:1 the master would have little urge to free them when at sea. His life and ship depended upon their subjection and he was usually party to an agreement to forfeit 40 pounds a head for all who escaped. Such little evidence as we have concerning the male convicts points to sustained periods of confinement below decks and the wearing of chains continuously. The women were rarely ironed and normally enjoyed much more freedom than the men. Under such conditions it is not surprising that the health of the men was seriously affected even when the mortality was below the average. In defence of the contractors we should note that the conditions were certainly not worse than those within many English gaols visited by John Howard. He found prisoners chained together and to the floor, rooms with little or no ventilation, and persons sleeping on rotting, sodden straw in cells that lacked water and sewers.

Agents of death more powerful than chains and confinement were also transported. Campbell declared that gaol fever (typhus) and smallpox caused the majority of the deaths on his vessels. At a time when the nature and the causes of these diseases were but dimly understood their introduction into ships in which the sick and healthy rubbed shoulders must naturally have been disastrous. But they were not the only dangers. In 1774 Messrs Stephenson and Randolph wrote to the gaoler of Salisbury declaring that they had suffered serious loss because of sore feet which had proved very fatal.[152] Other complaints such as scurvy, dysentery, and scorbutic diseases can easily be imagined where salt food was the normal diet. The government contractor, moreover, was compelled by his agreement to take all convicted felons whatever their state of health at the time, and we have already seen that 13 out of 69 prisoners taken from Newgate on a single occasion had to be taken to the lighter in carts because they were unable to walk.[153]

But a little thought raises a doubt whether even under these conditions the conveyed were worse off than many who remained within English gaols. In 1773 smallpox caused the death of 11 prisoners in Oxford gaol,[154] and of five in Bury St Edmunds.[155] Howard found gaol fever in more than a score of prisons; he declared that it caused more deaths than did executions.[156] In the Clerkenwell Bridewell he discovered feet that were "quite black" and in Hertford gaol mortified toes. Thus we can safely assume that the majority of diseases introduced into convict ships came from English prisons. The figures oppose the belief that they were the normal scourges of voyages to America, for the mortality would assuredly have exceeded ten percent.[157] Campbell's evidence supports this view; he affirmed that on occasion 50 to 60 out of 150 died. The reasonable inference then would seem to be that the reported average (ten percent) was the result of a high mortality rate for a few voyages and a relatively low one for the remainder.

The colonists were not unaware of this evil effect of the transportation. Official attempts to prevent the introduction of infection were opposed by the anxiety of ship-masters to avoid periods of quarantine, and of factors to sell their wares. The result is described by Governor Sharpe who, writing in 1767, asserted that it was notorious that distempers introduced into Maryland by convict ships had destroyed scores.[158] He declared it became the legislature to protect the community against the possibility of such occurrences. In fact its members had done this only a few months before by passing a Quarantine Act in December 1766.[159] Its provisions resembled those of the Virginia Quarantine Act passed only a month earlier,[160] which imposed a fine of 10 pounds a head for all convicts landed unless the ship-master had previously taken an oath that they were free from gaol fever or smallpox, because as its preamble stated, "it is represented to this Assembly that the gaol fever and small pox are propagated among the inhabitants of this Colony by the importation of convicts and indented servants".[161] In 1772 the fine was raised to 50 pounds.

The Maryland Act was opposed by the local factor Ringold, who for the occasion assumed the pseudonym A.B.[162] In the *Maryland Gazette* of 30 July 1767 he asserted that it was at least 400 to 1 that the convicts did no injury in the way complained of. This evoked a reply from another writer who adopted the pen-name "Philanthropos", which read, "For who but a man swayed with the most selfishness would endeavour to disarm the people of all caution against such imminent danger lest their just apprehensions should interfere with his little scheme of profit". The government contractor, Stewart, and probably Sedgeley, applied to Lord Baltimore for a rejection of the Act.[163] As they received no satisfaction they placed the matter before the Lords of the Treasury, who referred it to the King in Council.[164] In November 1767, however, Hamersley reported to Sharpe his belief that the contractors would not proceed in the matter with much vigour because Lord Baltimore thought himself bound to maintain so salutary a law and because they apparently feared further regulations against themselves if the facts were known. In return Sharpe expressed both his own and the Province's gratitude for the paternal part Baltimore had played in the dispute. But the official machine had been set in motion by the appeal to the Council. As a result, on 13 August 1767 Lord Hillsborough informed Sharpe that the contractors had complained of obstruction and ordered him to transmit an authenticated copy of the Quarantine Act.[165] This produced the reply that a copy had been forwarded in the preceding July, which sheds some light on the official capacity of the time. Finally, on 29 July 1768, the Commissioners for Trade and Plantations recommended a disallowance of the measure.[166] The colony soon renewed it. Consequently we may suppose that the contractors did not entirely avoid inspection after that date.

The dispute had one beneficial result: the contractors "finding that they could not immediately succeed in their application" introduced improvements into their vessels. Messrs Sedgeley & Co. furnished their ship with a ventilator which, said Sharpe, they might be ashamed of not having done long before. Stewart and Campbell made theirs quite airy by opening a range of ports on each side between decks "and by that means it seems the ships were kept healthy".[167]

A study of Governor Sharpe's correspondence leaves little doubt that he primarily blamed the contractors for the ill-health and mortality among the convicts. Reason, however, opposes the belief that they alone were responsible. There is little enough to cause the belief that they were humane but there is nothing to show that they were intentionally cruel. Ship life was not an easy one in the 18th Century and those engaged in carrying convicts were moved by the traditions of more than a hundred years. To them the transportation was a business, and profit could be secured only by satisfactory sales. The death of any saleable convict meant a reduction of profit. The government contractor's agreement forced him to take the healthy and the unhealthy. It is probable that county authorities made similar bargains. Thus many of the convicts were never saleable. The Government's payment of five pounds a head was based on this knowledge and can hardly therefore be regarded as a discouragement to humane treatment on the voyage. To kill convicts would cause nothing but loss.

The contractor, therefore, had two alternatives: to treat his charges well in the hope of receiving a good selling price, or to care for them in such a way as would, under normal circumstances, yield a satisfactory return. If he adopted the former method, the result was problematical and in any case he had to compete with the sellers of superior coloured labour. Under abnormal conditions he stood to lose if he tried the second method. Ordinary business practice, therefore, would urge him to weigh all the probable circumstances and then determine his actions according to the principle of diminishing returns. Only by endowing the contractors with a mentality entirely different from that of normal merchants can we reach the conclusion that they wilfully destroyed what they had to sell. A contemporary merchant, George Moore, who engaged in the transportation a few years later certainly advised his employees to "be attentive to their health and keep them clean".[168]

Even the contractor's resistance to the Maryland Quarantine measure can be traced to business grievances. Satisfactory voyages to America required cargoes both ways. Convicts formed a useful outward freight and usually, before the departure of his ship, the merchant arranged for a return cargo of tobacco or other goods. If, then, his vessel were forced to remain in quarantine for a long period his whole plan of business might be destroyed. The Committee for Trade and Plantations therefore spoke with some reason when it described the Act as obstructive to trade.

Modern governments could hardly free themselves from responsibility if similar conditions were discovered, but 18th Century Ministers lacked the highly trained and well equipped staffs that assist their present successors. Moreover it is not usual to inquire into well established institutions until defects have been exposed; but, as already stated, the facts apparently were not common knowledge. Those interested in the suppression of the slave trade might have taken an interest in the convict transportation also, if they had known the facts, but no Clarkson appeared to inquire closely into this trade; nor is it impossible that some of them would have considered an innocent negro worthy of more compassion than a convicted fellow countryman. The state of the gaols at the time does not foster the belief that people were moved by any general desire to alleviate suffering. It cannot however be regarded as a final argument in support of the view that the 18th Century Englishman was inhuman, for Howard found good gaols as well as bad and the *Annual Register* of 17 January 1763 describes how a jury in the Old Bailey was so moved by the misfortunes of a prisoner that it not only recommended him to mercy but also set on foot a liberal collection for him and his family.

The fact that contractors could sell their convicts is proof that there was no general opposition to the system in at least the Southern States of America. Slavery, it would seem, was gaining ground in Maryland and in Virginia, but its adoption can hardly be imputed to the greater humanity of the African trade. Blame, discovered in a later age, may therefore be widely distributed; the transportation was a product of a preceding age; only under more enlightened conditions was a more humane system possible. Nor must the transportation be judged by the voyages of extraordinary mortality. Germs, introduced into convict ships, could just as effectively have slain those who remained in English prisons. The *Maryland Gazette* contains many advertisements of the arrival of convicts. In general they are sarcastic. Had contagion and death been common features of the system the writers had then a wonderful opportunity to condemn it. In actual fact their reports frequently contain no reference to sickness. When salt provisions were normal food, suffering was inevitable. Crews, even of a later period, were sometimes so reduced as to be unable to lower the anchor. Naval expeditions suffered seriously also and it would be as reasonable to suppose that the contractors intentionally destroyed their convicts as it would be to imagine that governments purposely injured those who fought their battles.

The convicts were delivered to factors or agents. Little is recorded of them. The names of two survive, Messrs Thomas and William Ringold,[169] one of whom actively opposed the Quarantine Act already mentioned. William Eddis, who observed the system, has left the following account of the disposal of the felons:[170] "These unhappy beings are consigned to an agent who classes them suitably to their real or supposed qualifications, advertises them for sale, and disposes of them for seven years to planters, mechanics, and to such as choose to retain them for domestic service". This evidence is supported by contemporary press reports. Thus the *Virginia Gazette* of 18 March 1775 published the following announcement:

> "Just arrived the *Justitia*, Capt. Kidd, with about 150 healthy servants, consisting of men, women, and boys, among whom are many tradesmen, carpenters, and joiners, bricklayers and plasterers, shoemakers etc. The sale will commence at Leedstown on Wednesday, the 22nd inst. and will continue until all are sold".

Now, the *Justitia* was Duncan Campbell's ship and Campbell was carrying convicts in 1775. Only a few weeks later the same paper described some of those landed from the *Justitia* as convicts. The "healthy servants" were in fact convicted felons. Such camouflaging of the reality was a well established business trick begun in the hope of securing higher prices. How long the sale continued is not recorded but 50 years before, the disposal of the 106 convicts on the *Margaret* lasted from 27 August to 5 September and one buyer alone secured as many as 21 on the last day.[171] The method of classification is revealed by the record of the *Gilbert* frigate whose convicts were listed as follows:[172]

NAME	QUALITY	AGE	COMPLEXION
Wm. Wades	Barber	35	darke
John Smith	Carpenter	53	black
Ann Adcock		16	fair
Kate Crumpton		40	dark

The price of the sold was determined by their sex and their physical, mental, and mechanical fitness. Men who possessed useful trades brought as much as 25 pounds a head; an ordinary man sold on an average for ten pounds, while the normal price of a woman was eight pounds.[173] The old and infirm were given away; occasionally it was necessary to encourage the receiver by the addition of a premium. In addition to these prices the government contractor received five pounds a head for all taken on board and it is probable that county authorities gave a like bounty. Sydenham, at least, received four guineas a head for transporting two felons from Oxford gaol.[174]

Stewart died in February 1772. Duncan Campbell, who for some time had been operating with him, continued the transportation alone while he also applied for a continuation of the contract in his own name. His application was rejected on the ground that other merchants were prepared to transport felons "without putting the public to any expense". Campbell, therefore, sought a contract assigning to him the right to convey criminals from Newgate and the gaols of the Home Circuit but without the receipt of any government bounty. This also was refused. Stewart was the last of the government contractors in the American transportation. With his death the payment of the five pounds' bonus ceased and with it also ended the Treasury records of the convicts carried from London, Middlesex, and the Home Circuit. From that date the removal of the felons from the gaols in those areas was an affair of the sentencing courts. Whether they paid a bounty or not is not recorded. Campbell, in 1779, maintained that after Stewart's death he derived no profit save that gained by the sale of the convicts' labour.[175]

To state the number of convicts conveyed throughout the period is probably impossible. The Treasury warrants reveal the number carried by the government contractor during the years 1763 to 1772. According to them Stewart was paid 21,355 pounds for the receipt of 4271 convicts.[176] His average annual consignment was therefore 475. This figure is in close agreement with Campbell's given to the Committee of the House of Commons in April 1779 when he stated that he had carried 473 annually for a space of seven years.

Eight years later Campbell informed the Undersecretary, Evan Nepean, that he "always looked upon the number from the other parts of the kingdom as equal to those transported by himself".[177] What he meant by the word "kingdom" is not stated but if we assume the widest application it was his belief that nearly 950 convicts were taken from the British Isles annually. Two later reports of a Committee of the House of Commons make it almost certain that Campbell had only England in mind. Those two reports, issued in April 1778 and April 1779, based upon returns which the House had ordered to be sent in, declared that the numbers transported from England at the times of their preparation were 960 and 1000 per annum.[178] Unfortunately Irish records have been destroyed; but if we assume that the total forwarded from Ireland was only one-quarter of that of Great Britain[179] a minimum of more than 1200 convicts was taken annually from the gaols of the British Isles, and the stream, as far as it is recorded, was fairly steady, showing no marked increase as the period advanced.

Any attempt to measure the effect of the system upon the colonies and the convicts themselves is rendered difficult by a diversity rather than a lack of information. A Committee of the House of Commons appointed in 1785 to consider means of disposing of convicts reported that the former system of transportation to America answered every good purpose that could be expected of it.[180] Lecky believed that the colonies were a good school of reformation, causing many of the transported to rise to wealth and respectability.[181] Each put forward the commonly accepted 18th Century opinion that this success was due to disciplined labour amid new surroundings.

But in actual fact several evaded that intended means of reformation. Those who had the necessary money could buy their own freedom; the agent was prepared to sell their labour to themselves if they were prepared to pay for it. Thus the wealthy escaped prepared correction and according to Campbell many were able to do this.[182] Their punishment amounted to little more than banishment for a period. Fraud occasionally reduced the severity of the punishment. Consignees and convicts had an incentive to suppress the evil pasts of the latter. To be sold as an indented servant might produce certain advantages to both such as a better price, a shorter period of servitude, less social stigma and a greater freedom. Collusion of this kind, however, was opposed by stringent colonial laws which required oaths and certificates concerning the condition of passengers.[183] The number who ran away from those who bought them must also have been considerable; a single copy of the *Maryland Gazette* advertised the desertion of seven convicts from three masters, the first of whom offered a 20 pound reward for the restoration of his four. Some returned to their home land before the expiration of their period of servitude despite the threat of a sentence of death without benefit of clergy. In 1763 a Coventry magistrate declared that many had friends in America who purchased their liberty and defrayed the cost of their return.[184] Ten years later Sir John Fielding deplored the mercy shown to several notorious criminals convicted of returning from transportation.[185]

William Eddis, who was a contemporary, describes how few of those who survived the period of enforced labour settled in their own neighbourhood. The stamp of infamy, he declares, was too strong upon them. They therefore either returned to Europe to renew their former malpractices or, if they had imbibed habits of honesty and industry, removed to a distant situation in the hope that they might remain unknown.[186]

American writers have unanimously condemned the importation. Basil Sollers's considered opinion of the system as far as it applied to Maryland is that the convicts were looked upon as criminals and dangerous persons.[187] MacCormac, whose studies were confined to the same province, tells that the newspapers traced most of the thefts and robberies to runaway or freed convicts.[188] Fiske, by reference to earlier writers, found that some became "mean whites" and were looked upon as inferior even to the better negroes.[189] Williams traces the severity of the Maryland slave code to the fact that many of the convicts became slave drivers.[190] Even Ringold, who championed the system, admitted that the most wicked ran away to the northward.[191] But lighter shades can be found even in the pictures of American writers. MacCormac believed that the rigid discipline of colonial laws and the seven years' labour converted the greater part into respectable and self-supporting citizens, and Fiske's authorities conceded that sometimes they proved worthy creatures and entirely forsook their former follies. The Abbe Raynal reported that not infrequently they contributed honourably to the population and prosperity of their new country.[192]

The opportunities for advancement which the system allowed caused some English authorities to doubt whether the punishment was in any real sense a deterrent to crime; Judge Perrott, in 1766, asserted that in the case of common offenders it had ceased to be a punishment.[193] Seven years later Lord Chief Clerk Miller decided that in his part of the kingdom transportation to America had begun to lose every characteristic of punishment.[194] The *Annual Register* in 1775 reported that certain prisoners begged to be transported. Occasionally prisoners expressed a preference for death. Sir John Fielding, in 1773, informed the Earl of Suffolk that he had heard several criminals declare that they would rather be hanged than suffer transportation a second time.[195] A few years later Robert Webber, after receiving a pardon conditional upon transportation, requested the judge to confirm his former sentence.[196]

To generalise amid such a mass of conflicting evidence is clearly difficult and the critical reader may question such an attempt on the ground that it is concerned with colonial history rather than with transportation. That some convicts committed crimes and that a larger number stole and deserted are well attested facts but, until careful research has established the ratio between the guilty and the innocent, final judgement must be suspended. That many returned to the British Isles is almost certain. Ballagh satisfied himself that many of those in Virginia proved in the long run to be industrious. If this were the result of labour amid new surroundings then the transportation, from the British point of view, was undoubtedly successful as far as the reformed were concerned. That it failed to reform others needs no further demonstration, but it is notorious that the behaviour of a troublesome minority will cast a reflection upon the whole of a group. Had one percent of the total convict population of Maryland alone been guilty of homicide in any year the journals of the day would have been charged with tales of murder. Negroes, on occasion, murdered and deserted but slavery continued long after the year 1776. On the eve of the Revolution convicts were still being bought, and we must suppose that those who bought viewed their purchases as seven-year[197] units of labour rather than as potential thieves, deserters, or murderers.

As the Introduction to this thesis shows, attempts to end the system had been made and thwarted before the year 1763. After that year resistance centred mainly in Maryland and Virginia and worked through Quarantine Acts. To combat measures of this kind was more difficult since they appealed to reason and had the support of the Proprietor of Maryland. The "paper war" which that colony's Statute of 1766 provoked within the colony[198] shows that the champions of the Act were not concerned solely with the good health of the settlement. "Philanthropos" denied that the importation of the scourings of gaols could be an "eligible mode" of peopling a young country, while C.D. wrote, "Is this the way to rid ourselves of the false and bitter reproach, so commonly thrown at us, that we are the descendants of convicts?". In his opinion their introduction was the greatest grievance imposed upon them by the mother country. Pride of race must inevitably have abolished the transportation. Had the colonists as a whole been inspired by it the "grievance" would have righted itself, for the British Government did not force convicts on to anyone. The Government did not compel contractors to remove them. When the West Indies no longer desired English felons they were carried elsewhere. For the same reason they were not imported into New England.

Within the southern colonies there were many that resented their introduction but there were others who were willing to buy them. Within those regions society was divided into at least two classes:[199] those of the coastal area including merchants, lawyers, journalists, and well established planters; and those of the more distant, less settled parts of the country. The former class stood in no need of convicts; its planting section preferred slaves; but slaves were dear; thus back country men of little capital were forced to buy convicts. The former class who were powerful in press and assembly organised the opposition to the transportation; the latter for economic reasons continued to buy the so-called scourings of English gaols. MacCormac states that in Maryland the contractors always found a ready market in spite of sentiment against the system, and the contractors' correspondence which remains contains no complaint concerning a difficulty of disposing of such as were landed.

The date of the departure from England of the last convict ship prior to the interruption caused by the Revolution is uncertain. Campbell was transporting until 1775.[200] Basil Sollers found port-entry records of the landing of convicts in Maryland until the same year, but later than either of these was the arrival in James River during April 1776 of the *Jenny*, from Newcastle, with a cargo of servants including convicts.[201] Current English newspapers published the departure of convicts as late as December 1775, but we cannot be sure that they were landed. The *Jenny* was certainly among the last, if not the last, to discharge British convicts during the period. On 11 January 1776 the *Gazetteer* announced, "It is reported that there will be no more convicts sent to America whilst the country remains unsettled". No hint can be found in that article that the writer traced the colonial resistance to resentment provoked by the transportation; he apparently believed that the system would be renewed when peace was restored. Political disputes ended the importation of convicts into America, for its political leaders were not of that class which purchased convict labour. To men of the type of Franklin and John Dickinson the introduction of British felons naturally seemed an insult and an indignity which loosened the bonds of empire between the mother country and the colonies. Basil Sollers, after a careful study of the subject, came to the conclusion that transportation was a chapter in the economic history of Maryland. To the student of economic history, then, the American Revolution has this additional interest, that it furnishes him with an example of the suppression of an economic interest by political ideals.

3

The Hulks

A BOUT THE MIDDLE of the year 1775, the British Government was convinced that the American revolutionists were determined to offer an active resistance to the importation of both goods and convicts from Great Britain. On 15 July the *Morning Post* announced that the brigantine *Hannah*, loaded with salt, had been ordered back from South Carolina and not even allowed to cast her cargo overboard there. The *Daily Advertiser* of the following day reported that transported felons "on board a ship sent to America" had been refused admittance. These were but two among a number of similar statements published at the time. Their effect upon those who read them rather than their truthfulness concerns us. To them it was evident that Government had been deprived of one of its most effective weapons for the suppression of crime. As if inspired by this, if we can trust the press of the time, England was overrun by a crime wave of more than usual dimensions. Thus *Lloyd's Evening Post* of 1 September declared that perhaps there never were more numerous and more formidable gangs of house-breakers than had recently infested the city and its environs. On the 27th it suggested the keeping of bloodhounds to trace such offenders. The *Morning Chronicle* of 19 October advised foot passengers traversing St George's Field to keep the highroad as the byepaths were much in-fested with footpads.

The Government's measures to suppress these evils only increased its embarrassment as they merely added to the number in the gaols. Soon the state of Newgate caused the Lord Mayor of London to fear epidemics, particularly as the time was approaching when other prison-ers would be brought to it from other gaols for trial at the Old Bailey. He communicated his fears to the Secretary of State, Lord Suffolk who, already troubled by the prison problem, decided to make a pretence of transportation.[202] His decision was conveyed by the Undersecretary, William Eden, to the Recorder of London on the same day. It provided for the removal of convicts from Newgate by placing them on "a prop-er vessel in the river in the usual manner and as if in due course for transportation". The Recorder was directed to take the usual bonds from the contractor, Duncan Campbell, who shortly afterwards received a number of convicts on board the *Tayloe* which remained at anchor in the river off Limehouse.[203]

The relief thus provided was of short duration as the flow of accused persons continued. The *Gazetteer* of 4 December announced that upwards of 140 prisoners would take their trials at the coming sessions of the Old Bailey. The *Morning Chronical* asserted that every division teemed with offenders.[204] To add to the troubles of the authorities, "a multitude of debtors" surrendered themselves in the hope of gaining relief by acting in harmony with the recently passed Act 14 Geo. III, c.77, which gave to bona fide imprisoned debtors the right to petition on certain conditions. Because of some defect in the law, however, these voluntary prisoners were retained in their various gaols. The result is seen in the *Morning Chronicle's* announcement of 23 February 1776, that it was well assured that the number of debtors in confinement was never greater and that their distress exceeded description.

The war revived the old time practice of employing pardoned offenders as soldiers. On 12 January 1776 William Eden advised Duncan Campbell that a selection would be made from those on board the *Tayloe*.[205] Nine days later Campbell was ordered to deliver 17 named persons to the officer who bore these instructions.[206] Their pardons, conditional upon serving His Majesty "out of the Kingdom of Great Britain", bear the date 23 January 1776. On 20 May he was directed to deliver nine other convicts "now on board a vessel of yours in order to transportation".[207] They had been pardoned on the same condition.

The Government's desire to rid itself of the responsibility of retaining the criminals is further evidenced later in the year. On 5 June, Campbell received orders to deliver nine male and five female prisoners "for whom application had been made". No conditions were attached to their pardons. Two months later seven more were discharged because His Majesty thought their punishment had already been severe enough.[208] Finally, on 12 December, William Eden conveyed to Campbell Lord Suffolk's orders to deliver the twelve men and three women who remained on the ship,[209] which was consequently discharged a few days later.

The experiment had not been altogether successful. In March 1776 the *Gazetteer* reported that the master of the vessel "that had the convicts on the river" had informed Sir John Fielding of the escape of twelve, two of whom had "got clear away".[210] The captain of the *Tayloe* himself announced the escape of 32 on 6 October. But on that ground alone the Government could hardly have rejected the method, for it was notorious that the gaols frequently failed to retain prisoners. Twelve escaped from Reading gaol in January 1776.[211] The writer who exposed the escape of the convicts from the river believed that about

30 thieves were at the time "loose upon the public".[212] A more serious defect in the system was its inability to remove offenders from England. In the closing years of the American transportation convicts had been conveyed to the colonies regularly and without cost to the Government. The *Tayloe* method simply transferred them from one form of prison to another within the country and cast upon the public the expense of maintaining them. The natural result was an increasing accumulation of convicts in spite of conditional pardons, and the more frequent substitution of burning in the hand and whipping for transportation.[213]

That the Government should desire to economise in time of war and that convicts ought to labour were well accepted views. In the past the colonists had directed their labour, but that was now impossible. Within the kingdom itself were Houses of Correction whose original purpose had been the reformation of evil-doers by means of disciplined work but it was no secret that the inmates of those institutions usually occupied their time in anything but industry.[214] Moreover those Houses of Correction, or Bridewells, had never been designed to accommodate "desperate villains" but only minor offenders. Howard plainly declared that felons could not be retained within them.

Lord Suffolk's difficulty can therefore be readily appreciated. To maintain convicts at public expense without requiring some work of them would provoke the condemnation of both moralists and taxpayers alike and since neither Houses of Correction nor transportation could solve the problem at the time he decided to compromise. In other words to place convicts upon ships and force them to work within England.[215] To all who could observe it was clear that the Thames was silting up. A writer in the *Morning Post* of 26 July 1775 had pointed out the inconvenience due to the presence of mud and gravel below the stairs at London and Westminster and had urged others to support a movement "to recover those advantages which can only proceed from care and attention to the navigation". As the convicts were afloat on the river at the time the Government came to its decision it required little mental effort to create the idea that they might suitably be employed there.

The plan was introduced into parliament by Lord North on 1 April 1776.[216] He moved to bring in a Bill to authorise for a limited time punishment, by hard labour, of offenders who were liable to transportation. A few discordant notes were heard amid the almost general harmony which the proposal provoked. Mr Johnstone, in the Commons, saw no reason why felons should not be sent to the West Indies or the Falkland Islands.[217] A contributor to the *London Magazine* declared that it was a flagrant error "to preserve the breed" in England. He suggested sending them to the East Indies.[218] But another in the same journal supported the proposal on the grounds that the transportation had removed some of Britain's most ingenious inhabitants whose labour had encouraged colonial industry and made the colonists independent of British manufactures.

Meantime Lord North's Bill to establish the hulk system had received the Royal Assent on 23 May 1776.[219] Its preamble states:

"Whereas the transportation of convicts to H.M. Colonies in America is found to be attended with various inconveniences particularly by depriving this Kingdom of many subjects whose labour might be useful to the community and who, by proper care and correction might be reclaimed from their evil courses

And whereas, until some other more effectual provisions in the place of transportation can be framed such convicts, being males, might be employed with benefit to the public in raising sand, soil, and gravel from and cleaning the R. Thames, or being males unfit for so severe labour, or being females might be kept to hard labour of another kind within England".

The following clauses explain the system of punishment established by the Act. Males convicted of transportable offences and those who had received a Royal Pardon after the receipt of a sentence of death were to be kept at hard labour in the way described for any term not less than three years or more than ten. Such offenders were to be delivered to the care of an overseer, or overseers, appointed by the Justices of the Peace for Middlesex in their quarter or general sessions. These overseers were to have powers similar to those of sheriffs or gaolers. Offenders were to be clothed and fed; their meals to consist of bread and any coarse or inferior food; their drink to be water or small beer. To supply any other food or clothing to them, without permission, would incur a fine of 40 shillings. By good behaviour the punished might shorten their periods of servitude. Those refusing to work[220] were to be whipped or suffer such other moderate punishment "as may by law be inflicted in a House of Correction". Escape from confinement would double the term of servitude for the first offence; death without benefit of clergy was the punishment prescribed for subsequent escapes. Every offender at the end of his term was to receive a sum of money, not less than 40 shillings nor more than 5 pounds, together with decent clothing.

As in transportation the execution of the Act was entrusted to a contractor who also became the overseer. For some years Duncan Campbell was the only overseer. In accordance with the terms of the Act he was appointed by the Justices of Middlesex who, however, acted under the direction of the Secretary of State.[221] His contract was concluded on 13 August 1776, some weeks after the plan had begun to operate. A resume of its provisions makes clear the aims of the Government at the time.

For the space of three years, dating from 12 July 1776, Campbell undertook to provide a ship of approximately 140 tons burden and to equip it for the accommodation of 120 male convicts. He also agreed to supply six lighters, each of 40-50 tons burden, or of such smaller size as the service should require, and to equip them in such a way as to enable 12 men to work in each of them. He was to accept all convicts sent to him from the "sundry gaols" provided always that his total did not exceed 120, and feed and clothe them according to the conditions of the Act. "As often as should be requisite", the vessel and the lighters were to be washed with vinegar, fumigated, or otherwise cleansed and rendered wholesome. The overseer also promised to provide medicine and other necessaries to preserve the health of the convicted and, in addition, a sufficient staff to manage their labour. When the weather permitted, excepting Sundays, the prisoners, at least 12 in each lighter, were to be employed in raising sand etc. from the bed of the Thames. Should the conditions make such work "improper" they were to be engaged in some other manner for the benefit of the navigation of the river.

In all his operations Campbell was to obey the orders of any of His Majesty's Principal Secretaries of State and in addition return to one of them, ten days at least before any session of Oyer and Terminer and Gaol Delivery to be held at the Old Bailey, or oftener, a true account in writing of all his convicts and also of the profit[222] produced by their labour which he should receive "from Trinity House or from any other persons in any other manner". Such profit was to be deducted from the next half yearly payment made to him by the Treasury. That payment according to the agreement was to be at the rate of 3560 pounds per annum.

The first hulk was the *Justitia.* In his evidence before the select committee of the House of Commons in April 1778, Campbell stated that she was of 260 tons burden.[223] The first convicts were received on board in August 1776,[224] but prior to that date preparations for their accommodation were in progress. In July the first lighter was launched. According to a writer in the *Annual Register* this vessel could neither be called a ship, nor a tender, nor was it so flat or open as a lighter. It was calculated to hold 24 tons of ballast. On the starboard side was a flooring about three feet wide for the men to work on and a machine called a "david" with a windlass for the raising of the ballast. On 26 July the *Morning Post* reported that the lighters were ready to receive the convicts. On 30 July the same paper announced the arrival at Newgate from different country gaols of upwards of 60 convicts destined to labour on the Thames. According to the *Annual Register* these men, "chained by the leg two and two", began to work in the first lighter "about two miles below Barking Creek"[225] on 5 August.

During that month the newspapers reported the transference of various groups of prisoners from Newgate to the *Justitia*. But as if to demonstrate the temporary character of this form of punishment and the judges' belief in a return to the transportation system, guilty persons were still, throughout the month of August 1776, being recommended to pardon conditional upon removal to America.[226]

That the establishment of a single hulk would not permanently relieve the pressure on the gaols was realised from the outset. Two months after the passing of the Act 16 Geo. III, c.43 Lord Weymouth addressed letters to 23 of the English sheriffs declaring it was the King's intention to show mercy to those who, by imprisonment, had suffered adequate punishment for their respective crimes and directing them to report the number and the particulars of those within gaols under their jurisdiction.[227] As early as 21 January 1777 Lord Suffolk, on hearing that the number on the hulk exceeded that of the agreement, recommended a consideration of further provision for those sentenced to hard labour. Another contract was therefore concluded with Campbell on 15 April 1777. By this agreement he promised to provide a ship of 240 tons or thereabouts, and six lighters of between 35 and 40 tons for the accommodation and employment of another 130 convicts. The other conditions were the same as those of the first contract with one exception: the annual payment was to be only £3483 7s 6d, one-third of which was to be paid every four months.[228]

For a time Campbell used one of his Jamaica ships as a second hulk but her convicts were soon transferred to a former French man-of-war of 730-800 tons which he bought for the purpose. This hulk bore the name *Censor*.[229] Its size enabled it to meet the requirements of a third contract, entered into on 2 February 1778 and providing for the detention of yet another 130 convicts for a payment of £3483 7s 6d per annum.[230] At Campbell's request it was also decided that all three contracts were to end on the same day, viz. 12 July 1779.

While these agreements were still in force Lord North, on 23 March 1778, moved in the House of Commons to bring in a Bill to continue the system by renewing the Act 16 Geo. III, c.43 which, as we have seen, was only a temporary measure. A debate ensued which demonstrated that even at that early date some of the influential members of the House were opposed to the method.[231] Burke preferred transporting to Canada, Nova Scotia, or the Floridas. Sir Charles Bunbury contended that England still possessed colonies in America to which convicts might be sent. Sir Richard Sutton and Mr Thomas Townshend both condemned the system because it failed to suppress crime, the latter asserting that scarcely a night passed without robberies in Park Lane or the hearing of pistol shots. Mr Gilbert, however, probably expressed the views of many of his fellows by describing it as a temporary measure which he would support until something was substituted. To find a substitute and to inquire into the hulk system the House on the same day set up a committee whose report will appear on a later page.

The debate just referred to has the additional interest of revealing the humanitarian tendencies of its leaders. Burke feared the time would come when felons would be put to death on the principle of economy. Sir William Meredith disapproved of the hulk punishment because he believed it was more severe than transportation. Sir Charles Bunbury was convinced that it was more severe. Mr Whitworth, who had taken the trouble to visit the hulks and talk with the convicts, reported their sickly appearance. These men carried the House with them and were appointed members of the Committee of Enquiry, Sir Charles Bunbury being selected to act as its chairman.

The three agreements already described stipulated that 380 convicts were to be maintained on the Thames. In reality the numbers on the *Justitia* and *Censor* varied considerably. By pardons, deaths, and escapes prisoners were constantly passing from the hulks. Their places were as quickly taken by others from the gaols within which was always a "waiting list" of felons ready to be transferred to the Thames. Occasionally the number fell short of that demanded by the contracts. Thus, in his return for January-February 1778, Campbell claimed maintenance for only 369, but the following two returns show that he had in his charge 382 and 412 respectively.[232]

If contemporary opinion can be accepted, labour on the hulks was a form of punishment particularly dreaded. The Recorder of London helped to originate the fear by telling those whom he first sentenced to terms on the hulks that "if they were incorrigible they would be worked without remission to the utmost of their strength".[233] An article in the *Gentleman's Magazine* some months later told how warders marched among the workers with drawn cutlasses to prevent idleness and how the tasks allotted depended entirely upon the whim of the overseer. Little wonder was it then that many offenders arrived on the hulks in a state of most "astonishing depression". To dispel this melancholy and to inspire good behaviour Campbell, within the first few months of the system, adopted the plan of recommending the granting of pardons to the better disposed members of his criminal community. On 12 December he received His Majesty's pleasure to remit to James Corbet and five others the remaining part of their sentences, together with directions that their case was to be held up as an example to the others in his custody.[234]

The number pardoned was indeed astonishing; in April 1778 the Committee appointed to inquire into the hulk system elicited from Campbell that in a little more than 18 months he had secured pardons for about 60 offenders and that he wished to recommend 30 more.[235] Not all his recommendations were adopted. Occasionally they were deferred; thus in his February-April 1778 Report Campbell referred the names of six convicts to the Court of the King's Bench because they "showed strong marks of reformation". In the following report (April-May) the same six were still recommended for pardon. The next report (May-June) shows that the favour had been granted to five of the six.[236] The sceptical may suspect that these recommendations were due to a desire to avoid responsibility or to profit by a reduction in numbers. In actual fact, however, others stepped into the places of the released, and the returns for the year 1778 show that the total number increased considerably in spite of pardons. Further, additional convicts brought no financial loss to the contractor as he regularly transmitted accounts for the upkeep of those in excess of his agreement and they were paid.[237] That he was not ridding his vessels of the sick is vouched for by Mr Stewart Erskine, who commanded the hulks. His evidence proves that the pardoned were healthy.[238]

In spite of the severe penalties prescribed by law for escaping from the hulks several attempted to gain their liberty and some, at least, seem to have succeeded. On 7 November 1776 the *Gentleman's Magazine* reported the escape of eight after a successful mutiny. In April, according to the *Annual Register*, 14 of the workers "rose on their guard" when a lighter blew ashore on the Essex coast and made their escape, but a naval officer whom they met persuaded eight of them to return to duty. From Captain Erskine's evidence we learn that 24 had escaped before that date.[239]

Death reduced the numbers on the hulks much more than did pardons or escapes. Within the period August 1776 to March 1778, out of 632 convicts taken on board the two vessels no less than 176 died.[240] As however their deaths must have been in large measure the result of their condition on arrival and of their subsequent treatment it will be well to consider these matters before attempting to assess the blame for this extraordinary mortality.

The hulk convicts came direct from English gaols and we have evidence that even under normal conditions some of them were infected by disease. Howard reported smallpox in Gloucester Castle gaol "about Christmas 1778", and gaol fever in the Savoy during the period 1776-1779.[241] In the year 1777 Campbell, when proposing to use the *Censor*, declared that convicts on arrival were seldom or never free from gaol distemper. This is supported by the evidence of Mr Dodo Ecken, whom Campbell employed as surgeon on the hulks. When he first went on board in October 1776, few were ill and none had died. He found, however, that several country convicts had been admitted, some of whom were sick. Soon after, a putrid fever broke out; of nine who came from York four soon died. Another unpleasant fact he reported, viz. 20 out of 40 from Newgate were suffering from venereal disease. On 10 October 1776 Campbell reported 84 on board without any sickness. His November and January reports mention the spread of the infection throughout the whole ship, and the death of 11 prisoners, 9 of whom had come from the country.[242]

To establish the introduction of infection from without does not completely exonerate the overseer. Howard, who visited the *Justitia* in October 1776, saw many who looked sickly, and the unhealthy had told him that they had neither surgeon nor apothecary. A sufferer from venereal disease had received no attention; a few boards separated the sick from the healthy. The former also slept on boards, and a very sickly smell pervaded the vessel.[243] Conditions certainly were not satisfactory on the *Justitia* at the time, but it is well to remember that the system had been in existence only a few weeks when Howard visited the hulk and, as Campbell's report proves, the officials on board had had little cause to provide against sickness.

In October the overseer appointed Mr Dodo Ecken to care for the sick, showing that he also had realised the changed state of health of the convicts. Ecken, moreover, affirmed that Campbell supplied everything that he recommended and that the unhealthy had all that was needed. Further, in the fitting up of the *Censor*, Campbell sought the advice of Mr Banks and Dr Solander, whose experience in the *Endeavour* caused them to be regarded as authorities in such matters. When they suggested the use of hammocks he had tried them but found that they were unsuitable because of the chains worn by the convicts. In arranging the beds of the convicts he had adopted the method employed in military transport ships, viz. two tiers with 5 feet 10 inches between the tiers, allowing 18 inches in width to each man. As that had proved unsatisfactory he had substituted "one general platform on each deck", which plan he continued although he increased the space allotted to each convict to two feet. After experimenting with loose matting he had established the practice of nailing it down. At first the friends of the imprisoned had supplied some with blankets. To those who lacked he had given rugs and in addition each mess of six men was allowed a large sheet of canvas. In October he had supplied straw beds instead of the matting. The prisoners were then divided into pairs, each of which was allowed a bed 6 feet by 4 feet and a blanket. The beds folded against the sides of the ships leaving a space of 20 feet in the *Censor* and 17 feet in the *Justitia*. Each deck was provided with a row of large portholes which the convicts themselves could open.[244]

Dr Solander, who visited the hulks in the second half of 1777, declared that their holds were airy and clean. He condemned the practice of compelling the men to sleep in sixes, and considered that 18-19 inches was not sufficient space for a man.[245] These faults, as we have already shown, were soon remedied. Dr James Irwin, a surgeon general of Artillery who visited the hulks "merely on principles of humanity", reported that each ship had a hospital. That on the *Justitia* had been too small but it had been enlarged. The sick were allowed everything that was recommended, even wine. He found no fault with their diet or the ventilation of their quarters. He believed that the sick brought their diseases with them as they usually died within the first 12 days. To confirm the general improvement we may again quote from Howard. He visited the hulks a second time in January 1778. On that occasion he found the men "much better used"; the chains had been taken from the sick men, who seemed to have the utmost attention paid to them. He no longer detected the disagreeable smell.

The history of the food allowance resembled that of their medical attention. In 1776 Howard found biscuits mouldy on both sides, green, broken, and consisting largely of crumbs. At that time the daily ration for a mess of six men was five pounds of biscuit, half an ox-cheek, and three pints of peas, except on "burgoe" days (of which there were two each week) when they received three pints of oatmeal made into porridge, five pounds of bread, and two pounds of cheese. After hearing Howard's report he had substituted four and a half pounds of second flour bread for the five pounds of biscuit, and rice instead of the peas. For a time he had experimented with six pounds but had judged it to be too much. Five days in the week the men received four and a half quarts of broth. Their drink was one quart of small beer per man four days a week. On other days they drank filtered water from the same source as that used in his own house. In winter he supplied the convicts with salt provisions because of the fear that ice might prevent communication with the shore. He thought that their allowance was better than that of the Navy. Dr Solander had tasted the food and found it wholesome. Howard confirmed Solander's opinion after his second visit to the hulks.

To blame Campbell for the abnormal mortality on the *Justitia* and *Censor* is therefore to do him an injustice. All the evidence establishes his readiness to accept the advice of competent critics and his willingness to amend the faults they discovered. His personal interest in the hulks is demonstrated by his visiting them twice a week and remaining on board all day. His activity in this direction was in striking contrast with that of several owners of private gaols in England. They rarely or never visited their own prisons. Campbell admitted that he avoided the hospitals but in failing to enter them he was only doing what Howard found to be common practice in English gaols, and what the Rev. John Newton advised the first New South Wales chaplain to do. To those prisoners who came from gaols in the description of which Howard inserted the words, "No bread, no water, no straw, no sewer", the regular feeding, bedding, and medical attention of the hulks must have been a welcome surprise.

The official returns tell little about the position of the hulks. They simply describe them as stationed at Woolwich. The *Gentleman's Magazine* of the year 1777 gives the information that they were "hard by" the Woolwich Warren "close to the end of the Target Walk". Campbell, in his evidence before the Committee of 1778, stated that he had obtained authority from Trinity House to work below Woolwich and that the Board of Ordnance had granted him permission to employ the convicts on ground adjoining the Warren where he began to build a bank.[246]

The method of working is described in contemporary journals. In the *Morning Chronicle* of 7 October 1776 the "parties concerned in the employment of the convicts" denied that they were raising sand in one part of the river only to form shoals in other places. They explained that the soil raised was carried ashore in lighters at high tide and there discharged and not thrown into deeper water. A more detailed account of the operations appeared in the *Gentleman's Magazine* of May 1777. It told that the prisoners were sent in lighters about a mile below Woolwich. There they raised ballast and rowed it back to Woolwich Warren. Others then threw it from the lighters after which it was sifted and spread to form an embankment. One party was continually busy in turning round a machine for driving piles "to secure the embankment against the rapidity of the tides". The official returns for January–February 1778 reported that the convicts had been raising gravel from Barking and Woolwich shoals, wheeling the same to cover and raise the surface near the new Proof Butt which they were erecting, and in making a wide and deep entrenchment round the additional part of the Warren.[247] Some of the gravel, however, was conveyed to Greenwich where it was used in the preparation of roads in the neighbourhood of the Hospital.[248] Mr Thomas Powney, a clerk of work to the Ordnance Board, under whose direction the convicts worked ashore, estimated that their labour was worth 6053 pounds before the inquiry of 1778.[249]

Any criticism of the amount of work done naturally calls for a consideration of the physical fitness of the workers and the conditions under which they laboured. Some, at least, were unfitted for the work provided by the Law, for Erskine asserted that six or eight little boys were employed in cleaning the ship as they were too small to work ashore. Among the men also was one who was blind and another with only one leg.[250] Discipline was strict but in none of the evidence, nor in the Committee Report based upon it, is there any hint that the sick were forced to work or that the convicts were wilfully ill-treated. Howard declared that the captain and overseers were not strict. He found the men to be orderly. Campbell affirmed that he rarely had to punish and that the men worked cheerfully. Erskine reported that a few had been punished with the cat-o-nine-tails and a few desperate prisoners who had threatened to kill their keepers had been put into irons for a week or a fortnight, but on the whole their behaviour had been good.

Campbell informed the Committee of 1778 that he had encouraged them for a time to work without irons but they had made bad use of the privilege. A contemporary account[251] describes the workers as wearing fetters on each leg "with a chain between that tied variously, some round their middle, others right up to the throat", some being chained two and two, others, whose crimes had been enormous, wearing heavy fetters. Among them continually marched six or seven men with drawn cutlasses to prevent escape and discourage idleness. Erskine announced that the men were put down at 7 p.m. and rose at 5 a.m.. Those who swore were beaten with a rattan, a procedure which probably explains the absence of oaths noticed by Howard. He also declared that it was more difficult to keep them clean than to keep them at labour.

A considerable staff had necessarily to be employed to enforce this discipline. Erskine told that there were 40, besides himself, to take care of the convicts. Their control continued whether the men were on land or water. The general direction of the work was decided by Trinity House and Army Ordnance officials among whom, as we have already noticed, was Thomas Powney. From him we learn that the shore workers were granted by Lord Townshend, on Campbell's application, a pint of beer a day. Under its inspiration and their usual discipline he believed that they performed as much work as men on the highways. Campbell thought the same but believed that they could do more without their chains. Howard was of the opinion that the chaining of both legs hindered their work; he estimated that they did about one-third of the amount performed by voluntary labourers. This he attributed to a lack of planning rather than to laziness or refusal to work.

In stating this fault he apparently spoke with reason. That many of the convicts were often in a state of idleness is certain. Campbell stated that those not engaged ashore nor in the lighters remained idle. He admitted that in the winter, when the weather allowed work, they were employed from 8.30 a.m. to 2 or 3 p.m. only. Howard discovered that the men on the Warren left work between 1 and 2 p.m. and did no more work that day, but he visited the hulk in January. In April, according to Campbell, the convicts toiled from 7 a.m. until noon, and from 1 p.m. to 6 p.m. In summer their hours were longer. With such hours the most enthusiastic advocates of labour could have found little fault.

But weather conditions must have prevented work on the river again and again during the year, and there is no evidence to show that the officers, either of the hulks or of the Ordnance Department, evinced any desire to direct labour when conditions were unpleasant. Again common justice forces us to admit that the contracts did not require employment on the hulks; they simply stated that the convicts were to be employed in some other manner for the benefit of navigation when the weather opposed work in the lighters. Whether Campbell attempted to discover a method of improving the navigation of the Thames when conditions made employment on it impossible is not recorded. The Committee of 1778 apparently recognised the difficulty as it made no comment on this defect in the system. Its effect upon the morals of the small boys on board did not pass altogether unnoticed. Campbell himself thought it would be well to separate them from the older criminals, but there is no record of any such measures being adopted.

Another fault found by Howard was a lack of uniformity, and a dirtiness, in the clothing worn by the convicts. Some, he reported, had no shoes, some no shirts. Campbell by his contract was responsible for the clothing of the prisoners but he told the Committee of 1778 that he allowed them to wear their own if they chose to do it. Otherwise he supplied them with a kersey jacket, worsted stockings, a shirt, cap, and shoes. Erskine estimated that Campbell supplied two-thirds of the clothing worn. The overseer also asserted that he compelled the men "to shift every Sunday", evidence which had the support of both Ecken and Powney. Whether Campbell was guilty of a breach of contract in not providing all the clothing is open to question. The contracts did not prohibit the wearing of one's own clothes and there is no hint that Campbell encouraged the convicts to wear them. The Committee evidently accepted the overseer's interpretation of the agreements as it recommended no alteration in the method adopted.

Religious considerations weighed heavily with Howard. He noted the absence of a chaplain on the hulks and the entrusting of religious instruction to the occasional voluntary visits of one of Lady

Huntingdon's ministers. Campbell's defence was that prayers were read twice a week and oftener but as the Committee's report will reveal this was not considered satisfactory.

All this evidence and much more the Committee duly considered. On 15 April 1778 it issued its report,[252] which contained the following facts:

> One quarter of the convicts had died on the hulks, the greatest mortality being among country prisoners confined on board the *Censor* which was the more roomy vessel.
>
> Neither Act, nor contracts, made any provision for the attendance of a clergyman to officiate during prayers and at burials.
>
> No provision was made in the Act for the sitting of a coroner on the bodies of the dead.
>
> A hospital on a separate ship seemed desirable.
>
> The contracts provided for only 380 convicts while the yearly average of those sentenced to transportation had been 960, including 720 males.
>
> The Overseer had entered into three contracts, one for 120 convicts at the rate of 38 pounds a head,[253] the other two each for 130 convicts at £26 15s 10¾d a head.
>
> The value of the labour on Woolwich Warren amounted to £3350, that of the ballast raised to £2703 12s 6d.

The Committee therefore resolved:

(1) "From the beginning of the hulks there had been a progressive improvement in the accommodation, food, employment and means of preserving the health of the convicts sentenced to hard labour on the River Thames, and that the said hulks are at present convenient, airy and healthy.

(2) "That it will be proper by a new Bill to continue the present mode of punishing convicts on board the hulks by hard labour for a certain time".

This was, in reality, a complete exoneration from blame of a government nominee, by a committee whose appointment was inspired by humanitarian motives, and yet, if we can trust contemporary accounts, the hulks inspired a greater fear at the time than did the gaols.

The reason is not hard to discover. One of the most astounding features of 18th Century gaols was their lack of isolation and their freedom from discipline. Debtors often entered prison accompanied by their wives and children. Howard deplored the overcrowding which resulted from the admitting of "lewd women under the name of wives". The insufficiency of the food provided by so many gaols encouraged the admittance of relatives or friends. The granting to gaolers of licences to sell alcoholic drinks and the freedom which allowed outsiders to enter and buy, disposed of much of the monotony usually associated with prison life. Among the forms of amusement found in them by Howard were Mississippi and Porto Bello tables, billiards, fives, and tennis. On occasion the inmates were "universally drunk". Colquhoun believed that a majority of the serious crimes committed in the metropolis were planned in gaols.

How gloomy must life in the hulks have seemed when compared with that spent in such institutions. Visitors were not entirely excluded from the *Justitia* and *Censor*; the friends of the sick were allowed to bring them greens, milk, and dainties. For a time also others conveyed on board provisions of different kinds but this privilege was soon stopped because it offered to the evilly disposed, opportunities for providing the convicts with saws and other means of escape. In an impassioned speech uttered in the House of Commons shortly after the inquiry of 1778 a member, named Gascoyne, declared that people went in thousands to the hulks and gave the convicts money, "particularly ladies of the town who, as they get their money easy, were generous".[254] But Gascoyne's words were obviously partisan and must therefore be treated with caution. By some exaggeration the friends of the sick might possibly have been measured in thousands. None of the evidence laid before the Committee gives a hint that considerable numbers visited the hulks,[255] and a little consideration of the system and the conditions on board the hulks will dispose of the belief. Disciplined labour, when the weather permitted, was the punishment prescribed by the law and the contracts, and Bentham tells that visitors were not allowed to converse with the convicts without the overseer's order when such work was in progress.

Nor would it be reasonable to suppose that when the weather was unfit others would be drawn by inclination to board the hulks, for on arrival, little would be found to please them. No "tap" appeared among the equipment of the hulks; alcoholic drinks, save the small beer doled out four days a week, were prohibited. To many of the associates of the prisoners an atmosphere in which the uttering of an oath produced a beating by a rattan could hardly have been congenial. The fact that the convicts were put down at 7 p.m. each night would in any case have limited the hours of visitation and in spite of Gascoyne's words, reason suggests that the so-called "ladies of the town" would have preferred their regular haunts to quarters in which they came under the unobstructed gaze of prison officials. The prohibition of Sunday labour may have offered to the friends of the convicted an opportunity to visit them but even if we assume that this was the case we are still forced to conclude that life on the hulks, when compared with that within the gaols, was a form of punishment in which isolation was a noticeable feature.[256]

In another important respect the hulks differed from the gaols of the period. Within the latter the possession of wealth could make life less disagreeable than it might otherwise have been. Gaolers were ever ready to provide superior meals and quarters to those who were willing to pay for them, but the construction and the discipline of the hulks forbade such favouritism. Within them, all lived and slept on decks open to all. Dignam's experience demonstrates this. He had hired a boat at a guinea a week for his black servant to bring him meals. The first day he was on board he ordered a dinner from Woolwich. When it arrived the overseer directed the servant to take it back and give it to the first poor man he met.[257] Causes of this kind and rumours of excessive toil rather than actual cruelty explain the unpopularity of the hulks among those whom the law classed as criminals, and drew from them on occasion the statement that they would rather be hanged than go on board the hulks. The Committee viewed the system in a different light; to it prohibition, discipline, and labour were valuable agents in reforming the fallen, a belief which the convicts' detestation of the hulks possibly confirmed. It is not surprising therefore that the Committee recommended a continuation of the system.

Parliament accepted the resolution of the Committee; a new measure continued punishment by hard labour until 1 June 1779,[258] thus reaffirming the temporary character of the system. On 1 August 1778 the Government concluded a fourth contract with Duncan Campbell.[259] Its provisions were the same as those of the third, and in common with the first three it was to expire on 12 July 1779. The number of hulks was not, however, increased as Campbell substituted for the *Justitia* another larger vessel bearing the same name. The new hulk, described as "a roomy old East India ship",[260] was probably larger than the *Censor* as the returns show that the overseer maintained 260 convicts on her while the *Censor* provided for 250 only. This is confirmed also by the evidence of Dr William Smith who later declared that he thought the *Justitia* "very well calculated" but the *Censor* too small.[261]

Labour on Barking and Woolwich shoals and in the vicinity of the new Butt continued during the year that followed the inquiry. The official returns show that 35,410 tons of ballast was raised over a period of ten months,[262] but the condition and the behaviour of the convicts were such as to bring discredit upon the system generally. The return for the months May and July stated that 20 had escaped while one had been shot.[263] The *Gentleman's Magazine* ascribed the escapes to a mutiny of 36 convicts on 7 June which caused a "terrible battle", in which one was killed and 19 or 20 gained their freedom. In October a like insurrection caused the deaths of two and the wounding of 13 prisoners.[264] According to the same magazine this rising had been organised by 150 convicts but the officers, being forewarned, had "put

48

the only place where they could escape into a state of defence".[265]
Thus, with the casualties mentioned, the convicts had been forced to submit.

Sickness and death continued their ravages in the hulks. The maximum was reached in January 1779 when in a little more than a month, 28 died and 37 were reported to be sick. Speaking in March 1779 Campbell declared that 132 had died in the course of a year. The mortality was not equally distributed between the two ships. In December the overseer reported the appearance of gaol fever in the *Censor* and the adoption of every means to check its progress, but that report told of the death of 25 convicts. In the following month the mortality, as already stated, was higher. In February 1779 ten more had died in addition to two who had been drowned; 31 were still on the sick list, but "the malignancy of the late disorder was much abated". Nevertheless the following report (February-April 1779) shows the removal of 21 by death and a sick list of 20. Another inquiry into the system was certainly needed.

The state of the gaols meantime provided grounds for an inquiry of the kind. In July 1778 the Mayor of London had written to Campbell describing the crowded state of Newgate and the impossibility of accepting from other gaols prisoners who were supposed to take their trials at the next sessions of the Old Bailey.[266] As the gaols generally seemed to be in a similar condition the House of Commons, on 16 December 1778, ordered returns of felons confined within the gaols of London, Middlesex, and the counties of the Home Circuit, and appointed a Committee under Sir Charles Bunbury to consider and report on the same.[267] In addition to carrying out these orders the Committee conducted a second inquiry into the state of the hulks. Its finding was announced in the House on 1 April 1779.[268] Its conclusions concerning the gaols, in so far as they interest us, were that the means of employment provided by those institutions for prisoners sentenced to hard labour were "generally unprofitable if not altogether neglected" and that the whole arrangement of the prisons was ill suited to the economy of the State and the morality and health of the prisoners.

The information elicited concerning the hulks differed little from that obtained in the preceding year. One hundred had been pardoned since the inception of the system. Ninety of the 132 who had died had been infected by putrid fevers which in the majority of cases could be traced to gaols; sometimes, apparently, ill health had arisen within the hulks themselves since eight or ten had died from no other known cause than lowness of spirits.[269] Three paid surgeons attended the convicts; the coroner was sent for immediately a death occurred. A

Methodist minister attended occasionally to the needs of the prisoners; no clergyman entered the hulks. The convicts were provided with "religious books and were allowed to read them by candlelight". Since the insurrection the bread allowance had been increased to 6 pounds a week per man. Sometimes, as an indulgence, they were allowed salt provisions on Sundays. Thirteen or 14 were very little boys not fit to wheel a barrow; 27 of the total were under 17 years of age. Thirty-one were infirm and unfit for hard labour; several were without the use of an arm or a leg.[270] A member of the House, Sir Robert Mackworth, who had visited the ships described some of the inmates as lame and very decrepit and therefore "very improper objects".

The finding of the Committee was:

That the Act which was a temporary expedient intended only for the most daring and dangerous offenders had been extended to several criminals whose youth, infirmity, and crimes might have been more properly subjected to some other mode of punishment.

That the mortality might be attributed in some cases to the very disordered constitutions of the convicts due to former profligacy. In other cases it might have been occasioned by extreme dejection of spirits, but it had chiefly arisen from epidemical diseases "especially to be expected in vessels instituted to collect the refuse of the several gaols of the kingdom".

That the mortality had been increased by overcrowding, effluvia from the sick, the contiguity of the beds and by a want of cleanliness[271] which was extremely difficult to be enforced and perhaps too by some circumstances in the food.[272]

That the labour done appeared to be of solid value to the public and might be estimated at rather more than one-third of the annual expense.

That the execution of the Act appeared to have received continued improvement from the first institution and that further beneficial alterations might be made in it if it were prolonged.

That it seemed expedient to have a hospital apart from the hulks and also a separate vessel to lodge felons on their first arrival in order to prevent their introducing the gaol distemper from the different prisons.

That a large piece of ground should be enclosed for a garden to supply vegetables and to provide labour for those unfitted for more severe work and a place of recreation for the convalescent and the well behaved.

That a clergyman should attend to perform divine service and bury the dead.

That provision should be made for the inspection of the hulks by some official or magistrate who might also examine other places of confinement.

That as the separation of the ill disposed conduces to reformation and health and as it is expedient to avoid expense by distant removals it seemed advisable to authorise the employment of convicts on other navigable rivers and also in the repairing of seaports, embankments, and in other public works, or in garrisons.

That two or more magistrates should have authority with the approbation of the prosecutor to release any youth under 15 years of age, accused of misdemeanour or petty larceny, on condition of service in the land forces of the East or West Indies, or in the Navy, for a term of three years or upwards.

That to prevent those discharged from returning to their evil habits through want of employment it seemed expedient in addition to the provision of clothing and money allowed by the present Act to vest a power in two magistrates upon a certificate of good behaviour, certified by the superintendent, to remit one-sixth of the term of imprisonment of any convict on condition that a reputable tradesman should agree to employ the discharged person and give security for his good behaviour for one year.

These resolutions were approved by the Commons;[273] on 31 May 1779 the hulk system was continued by the Act 19 Geo. III, c.74 for the space of another year. Many of its clauses reveal the effect of the Committee's finding; thus it directed that male convicts, on arriving at the hulks, were to be washed, deprived of their clothes which were to be burnt if necessary, and confined for at least four days in some secure place or vessel for the detection of infection. A hospital and a large piece of ground for a garden were to be provided. Within the latter, invalid offenders recommended by the Surgeon were to be employed in raising vegetables. Felons liable to hard labour might be employed not only upon the Thames, but also upon any other navigable river, port, or harbour, or on public works upon the banks of the same. As prescribed by the previous law they were to be sustained by bread, coarse meat, or other inferior food, water, and small beer. A chaplain was to read morning and evening prayers and preach a sermon every Sunday, Christmas, and Good Friday. The hulks were to be inspected once a quarter by an official to be appointed.

The persistent faith in the transport system was, however, demonstrated in the same Act, for one of its clauses provided that felons convicted of offences punishable by transportation and those pardoned on condition of the same might still be ordered to be transported to any parts beyond the seas either in America or elsewhere. The same Act also made provision for the erection of two penitentiary houses[274] for the punishment of those unfitted to labour on the Thames and like places, by solitary confinement, well regulated labour, and religious instruction.

A fifth contract was signed by Campbell on 5 November 1779. It provided for the disciplining of 510 convicts on two hulks[275] of 600 tons or thereabouts together with 24 lighters, a receiving ship of 80 tons, and a hospital ship of about 220 tons. The convicts, on arrival, were to be washed and their clothes burnt if infected. In addition to the medicine mentioned in the earlier agreements the overseer was now

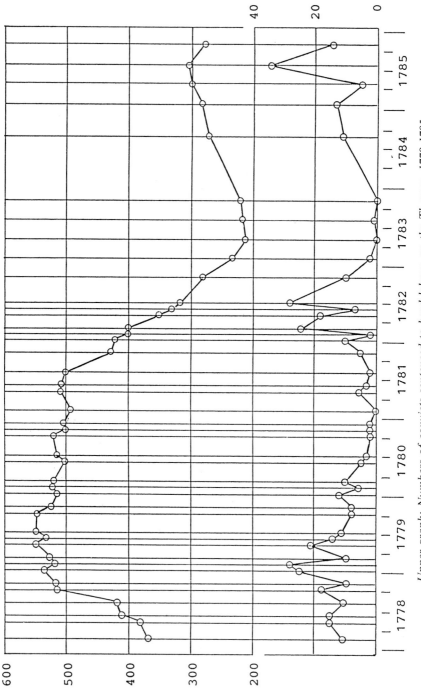

Upper graph: Numbers of convicts sentenced to hard labour on the Thames, 1778-1785.
Lower graph: Mortality among convicts sentenced to hard labour on the Thames. Note different vertical scales.

definitely required to provide surgeons to attend to those under his charge. In return for fulfilling these conditions Campbell was to receive from the Treasury £14,810 2s 6d clear of all deductions during the year in which the contract was to be effective.[276] In the following two years similar agreements were concluded, but for 460 and 440 convicts respectively,[277] after which no contract is recorded until the year 1785 although in the interval Campbell had been directed to prolong his duties and continued to forward his returns to the Treasury. The graph on p.52 demonstrates that during the years 1779 and 1780 the average number of felons maintained on the Thames exceeded 500 but that from July 1781 a rapid reduction began. The following table in part explains this:

DATE	DEATHS	PARDONS	DISCHARGES	CONDITIONAL REMISSIONS
1781 May-Jul	3	3	18	64
Aug-Oct	5	7	20	–
Dec	10	13	8	–
1782 Jan	2	0	10	–
Feb	24	18	17	1
Apr	18	2	24	1
May	7	10	15	1
Jun	29	17	14	–
Oct	11	1	38	1
1783 Jan	2	16	11	–
Apr	–	15	21	–
Jul	2	4	14	–
	113	106	210	68

These figures show that in the course of two years various causes removed 497 convicts from the hulks. The discharges can be explained by the practice of imposing sentences of three to seven years during the period 1776-9. The plan of remitting a part of a sentence as a reward for good behaviour accounts for the number of pardons recorded. Under ordinary circumstances others would have stepped into the places of these and of the dead, but the times were extraordinary. The continued hostilities in North America continued to absorb many who might otherwise have been retained in England, and in 1780 Holland declared war on Great Britain. This caused the sending of a convict force to the west coast of Africa in the following year to assist in taking the Dutch forts there.

The declaration of peace with the United States of America revived the possibility of a convict trade with North America. Even before the definite declaration, preparations for the exportation had begun. Transportation to America again became a regular sentence. On 3 January 1783 George Rose, of the Treasury, informed the Undersecretary,

Evan Nepean, that the overcrowding of Newgate and the appearance within its walls of an infectious distemper rendered the immediate removal of the inmates "without waiting to settle the terms of transporting them to America" highly important.[278] He had therefore accepted the terms offered by Duncan Campbell to retain those who were about to be transported. They were, the use of the *Censor* as a temporary place of confinement at a cost of 150 pounds a month to be paid for the ship and staff, one shilling a day per convict for maintenance, and ten shillings per convict for clothing. He also declared that their lordships had learned that it was absolutely necessary that Campbell should enter into a contract for the transporting of convicts before their delivery to himself and they had consequently "agreed to adopt some method of sending them to their destination in order to bear him harmless for not performing the conditions of his contract so entered into". The agreement was acted upon; a little more than three months later Campbell presented an account for furnishing a vessel for the temporary reception of convicts ordered to be transported to America amounting to £886 6s 0d.[279]

The *Censor* was engaged to retain 250 transportable felons. The number, in reality, varied considerably owing to deaths and the delivery of large numbers for transportation. Thus on 12 August 1783 Campbell was directed to deliver to George Moore 56 convicts for removal to North America.[280] On 24 August 1783 Lord North renewed the agreement with Campbell[281] which suggests that the former contract had expired owing to the removal of some or all the convicts. On 23 January 1784 Lord Sydney repeated this action;[282] thus the *Censor* was maintained as a depot for the temporary retention of convicts about to be transported who, at this early date, were clearly distinguished from those on the *Justitia* by the fact that they performed no labour.

The Americans refused to accept British convicts; consequently other places had to be sought. Prior to such attempts the law had been amended to enable the removal of offenders to those places. The more general sentence of transportation beyond the seas was in common use in 1785.[283] The authorities, therefore, had good reasons for retaining the *Censor* for the use already described as by that means a supply of convicts would be at hand when the desired site was discovered and in the meantime the pressure on the gaols was reduced. The respective figures for the two vessels during the years 1785 and 1786 are shown on the next page.

A difficulty in discovering a suitable site for a convict settlement soon produced an accumulation of transportable felons which could not be accommodated in the *Censor*. The surplus was therefore trans-

DATES	NUMBERS		DEATHS		PARDONS		DISCHARGES	
	J.	C.	J.	C.	J.	C.	J.	C.
1785 Jan-Apr	300	261	5	17	3	0	31	0
Jul	306	262	34	14	9	0	29	0
Oct	278	258	14	6	2	0	9	0
1786 Jan	264	253	12	7	2	1	1	0
Apr	293	259	11	12	2	2	23	0
Jul	280	255	8	6	3	2	18	0
Oct	292	255	1	5	2	0	26	0

ferred to the *Justitia*, which from that decision contained both classes of convicts, viz. those sentenced to hard labour and those awaiting transportation. The Government's desire to transport, rather than retain, convicted felons is demonstrated by a relative increase in the number of the latter. The October-January return of the *Justitia* shows that more than 220 of the 264 on that vessel were confined for short periods of hard labour; a year later the number had fallen to 146.[284] The same desire to be rid of felons is indicated by the disinclination to pardon those on board the *Censor* illustrated by the figures shown.

Long before this, however, the idleness of these convicts had impressed itself upon the Government. The Act 24 Geo. III, c.12, passed in the year 1783, after citing the difficulty of transporting criminals, provided that male transportable felons might be removed from gaols to appointed places on land or navigable rivers within England or Wales by a written order of His Majesty, notified by a Principal Secretary of State, or by an order of three Justices of the county. They were to be clothed, fed, and disciplined, and where the same could be safely done, permitted to labour. To encourage such voluntary work they were to be paid one half of their earnings. The Court of the King's Bench was by the same measure authorised to change the destinations of those already sentenced; time spent in places of detention was to be deducted from the period of transportation.

Almost immediately Campbell exposed the impracticability of the measure by asking for definite instructions on how to effect it.[285] The results were a speedy repeal of this benevolent measure and the passing of another Act, 24 Geo. III, 2nd session, c.56, which gave to overseers the power to keep such convicts at hard labour. The change had not been effected without comment; the reluctance of the Commons caused the Solicitor General, on 11 March 1784, to offer a detailed explanation of the reasons that necessitated the change. In this he argued that he could not conceive it improper to make convicts work for their subsistence.[286] The immediate effect of the new measure was to make those convicts already on the *Censor* liable to hard labour.

On 20 November 1784 Campbell was appointed overseer of labour on the *Censor* hulk with orders to employ her convicts on the River Thames in the same manner as he employed those on board the *Justitia* .[287] As the working costs of compelling convicts to labour were higher than those of keeping them in idleness a new agreement was concluded guaranteeing a quarterly payment to the overseer of £1625 in return for the maintenance and employment of 240 convicts.[288] About the same time he was also allotted a quarterly payment of £1818 3s 6d for his services in controlling 250 felons on the *Justitia*,[289] the relatively greater expense being due in part to the cost of the receiving and hospital ships being attached to the *Justitia*. Thus by the beginning of the year 1785 provision had been made for punishing 490 convicts by hard labour on the River Thames at a minimum annual cost of £13,772 14s 0d. A reference to the table on page 55 shows that the number actually employed was normally in excess of that total.

The *Censor* convicts resented their compulsory labour; the January-April 1785 return declared that the men had unanimously refused to work, "pleading the hardship of being put to labour here" and of transportation to follow. Their resistance was temporary; good order was restored by the "exertion" of the officers without bloodshed and the felons returned peaceably to duty. The overseer's reports suggest, however, that they worked less strenuously than those condemned to labour only. They read, "The convicts in the above return which have been ordered on board the *Censor* hulk are by His Majesty's commands under the same regulations as those ordered to hard labour on the Thames and have been occasionally employed in the same works".[290]

The health of the convicts received more attention in the years that followed the Act 19 Geo. III, c.74. The presence of the receiving and hospital ships provided the means to separate the infected from the healthy. This separation possibly explains the decline in the death rate during the years 1780 and 1781 shown by the graph on page 52 but the extraordinary increase during the following years tends to discount the theory. Both ships were in existence in 1785 when as many as 48 died during the brief period April to July.[291] The irregularity of the curve however suggests that the mortality was not a result of seasonal changes, nor of inattention on the part of the keepers, but that it was due to infection irregularly introduced into the vessel. Whether the officers and crews were attacked by disease is not recorded but as early as March 1777 Campbell complained that the fear inspired by distempers made it difficult to maintain the complement of officers and men on any terms.[292] There is no hint that either Campbell or Erskine was affected. One means of preserving health, provided by the Act 19 Geo. III, c.74, was the creation of a garden. There is no proof that one was established at the time although there is evidence that Campbell questioned the Treasury concerning the formation of a garden.[293] The Bentham papers show that one was in existence at a later date.[294]

After the passing of that same Act the spiritual and moral welfare of the convicts received regular attention. Within a few weeks of its passage Campbell enquired of the Treasury whether he would secure a chaplain "on the best terms" or have one appointed for him by the authorities.[295] What method was adopted is not explained, but receipts for the years 1784 and 1786 show that the Rev. Charles Lorimer was then chaplain and that his salary was at the rate of 100 pounds per annum.[296] One practical means of reform apparently was not applied in the hulks. Within them were several boys of 13 and 14 years of age who were supposed to be undergoing punishment by hard labour on the Thames. Campbell in his evidence before the Committee of 1778 had stated that he thought means might be adopted to prevent them from speaking with the older criminals but the difficulty of such prevention must have impressed him at the time. He was not responsible for their presence; the courts were to blame for that. The Act 19 Geo. III, c.74 had ordered the overseers of Houses of Correction to lodge convicted felons in separate cells during the night time but the construction of the hulks made any such action impossible. Morally the results were disastrous and for this reason the system was roundly condemned by a Committee of the House of Commons in 1785.

The appointment of this Committee was not inspired by the state of the hulks but by a rumour that the Government intended to ship off a large number of convicts to Lemaine, an island in the River Gambia.[297] The rumour was well founded for the Government had for some time been arranging such a transportation. Owing to delays the chance of despatching them in time to arrive during the dry season had been missed. It had therefore turned to Campbell to provide means for maintaining the convicts until a more favourable season returned. He supplied another hulk, the *Ceres*,[298] a ship of about 700 tons, at a cost of 175 pounds a month for the first three months, which sum was then to be reduced to 150 pounds, together with one shilling a day per man for maintenance and ten shillings a head for clothing. Only ten days before the introduction of the rumour into the Commons by Lord Beauchamp the *Ceres* had been declared ready to receive her convicts.

The Committee was entrusted with the task of inquiring into both the hulk and the transportation systems. One result which will be explained later was the rejection of the Lemaine project, another was the issue of a report, which declared:[299]

It appeared to the Committee that the extraordinary fulness of the gaols made separation of the prisoners impracticable and that by constant intercourse the prisoners corrupted and confirmed each other in every practice of villainy; that the hulks, however necessary as a temporary expedient, had singularly contributed to these mischievous effects; that they formed distinct societies for the more complete instruction of all newcomers who after the expiration of their sentences returned into the mass of the community not reformed in their principles but confirmed in every vicious habit; that when they regained their liberty no parish would receive them and no person set them to work; that being shunned by their former acquaintances and baffled in every attempt to gain their bread the danger of starving almost irresistibly led them to a renewal of their former crimes.

As a means towards moral reform the hulks were discredited after that report. No blame for the failure of the experiment seems to have been attached to Campbell; the system, not the overseer, was at fault.

The possibility of convicts' experiencing a difficulty in gaining a livelihood after dismissal from the hulks had been foreseen some years before and steps taken to make their return into industry less difficult. The Acts 16 Geo. III, c.43 and 19 Geo. III, c.74 had each provided for the issue of decent clothing to the convicts at the time of their liberation. By the former Act each was also to be allowed a sum of money which varied from 20 shillings to 5 pounds at the discretion of the overseer, who was to determine the amount according to the convict's behaviour. The latter Act reduced the maximum to 3 pounds but also guaranteed to those who "engaged in proper employment" for one year after their liberation an additional sum "equal to that paid to them at the time of their demission".

The members of the Committee of 1785 were not the only Englishmen of the time who were convinced of the failure of the hulk system. In the month in which its report appeared the Lord Mayor of London wrote to the Secretary of State urging the absolute necessity of a return to the transport system, "the continuation of which for the last ten years would have greatly diminished the number of thieves and those of the worst sort in the City". Labour on the Thames in his opinion only produced "a torrent of those wretches, more hardened than ever" which obviously accounted for the alarming increase of crime. The Government was probably in fervent agreement with the Lord Mayor in his advocacy of transportation. Its immediate difficulty was to find a site to take the place of Lemaine which the inquiry, while still unfinished, had proved to be a very unpopular area for settlement. Soon it was actively engaged in an attempt to ship convicts to South Africa.[300] Meantime it was acutely conscious of the overcrowding of the gaols; thus in spite of the recorded condemnation of the hulks their number was increased.

The first of these, the *Dunkirk*, was the result of circumstances entirely accidental. Early in the year 1784 the ship *Mercury* , employed by

George Moore in an attempt to land convicts in America, was seized by the criminals on board. The mutineers attempted to land in Torbay;[301] they were only partially successful as some 70 to 80 were seized and lodged in Exeter gaol. This extraordinary accession of criminals produced a most emphatic appeal for relief which was answered by transferring the criminals to a former guardship, the *Dunkirk*, lying in Plymouth harbour. The number was soon after increased to 100. There they remained in charge of Mr William Cowdry and certain turnkeys, assisted by a guard selected from one of the Plymouth regiments.[302]

Cowdry's correspondence suggests that he was not devoid of human sympathy. He persuaded the Secretary, Lord Sydney, to provide his charges with fresh clothing because that in which they appeared was insufficient "to defend them against the approaching winter" and "was so infested with vermin that it must be thrown away".[303] He stressed the importance of having a surgeon on board every day,[304] and his use of tar oil as a disinfectant, instead of vinegar, may also be regarded as another example of his personal interest in his convicts. His efforts seem to have been successful as in March 1786 he reported that the men were very healthy and he believed could be easily managed from that date "if they were used properly", although the dangers and fatigues he had gone through were inconceivable. Unfortunately for Cowdry he lacked financial resources; consequently the Government overlooked him when it entered into a contract to convert the *Dunkirk* into a regular hulk. That agreement was concluded with Henry Bradley, "of the city of London, Merchant", on 10 March 1786.[305] Bradley thus became the overseer of the *Dunkirk*, which continued to receive convicts for some years.

Meantime the complaint of the Lord Mayor of London was reinforced by others from the counties. The Justices of the Shrewsbury Sessions described to Lord Sydney the great number of convicts in their county gaol, 31 in all, some of whom had been sentenced two years before.[306] The Grand Jury of Leicester urged speedy relief from overcrowding to prevent fatal consequences. The request was accompanied by a petition from the imprisoned themselves who stated that they had been compelled to exist for nearly three years on two-pence worth of bread a day. Some of them were bare-footed, others bare-legged; some had "never a shirt to their backs"; the whole of them were almost eaten alive by vermin. They implored the Government to transport them.[307] The report of the Committee of 1785, issued on almost the same date, did not minimise the difficulty. The following month the Admiralty was ordered to provide for an exploration of the coastal area of South Africa in the neighbourhood of the River or Bay of Das Voltas "in order to fix upon a proper site for a settlement".[308]

About the same time new measures were adopted to produce a more immediate relief. Defence works at Portsmouth and Plymouth provided a temporary solution.

On 14 September 1785 Duncan Campbell was instructed by Lord Sydney to visit Portsmouth to report on the possibilities of the ship *Firm* as a hulk and of employing convicts on works about Cumberland Fort. Six days later he informed Nepean that the *Fortunee* was to be preferred to the *Firm* as the latter would only with difficulty be got over the bar into Langston Harbour. As for the proposed work, he believed the convicts would be competent to perform it.[309] In November the Treasury was therefore directed to contract, or otherwise provide, for the superintendence and security of 300 convicts to be employed at Portsmouth and of an additional 200 at Plymouth. With the directions went a statement describing the urgent need of a speedy removal of the convicts and promising an immediate despatch of those destined to remain on the *Fortunee* as soon as that vessel was ready to receive them.[310]

In actual fact the convicts were not allowed to remain in Newgate until that ship was ready to receive them; on 8 December 1785 two hundred were conveyed in waggons from that prison to Portsmouth and placed on board the *Firm*.[311] Early in February the number was increased by another hundred carried from the same prison in the same way.[312] There they remained until 20 February 1786, when they were removed to the *Fortunee* moored in Langston Harbour[313] under the charge of Duncan Campbell, who received the contract for that vessel. In accordance with Bradley's contract also the numbers on the *Dunkirk* were increased to 200, the additional hundred being obtained from the neighbouring parts of England and Wales.

The agreements which established the *Dunkirk* and the *Fortunee* differed in certain ways from those which set up the earlier hulks. The Government supplied each of these later hulks and promised to provide all necessary boats in addition to paying the overseer 125 pounds a month to employ a ship's company of 1 master, 3 mates, 1 boatswain, 1 carpenter, 1 clerk and steward, 1 cooper, 2 quartermasters, and 23 able bodied seamen "at the least". Bradley, in addition, was to receive one shilling a day for every convict maintained, Campbell only eleven pence.[314] Each contract was to continue for a year from the date of the mooring of the hulk and for ever thereafter, until terminated by a three months' notice from either party. The convicts on both were of the *Censor* or *Ceres* type; they were there to labour while they awaited transportation.

The *Dunkirk* was distinguished from all the other hulks by containing a number of women convicts. Their introduction was probably accidental, certainly not due to any desire to employ them at hard labour as the men were employed. Women, as well as men, sailed to America in convict ships. The *Mercury* had carried convicts of both sexes and it is possible that the convict women on board the *Dunkirk* were some, or all, of those who had set forth in the *Mercury*. A clothing account of 1 December 1784 shows that Cowdry supplied apparel to nine women convicts.[315] Later when the Government adopted the plan of transporting convicts to New South Wales the *Dunkirk* became a regular depot for some of the women who proceeded with Governor Phillip. There is no evidence that their presence produced any immorality; the two sexes apparently lived apart, which would have been impossible on the *Justitia* or *Censor* .

The *Dunkirk*, from the assumption of Bradley's command, remained a healthy ship. During the period March–December 1786 only six deaths are recorded out of an average of 212 convicts. The *Censor* for the corresponding period lost 23 out of an average of 256. Campbell's experience on the *Fortunee* was less happy. Before the signing of the contract and while the felons were still on the *Firm*, gaol fever attacked his convicts. That many of them should have been sick is not surprising. Captain Hill, whom Campbell placed in charge, complained that they were almost naked, that the ports could not be opened, that the men had nothing to lie on save the decks and could not be kept dry because of defects in them and a lack of tarpaulins.[316] The record of the mortality is lost; possibly not many died, as the February–May 1786 report shows 294 aboard. The interest in the episode lies in its effect on outsiders. Over 100 patients were admitted into Haslar hospital, suffering from gaol fever supposed to have been caught from persons on the *Firm*, and eight of them died. After transference to the *Fortunee* these convicts remained unhealthy; 27 deaths are recorded during nine months of the succeeding year. In justice to Campbell it is only fair to point out that the *Fortunee* was always a crowded ship, her convicts during that period averaging 317. Infection once introduced into a vessel was not easily removed. Thus Campbell was in this case a victim of circumstances.

Mutinies marred the later history of the hulks. In his February–May 1786 report Campbell stated that Captain Hill had been compelled to have recourse to firearms because of an attempt to seize his ship. Two convicts had been killed and nine wounded, of whom one had died.[317] During the period April–July those on the *Censor* also rebelled, necessitating the shooting of three of the mutineers.[318] In describing the incident the *Gentleman's Magazine* told how Captain Erskine remonstrated in vain with the convicts but was forced to fire upon them because they seized and "instantly hung up" one of their own number who had shown signs of deserting them. The Coroner's verdict in the case of the three men shot on the *Censor* was "justifiable homicide"[319] and it is probable that the same decision was arrived at in respect of the *Fortunee's* offenders.

The type of work performed on the *Dunkirk* and *Fortunee* can be illustrated by a reference to the returns of the latter vessel during the period November-February 1786. Then they were employed by the Master General of Ordnance in digging moats, raising glacis, and constructing other works under the direction of the engineers appointed to superintend the fortifications at Cumberland Fort.[320]

The five hulks already described failed to solve the gaol problem in spite of the fact that the numbers on board them normally exceeded those required by the various contracts, as the following figures prove:

HULK	REPORT FOR 1786	NUMBER ON BOARD	CONTRACT NUMBER
Justitia	July–October	292	250
Censor	July–October	255	240
Ceres	July–October	311	250
Fortunee	August–November	336	300
Dunkirk	June–September	214	200
		1408	1240

The gaols continued to be overcrowded. Two other hulks, the *Stanislaus* and the *Leon*, were added to the number, making a total of seven; but this was subsequent to the adoption of the transportation to New South Wales, which caused the decline of the hulk system. The successful removal to the antipodes of what were described as serious offenders abolished the need for maintaining the hulks as prisons for their detention. Some of them remained as places in which less serious offenders could be employed at hard labour for some time after the conclusion of our period. The effect of the New South Wales transportation is shown in the following table:[321]

NUMBER OF CONVICTS ON THE HULKS

YEAR	HILARY	EASTER	TRINITY	MICHAELMAS
1790	2053	2098	2151	2069
1791	2083	944	900	916

The stoppage of the American transportation had called the hulks into existence; the discovery of a satisfactory substitute caused their usefulness to decline. The great reduction in numbers after the Hilary term of 1791 was a result of the discharge of three of their number, the *Justitia*, *Ceres*, and *Dunkirk* in March of the same year; the remainder lingered for greater periods.

No criticism of the hulk system is adequate which does not take into consideration its origin and purpose and which fails to pay regard to contemporary thought and events. For example the shooting of prisoners was fatally common at the time. Blunderbusses were frequently used to quell gaol disturbances. According to the *Gentleman's Magazine* of September 1781 a riot in the New Prison, Clerkenwell, was suppressed by the shooting of three and the wounding of twelve others. In 1784 a disturbance occurred among the women of the Clerkenwell Bridewell. The warder fired a blunderbuss among them and killed one.[322] In that respect the gaol and the hulk systems stand equally condemned.

The labour results of the hulk system were certainly disappointing. Colonists had been able to employ convicts profitably, and when the hulk plan was suggested its advocates probably expected that a profit might be secured for the community by employing them on public works. In reality the labour performed did not repay the expenditure on the system.[323] But material profit had not been the only aim in the setting up of the first hulk. Moral benefit had assuredly been received by some who went to America, and the supporters of the hulk system hoped for similar results in England. Experience proved that the effect was otherwise. The majority of the convicts who had crossed the sea had laboured under discipline of some kind, but far from their former evil companions and often entirely separated from other convicts. Those in the hulks lived constantly in the company of similar or worse criminals, and that alone was sufficient to produce the evil result described in the Committee Report of 1785.

That same report however made plain the fact that the system had been adopted only as a temporary expedient. At no time had the Government intended that it should permanently replace transportation. The increase in the number of hulks after the year 1783 is not a proof of public support of the system of punishment they provided; rather it indicates a desire to return to transportation, which could be facilitated by the establishment of depots from which criminals could be easily removed. On 11 March 1784, during the debate that preceded the Act 24 Geo. III, c.74, the Solicitor General plainly stated that convicts, while on the hulks, were in the eye of the law in a state of transportation; they were supposed to be "on their way to America".[324] Because of this the hulks span the gap between the American and the Australian systems of transportation and as such must be considered in any treatment of the transport form of punishment.

Obviously the system was more expensive than the carriage of convicts to America. Merchants had competed to conduct that transportation at no cost to the public in the closing years of the American colonial period. The hulks necessitated a heavy regular expenditure of money paid to contractors, chaplains, coroners, juries, and to the convicts themselves for clothing and gifts at the time of their dismissal. In the third quarter of the year 1786 (i.e. when the Government decided to adopt a transportation to New South Wales) the regular quarterly expenditure on the five hulks then in existence[325] was £8015 8s 6d. Thus, regardless of incidentals, the annual rate of expenditure was £32,061 14s 0d. If we deduct one-third of this to represent the value of the work performed by the convicts we are left to conclude that the system cost the country more than £20,000 a year without removing its evil-doers or solving the gaol problem, for at that time both the hulks and the gaols were crowded.

Tradition has caused these vessels to be associated with cruelty and suffering. Tales of excessive toil and brutal inhumanity circulated by discharged prisoners and others, and magnified in transit, have cast a shadow over them which three inquiries, conducted by Committees of the House of Commons, failed to substantiate and which later research has not been able to confirm. That their prisoners laboured is true; that they wore irons is equally certain; but what the evidence shows is that they lived under a military system of discipline which provided them with regular food, clothing, open air, and medical attention and therefore made their lot in those respects pleasanter than that of law breakers confined within a majority of contemporary prisons. It was not charges of inhumanity, but the realisation that it was not a satisfactory substitute for the transport method, that caused the decline of the hulk system.

4

West African Military Experiments

B Y TRACING THE DEVELOPMENT of the hulk system throughout the decade that followed the outbreak of the Revolutionary War in America a chronological presentation of other attempts to reduce the number of convicts within British gaols has been postponed. The delay, which has been intentional, is a result of differences within the attempts themselves. The hulks, although unsatisfactory as a means of punishment or gaol relief, remained and developed throughout the whole period — the other attempts, which were tentative in nature and more or less disastrous in their results, were discarded when experience demonstrated their futility. To emphasise this contrast the strictly chronological method has been avoided.

The political setting of these African experiments has been adequately presented in other easily accessible works.[326] It will suffice for the purposes of this chapter to state that the Dutch and the English were rather precariously established in various forts along the West African coast. During the intervals of peace prior to the Revolutionary War, as factors for rival companies they had actively competed in the purchase of slaves and other commodities. In this competition each, also, had striven to preserve or enhance its reputation at the expense of the other among the coastal populations which, events will show, lacked much of that submissiveness sometimes attributed to native peoples. In time of war between their respective nations they supplemented their commercial rivalry by military and naval aggression aimed at the seizure and confiscation of the other's possessions. Peace between the two powers was broken in 1780 by the entry of the Dutch into the American Revolutionary struggle. Hostilities in West Africa were a natural corollary of the declaration of war.

Before the rupture of peace the British Government's interest in the defence of West African forts had been indirect and intermittent. Ships of war had visited the coast during the healthy season, but the naval operations of the American conflict had caused a neglect of the African coast. The confidence which these warships had inspired within the occupants of the British forts was consequently less emphatic than it might otherwise have been. Thus Richard Miles, Governor of Cape Coast Castle, wrote in the year 1779, "I do assure you the non-appearance of any of H.M. ships in this quarter for near these two years past hurts the English very much in the eyes of the natives".[327]

The Government was financially interested in the forts. For some years parliament had voted annual sums of money to the Company of Merchants trading with Africa, or to its Committee, to assist in their maintenance. This practice had almost developed into an annual parliamentary contribution of 13,000 pounds towards West African defence.[328] In 1778 the Company, moved probably by impending danger, proposed a more ambitious protection for the coast generally, necessitating an annual expenditure of 55,932 pounds on the following establishment:[329]

FORTS	EUROPEAN TROOPS	GUNS
George	58	40
James	72	50
Appolonia	21	20
Dixcove	29	30
Succondee	33	40
Commenda	40	40
Cape Coast Castle	118	100
Annamaboe	40	40
Tantumquerry	28	30
Winnebah	29	30
Accra	31	50
Prampram	15	16
Wydah	40	50

Not all these forts were on the Gold Coast, which is the principal centre of interest in this study; the first two were situated respectively on the Senegal and Gambia Rivers but all the remainder were described as being under the Governor and Council of Cape Coast Castle. The presence of a healthy, properly equipped force of this magnitude would have destroyed all European opposition there. Subsequent paragraphs, however, will demonstrate that the British forces on the coast fell lamentably short of this ideal.[330] The explanatory statement attached to the proposal emphasised the difficulty of even preserving the lives of British soldiers in the area and therefore recommended the employment of "black soldiers", chosen from distant parts, whose tribal and language differences would prevent them from associating with the local natives. As a result the Company would acquire "a certain and infallible method" of keeping the garrison well manned "which the mortality among Europeans made uncertain".

Few Englishmen had in fact been sent to act as soldiers on the coast for some time. Their comparatively small numbers and their acclimatisation probably explain a statement made by Governor Miles in 1779 that only two Europeans had died within the last two years. This was not their normal condition, for a report two years later told that almost every officer in the castle was "laid up with some complaint or other". The interest in the 1779 statement lies in its preceding the organisation of the convict force that sailed to the Gold Coast. It therefore provided an answer which might easily have been directed against any who charged the Government with inhumanity in sending criminals to certain death.

The low rate of mortality of the years 1778 and 1779 failed to produce real confidence on the coast. In the former year the Governor and Council of Cape Coast Castle described their "deplorable" condition. The Castle itself, having only 45 effective men, could not reinforce the outer forts, yet Annamaboe, a fortification "of the most consequence to the nation", had a garrison of ten mulatto soldiers, and almost every fort on the coast was "equally short".[331] The account ended with the remark that if the Government regarded the settlements as objects of consideration it was time they were placed upon a different footing. The advice bore little, if any, fruit for two years later the Governor and Council were unable to avoid a public exhibition of their impotence. The natives of Annishan, "a set of banditti and thievish people", seized a boat belonging to Captain Kendall and put a company slave into irons on the pretence that they were owed some money. To pacify the natives they were compelled to pay them the equivalent of 31 pounds.[332]

In addition to military weakness a serious shortage of labour troubled the Company's servants. In the Castle there were only 16 canoe men, and in all the other ten forts only five; yet it was estimated that 160 were needed. [333] Canoe men were indispensable for without their aid communication with the outside world was uncertain. The fear of possible isolation had even caused the Company's officials to include in their means of defence a system of bribery which purchased peace from chiefs who otherwise might have been dangerous. Governor Miles reported that the English paid ground rents for their forts and annual stipends to the principal natives. In 1781 instructions to reduce expenditure provoked the following pathetic reply from the Castle: "Owing to the weakness of the Company's position it is necessary to keep black men of power in our pay that we may live at peace with the natives who would otherwise molest us, knowing we have not sufficient power to protect ourselves".[334] Thus apart entirely from any fear of European menace the British forts were in need of reinforcement both by troops and by labourers when the peace with Holland came to an end in 1780.

The 12 Dutch forts, studded along the same sea board, lay cheek by jowl with those of the English. Elmina, their chief post, was separated from Cape Coast Castle by a distance of about five miles; on other parts of the coast the competing establishments were within range of each other's guns.[335] The balance between the rivals was as a rule finely adjusted; the appearance of a reinforcement might easily produce a speedy capitulation of a number of the enemy's less important forts. The past had demonstrated that sea power was a determining factor in any struggle between the opponents. Unfortunately for the resident British the American operations had withdrawn all British warships from the coast.

The transportation of convicts to West Africa had been suggested while they were still being conveyed to North America in 1769, and the proposal had received the support of George III himself. In May of that year the Recorder of London (James Eyre) informed the Earl of Rochford that as the King had been pleased to pardon a convict on condition that he served in Africa it had occurred to him that many others might be disposed of in the same manner "with advantage to the public instead of being transported in the usual way".[336] He therefore forwarded the names of 18 convicts who, in his opinion, might be used as soldiers in the same area. To encourage the convicts to accept the proposed condition he recommended a reduction in their periods of servitude to five years. Rochford, in acting upon the suggestion, informed the Secretary at War that the King, considering the extreme unhealthiness of the climate on the coast, desired that troops which necessity required to be stationed there should be such men "as must look upon that duty as a mitigation of their sentences" rather than well deserving volunteers.[337]

The proposal provoked a speedy protest from Mr R. Browne, the agent of the Senegal Settlement. He denied the justice of compelling faithful officers to work with criminals and pointed out that as the whole garrison consisted of 60 men the non-criminal element would be forced to keep watch on the convict section. Should the step be taken he would be pleased to be able to insure his property at 75 percent. In any case the season was not the right one for the sending of troops, "wherefore it may be alleged that these villains are the best sacrifices for death". He suspected, however, that some would survive and what they would do to the merchandise there, "scarce ever less than £30,000 worth", he left to the imagination of the Secretary at War.[338] In truth he had little to fear as a medical examination of the 18 showed that four had distempers, eight were "undersized and limbed", only six were fit for service.[339] Possibly they sailed in H.M. Sloop *Weazel*, which at the time was preparing to sail to Senegal.

A second proposal to employ convicts in West Africa was made by Matthias McNamara, Lieutenant Governor Commanding Senegambia, in the year 1776.[340] His five years' experience, he declared, had convinced him that no place was more suited for convicts than the River Gambia. He recommended Vintan, situated about two leagues up the creek bearing the same name, as a site for settlement. To ensure the safety of the settlers he advised the sending of a large body of convicts. In the course of the first two or three years numbers of them would become inured to the climate and be able to build houses and cultivate the soil. A natural attachment would soon spring up between them and the natives, leading to an expansion into other parts of the country. The cost of the plan might be partly offset by the Government's becoming involved in secret trade, carried on very privately as "should our merchants trading in this province be acquainted with it they probably would report it in a very unfavourable light to the natives which might be very prejudicial to us and perhaps frustrate our intentions". Two motives probably inspired McNamara's proposal: a dislike of the Company, shown by his suggestion of secret trade, and a desire to gain favour in the eyes of the Government, whose anxiety concerning convicts was well known. He soon needed the Government's good opinion, for an inquiry into the affairs of his command, a few months later, revealed perjury, licentiousness, relaxation of discipline, and disorder in every department.[341] Thus it is not surprising that this suggestion failed to stir the Government to action.

Another serious proposal to establish convicts on the Gambia was made by John Roberts, Governor of Cape Coast Castle, in January 1779. Two aims prompted his "Observations": economy, which he believed could be effected by removing the convicts from the hulks, and the encouragement of trade by the establishment of a colony.[342] The site of his intended settlement was Yanimarew, an island about 400 miles up the River Gambia. His description of the area is strongly reminiscent of those prepared by 16th Century advocates of colonisation and recorded by Hakluyt. The local king and his leading people would easily be persuaded to grant sufficient land. In the first instance it would not be prudent to experiment with more than 150 men and 60 women "as most of them would have the seasoning sickness". Their arrival in November or December would "perhaps produce little mortality before the rain set in". The products of the country should meet every demand; they included elephants, camels, sea horses, gold, dyewoods, cotton, tobacco, sugar etc. and "vines, coffee, cocoa, and ginger would no doubt answer". When the first settlers had become seasoned they would be able to support others who could then be sent. By marriage with the natives the numbers of the colony would soon increase and a generation would arise to whom the climate would be natural. Among the articles for the undertaking of such an experiment he suggested 16 six-pounders, 12 three-pounders, 24 swivel guns, 200 muskets, and 1000 gallons of rum.

Two months later the 1779 House of Commons Committee reported its findings concerning the hulks and transportation.[343] It had considered the practicability of removing convicts to West Africa. John Roberts had been questioned; he had stated afresh the views he expressed in his "Observations"; had declared that the cost of maintaining 210 convicts for the first two years would be £7049 7s 10d and £2816 respectively and his belief that in the third year the settlement would be self-supporting.[344] Mr Thomas Perkins, who had been a thousand miles up the Gambia to buy slaves, confirmed Roberts's opinion. He estimated that sufficient land could be bought for 100 pounds, and that not above 20 out of 200 would die from the seasoning sickness. Mr Robert Stubbs after a four year residence supported the evidence already given but believed that Podore, 70 miles up the Senegal, would be a more suitable site. He admitted however that the climate would be fatal to a number of them; Dr Thomas Wallace who had spent four years on the Gambia and Senegal Rivers apprehended that not above one-sixth would die in the process of becoming seasoned.

Others were less optimistic. Richard Camplin handed in a return of the mortality on the coast during the period 1755-76; this showed that out of 746 who had been sent to the forts, 334 had died, 371 had been discharged or deserted; of many others they had no account whatever. So serious had the mortality been that the Africa Committee had sent out only seven officers during the last three years and had adopted the practice of manning its forts with mulattos and the children of European soldiers born in the country. Colonel Charles O'Hara, who had lived for some years in Senegambia, upheld the view that Podore was one of the healthiest places on the River Senegal but could hold out no hope for the security of any settlement there. The ruling chief would probably sell enough land for 100 pounds but authority was always changing hands in the area; "the Moors and Blacks in Africa considered white men as their property". His ten years' experience had shown that above one-third of the male settlers died; women hardly ever survived.[345]

After a consideration of this and other evidence the Committee made the following observations:[346]

> "That it is not in the power of the executive government, at present, to dispose of convicted felons in North America, and that every plan of transportation, hitherto suggested, appears to be attended with many difficulties.

That the sending of atrocious criminals to unhealthy places where their labour may be used and their lives hazarded, in the place of better citizens, may in some cases be advisable and in the instance of capital respites is indisputably just".

Military operations on the West African coast had begun before the entry of the Dutch into the war. In May 1779 Goree fell into the hands of the English who, however, had lost Fort St Louis on the Senegal to the French two months earlier.[347] In the following year Captain Wall, who was in charge of Goree, was ordered to attempt the recovery of Senegal but nothing was accomplished.[348] The decision of the Dutch to ally themselves with the anti-British powers in December 1780 only increased the difficulty of an already serious problem and necessitated urgent measures for the preservation of the English forts on the Gold Coast.

The extent and the duration of the military operations had already made the raising of troops a difficult task. The Government was therefore prepared to accept the offers of any officers who volunteered to undertake the duty. A week after England's declaration of war on Holland an offer to raise an independent company, made by Captain Kenneth McKenzie, was accepted with the proviso that he was to enlist men who were of a minimum height of 5ft 4in and between the ages of 18 and 40 years only.[349] His efforts were successful; on 11 April instructions were issued to place his company on the establishment as from 7 February last inclusive.[350] How his success was secured is not recorded. In his defence at a later date he declared that the operation had entailed considerable expense, which suggests that the enlistments had not been due entirely to patriotic fervour. His behaviour on the West African coast opposes the belief that they were a result of personal charm. Circumstances, however, caused him to be in charge of *two* companies when he reached the Gold Coast. The second company had been raised in a similar manner by Captain George Katenkamp. It had been placed on the establishment as from 27 March 1781, i.e. some six weeks after McKenzie's.

The composition of the total force at the time of its arrival at Cape Coast Castle is uncertain. The total strength of an independent company was 116, composed as follows: 1 captain, 2 lieutenants, 1 ensign, 5 sergeants, 5 corporals, 2 drummers, and 100 privates. Two complete companies would therefore have contained 232 ranks of all kinds. A Treasury Minute of 7 April 1781, however, mentions only 200 privates and 6 officers.[351] It is possible that the non-commissioned officers were overlooked in this Minute, for Governor J.B. Weuves in reporting the strength of McKenzie's companies in March 1782 gave a total of 212. "A detachment of 200 men", the description commonly applied to the force, probably referred to the privates only.

Ensign Clarke's evidence points to the presence of only one lieutenant and one ensign in each company at the time of departure.[352] Of these Captain Katenkamp died at sea. Lieutenant Mawby of McKenzie's company was slain in a duel at Goree. His opponent, Lieutenant Cranston, returned to England almost immediately after arrival on the coast, leaving Ensign Clarke, who arrived after the force had landed, the sole surviving officer in Captain Katenkamp's company and second in command because Ensign Hawkshaw of McKenzie's company died also.[353] On 29 April 1782 Governor Weuves in urging a speedy reinforcement declared that Captain McKenzie, who at the time was dangerously ill, was the only one left to command the detachment.[354] The point is of interest because the behaviour and the efficiency of any military establishment depend in large measure upon the number and the quality of its officers.

How many convicts were included among the ranks is likewise uncertain. Governor Weuves's correspondence at times suggests that he believed the entire force was composed of criminals. In describing the difficulties introduced into the forts by McKenzie he wrote, "add to which his corps is composed of all the felons that were discharged from the hulks". In this he probably was guilty of exaggeration, but we can sympathise with him for he never received a list which would have enabled him to distinguish between the volunteers and the pardoned. His successor, Miles, as late as 30 August 1783 was compelled to accept the word of a sergeant that seven of the remnant were volunteers, although, as he pointed out, he could not be certain because the sergeant himself had been a convict.[355] This was neither the first nor the last time that convicts left England without any record of their crimes and sentences. Remissness of this kind had provoked special legislation in the American Colonies; Governor Phillip complained after arrival in New South Wales that he was ignorant of the offences and sentences of his transported felons. Sceptics might almost be pardoned for believing that the omission was intentional to hinder the return of the dismissed, but there is no evidence to support the belief.

McKenzie himself establishes the numerical superiority of the convicts in his companies. In his defence he stated that "the greatest part" of the troop he had raised was drafted into the American service by order of the Government and "their places filled by convicts, both civil and military, taken out of the Savoy, Newgate, and the Hulks".[356] In July 1782 the whole of his assisting officers were convicts.[357]

Miles vouched for the numerical superiority of the convict element in the remnant existing in 1783 for he was certain that 17 of the remaining 24 were convicted felons. The Companies' Returns unfortunately do not distinguish between the free and the unfree; direct evidence is yet to be discovered to establish the ratio between them, for the warrants of conditional pardons are not definite enough to permit even an approximation. The two volumes of pardon warrants (S.P.44/95 and 96) show that more than 130 pardons were issued in the first six months of 1781 on condition of service on land or sea, but unfortunately in most of these the destination is indicated merely by the word "Abroad". Thus a list of pardoned convicts sent by Lord Hillsborough to the Secretary at War on 3 May 1781 contains 29 names divided into three groups labelled Abroad, East Indies, and Coast of Africa. Within these were 15, 4, and 10 names respectively but it is significant that the leading name within the first group is that of Murray McKenzie who afterwards played a conspicuous part in the forts of the Gold Coast. Such evidence as we have, therefore, supports the view that convicts formed a very influential part of the expedition that proceeded to the West African coast. It is as a new experiment to solve the crowded gaol problem that the military operations against the Dutch forts command our attention.

Failure was predicted even before the expedition sailed. Richard Camplin, an already quoted member of the Africa Committee but one whose views were not always in accord with those of his fellows, declared that a committee of the House of Commons had considered the feasibility of employing convicted felons in the forts ten years before and had condemned the proposal.[358] Their reasons, according to Camplin, were a possible destruction of the forts due to the smallness of the number of Europeans serving in them and the probable abolition of all English influence, which was maintained only by the respectability of the Company's servants. The behaviour of some of the convicts caused him to predict a like result on this occasion for, as he said, if the "devilish spirits of those within the Savoy, when in the capital and surrounded by the King's Guards" could not be tamed, what chance would an African Governor have when attempting to command them?[359]

Possibly the Government suspected some trouble but the case was clearly an urgent one for only in the preceding December the Governor and Council at Cape Coast had described their impotence in dealing with the natives alone[360] and in March, Miles, who was in England, declared his belief that a 50-gun ship and a sloop of war could take possession of all the Dutch forts.[361] It need not surprise us then that in April 1781 Lord Germain should have advised the Africa Committee that His Majesty, having taken into consideration the exposed state of the British trade and settlements on the coast of Africa, had decided to send a detachment of 200 men under the convoy of two of H.M. ships of war.[362]

By 15 June 1781 the two companies were embarked on board the *Mackarel* transport (at Gravesend) which received orders to proceed to Spithead and place itself, together with the storeship *Ulysses*, under the command of the convoying ships of war.[363] Almost at the last moment it was discovered that the two vessels were not capable of conveying all the necessary supplies for the expedition although the Government apparently believed that the force took with it nine months' provisions.[364] In company with the two warships *Leander* and *Alligator*, the *Mackarel* and *Ulysses* sailed on 4 August 1781.[365] At Goree the force was delayed by the proceedings of a court martial consequent upon the duel between the two officers already related. A shortage of water then forced the ships into Sierra Leone; not until 5 February 1782 did they reach Cape Coast Castle.

There Captain Shirley of the *Leander*, Captain McKenzie, and the Governor and Council of the Castle unanimously decided to attack Elmina and St Jago. Reinforced by 42 volunteers from the 75th who had accompanied the force from Goree, a detachment of 15 from the Castle, and 70 sailors collected from ships in the Cape Coast Roads, the 212 Independents and Marines were decisively beaten, the engagement ending in a "precipitate retreat" and the loss of the only field gun employed against the enemy.[366] Then turning their attention to the other Dutch forts Shirley, without the aid of the Independents but assisted by the men of the 75th and a few volunteers,[367] took possession of Mouree, Cormantyne, Apam, Berracoe, and Accra. The last alone offered any resistance; it fell after a siege of about 19 days.[368]

The behaviour of the two Independent companies, almost from the time of their appearance on the coast, was extraordinary. Thirty-nine of them deserted to the Dutch, whose spirited resistance at Commendah in June 1782 was partly attributed to the military activity of these deserters. Twenty-eight others, after being placed on a captured Ostend vessel, put to sea on 13 April and vanished, it was supposed, to become pirates, taking with them a cargo estimated to be worth 5000 pounds.[369] Governor Weuves plaintively complained that the troops had become the terror of the Company's servants rather than a means of protection. Being under no discipline (i.e. during Captain McKenzie's illness) they broke into the Castle stores, flew to arms at once on being checked, refused to be distributed among the other forts, and were entirely beyond his control because, at the time, he commanded only between 24 and 26 effective men, the majority of whom were mulattos. When he complained to McKenzie, that officer declared that the men had become desperate and he could not trust himself among them.[370]

74

Governor Miles, who arrived at Cape Coast Castle on 29 April 1782, found those who were still alive in a "truly sickly state indeed", with "no arms . . . not even a musquet among the whole of them". Captain McKenzie had reported that some of them had sold their arms while before Elmina, the others had disposed of theirs during his sickness.[371] He included one of that commander's returns to show the state of the companies "since 20th March, 1782". It was as follows:

FORT	WELL	SICK	DEAD	DESERTED
Cape Coast	16	6	17	15
Mouree	9	3	12	16
Annamaboe	-	-	4	7
Cormantyne	4	2	13	-
Apam	3	1	1	-
Accra	3	-	3	-
Commendah	14	-	15	1
Totals	49	12	65	39

His comment on the 61 who remained was, "such wretches as they are my eyes never beheld; miserable and filthy to the last degree; a disgrace to the very colour". Continuing, he declared that they were not sufficient to garrison the captured forts, much less to be of service; not one of them had appeared in the field at the taking of Commendah, which had fallen on 28 June. Five, left to defend Cormantyne, had deserted after breaking every lock and unhinging every door in the fort and throwing the powder into the well. The natives had allowed them to do it and then brought them to the Castle for a reward. Writing in September he stated his belief that not more than 25-26 of the original 200 were alive. This probably was an underestimate as in August of the following year he reported a remnant of 24,[372] but long before that date all the non-commissioned officers of the force were convicts.

The commander's behaviour was equally extraordinary. Although at first accused of being afraid of his own men he was later charged with forcing them to submit to the grossest inhumanity. Ensign Clarke declared that he had visited Nassau (or Mouree) Fort where he had found 16 men almost entirely naked, emaciated, and eaten with vermin. He had taken them by sea to Cape Coast Castle. Clarke's evidence, which usually must be distrusted, has here an appearance of truth since McKenzie's Return shows 16 men, described as "well", at the Castle. A footnote written within the Castle, however, suggests that the men were not well as, some time after, 12 of them were only in the convalescent stage. The Council also charged him with ordering from Commendah to Headquarters 12 men whom the Governor had declared unfit to move. He enforced his orders and the unfortunate invalids were found "crawling over rocks" by some of the Company's officers.[373] His most famous exploit was to blow one of his men, named Murray McKenzie, from the mouth of a cannon without even the semblance of a trial, on the ground that he was conspiring to cut his commander's throat.[374] His excuse was that as he was the only officer and the matter was urgent a court martial was impossible.

Both Clarke and the Company's officials accused McKenzie of using his soldiers' supplies for his own ends, but in an inquiry conducted by Captain Butchart of H.M. *Argo* four of the NCOs affirmed that McKenzie supplied them with provisions and liquor in plenty.[375] Such evidence may be suspected but it is worthy of notice that the same four witnesses unanimously declared that they had not received a farthing of their pay since leaving England.

He was accused of drawing on the King's stores for upwards of 1200 pounds and then, only a few weeks later, for two months' provisions when his total force did not exceed 60 men. Other charges were the theft of a bottle of gold dust from the Ostend ship, and the forging of the soldiers' signatures on their pay lists. More interesting from our point of view was the glaring incompetence imputed to him. Miles solemnly declared that he was "the most unfit man in the world to command there or anywhere else". Ensign Clarke ascribed the failure at Elmina to the captain's desertion[376] while Shirley claimed that it was due to "the notorious conduct of Capt. McKenzie" about which he begged leave to remain silent. The Council accused him of discouraging discipline by failing to appear in correct military dress.[377] Council and Governors alike blamed his refusal to accept advice which had two serious effects: it reduced British prestige on the Coast as the natives would not believe that any British subject was independent of the Castle, and it led to his seizure of two neutral ships contrary to the advice of Shirley and the Governor.

McKenzie's defence was that the Castle obstructed him in all his attempts; further that the "Etiquette of the King's service was such that he could by no means place himself in any shape whatever under the command of the Governor and Council".[378] The disputing led to his isolation in Mouree Fort, and to his capture by the natives, who beat him unmercifully and "turned him out of the town as naked as nature formed him" on the ground that he had robbed them of their fish.[379] Then after persuading two of the Company's servants to desert with the intention of joining himself in certain "plantation schemes", and after arousing a suspicion that he was arranging to run off with a schooner, possibly with the intention of engaging in piracy, he was arrested by Captain Wickey of H.M. *Rotterdam*, sentenced to death in the Old Bailey for the murder of Murray McKenzie, and then pardoned in

December 1785 after an imprisonment of a little more than two years.[380]

Ensign Clarke's career, if not quite so dramatic, was at least extraordinary. Within ten days of his arrival on 30 April 1782 he was charged with refusing to obey his commanding officer's orders. On 14 May McKenzie desired the Governor and Council to place him under arrest. Four days later, because of a claim by McKenzie that Clarke should be delivered to himself, the Ensign resigned his commission. On 9 June, however, he appeared in the Castle at the head of 13 armed Independents, ordered the Company's troops to lay down their arms, and declared his intention of arresting McKenzie.[381] After such mutinous activity it is not surprising that he also went home under arrest.

These were the officers who directed the operations of the convict-tainted companies on the Gold Coast. That they lacked many of the characteristics of truly great commanders is obvious. Whether the NCOs contributed to the soldiers' sufferings or not is unrecorded. The Company's influence was apparently small. Clarke directly accused it of withholding stores that should have been applied to the Independents, but Clarke also accused McKenzie of effecting the poisoning of one of his own officers and hinted, moreover, that he was responsible for the death of Captain Katenkamp, charges that were not considered seriously, so we need attach little importance to his words. In one respect the Castle seems to have added to the comfort of the soldiers; its hospital did minister to some of their wants and its correspondence suggests that it was prepared at times to oppose McKenzie by attempting to alleviate the sufferings of the troops. When Sergeant Varley, who was confined to the Castle hospital, was demanded by McKenzie the Castle refused to surrender him, stating that the surgeon had pronounced his condition critical and that the order had not been delivered in writing.[382]

To distinguish between the behaviour of the volunteer and of the convict soldiers is impossible as the records fail to do it. No hints remain to show that the malpractices of the troops originated with the convicts and were opposed by the other element in the force, or that the volunteers were led into evil by the pardoned. Reason suggests that the latter engineered a movement which the treatment of their officers hastened. The desertion of such large numbers can probably be explained by ill-treatment within their own companies and a desire to return to their homeland. The convicts were probably convinced that the Government had no intention of sending them back to England after the war. Governor Miles supposed that they were not to be returned when operations ceased, for he retained them when he sent off the supposed seven volunteers who went as witnesses against Captain McKenzie. But on the same day he reported the arrival of "say 12 soldiers and 5 convicts" from Goree, some of whom claimed to be volunteers and demanded their discharges while others alleged that their sentences had expired. He did not know what to do and he desired a "certain list" as a rule to go by.[383] Had he seen the orders sent to the commanding officer at Goree his doubts in one direction at least would have been dispelled for they definitely stated that it was not His Majesty's intention to return the convict soldiers.[384]

The pardon warrants are not explicit in the matter. That dated 8 June 1781 and relating to the conditional pardoning of 54 offenders required them to enlist and continue to serve in the land forces. Another of 17 February contains the extraordinary proviso that the pardoned were to serve on land or sea in the service of the East India Company for "at least 12 months".[385] The only result among the convicts must have been a belief that the Government intended them to perish in West Africa. Thus one means of encouraging good behaviour was lost. Miles detected the weakness in the system; in December 1782 he wrote, "While they have a prospect, however distant, of visiting their native country and particularly knowing it to depend on the officers they live under, that consideration may induce them to behave well, but, deprived of all hope they naturally shake off all care or concern about it and of course grow desperate".[386] As for the men, desertion seemed to provide the only prospect of leaving the Coast. It offered, moreover, the possibility of a higher status in society as their records did not go with them. Patriotism and the desire to live were in conflict; life on the Gold Coast depended, not infrequently, upon escape. For convicts, that could be effected by desertion only.

A little military experience will convince even the sceptical that certain requirements are essential in any force to preserve its effectiveness. Among these are humane discipline and regular food, clothing, and pay for services rendered. Enough has already been written to demonstrate the weakness of the discipline employed in the two Independent Companies. All accounts vouch for the deplorable state of their clothing. "Almost entirely naked and filthy" is the description commonly applied to them. McKenzie possibly was not entirely to blame for this as the nine months' provisions that were supposed to accompany the force evidently did not.[387] But whether he was guilty or not, the effect upon the soldiers must have been to discourage that pride and esprit de corps which have urged others to do great things.

Despite the evidence of the four NCOs already given there is evidence to support the belief that the men were not regularly fed. Miles accused McKenzie of starving his soldiers;[388] Clarke contended that the Company withheld supplies from them.[389] Possibly their breaking into the Company's stores was not without some justification. As for their pay, the same four NCOs denied that they had received a penny in 12 months. The seven witnesses whom Miles sent to England assured him that McKenzie had forged signatures in respect of pay; they pointed out that Murray McKenzie's receipts were evidenced by marks only while everybody knew he could write.[390] The amount and the nature of their pay had not been as clearly stated as it might have been. The Africa Committee certainly suggested that they should be paid in kind, a practice which at the time was provoking complaints among its own soldiers who declared that they lost 15 percent of their salaries by the method.[391] If, therefore, they were paid in that way they had some reason to grumble, but there is no hint that they received even that favour. Thus as an experiment in the employment of convicts the test was not fairly conducted. Even under competent, sympathetic officers, trouble might have occurred; under the conditions which existed unsatisfactory behaviour was the natural result.

The experiment removed from England a number of prisoners and therefore temporarily reduced the pressure on the gaols, but in a way that brought little credit to the Government or its officers. Little direct blame attaches to the former. No intended cruelty appears in its correspondence; before the expedition was begun Miles was consulted concerning the feasibility of the project and as we have seen, a report from the Coast declared that only two Europeans had died during a period of two years. Moreover in the year 1779 a Committee of the House had emphasised the justice of sending "atrocious criminals to unhealthy places where their lives might be hazarded in the place of better citizens". The Secretary of State probably suspected that some of the felons would die but in war time that was to be expected in any field of operations. There is no evidence that the convicts were forced to leave the hulks; their pardons were conditional. Moreover they only went where others volunteered to go.

Whether cruel or otherwise the experiment did not solve the gaol problem; nor did it effect anything of permanent value on the West African Coast. There its results were negative rather than negligible. In September 1782 Miles complained that the introduction of the two companies had created a spirit of anarchy among the natives "which he feared would not be got rid of". In the following year he admitted that an officer and 20 men might threaten their existence.[392] Even the captured forts were evacuated.[393]

The Independent Companies were disbanded on 24 September 1783.[394] The surviving convicts remained on the Coast. Ten years after the setting out of that expedition the Committee considered a petition for discharge from five of them. No correct information could be found in the Secretary of State's office concerning three of them; the other two had been pardoned on 30 April 1781 on the condition of serving as soldiers. It therefore decided that it could give no directions in respect of their discharges.[395]

The disaster did not terminate the practice of sending convicts to the Gold Coast. In October Evan Nepean informed the Africa Committee that the Government intended to send certain convicts, including women, to the area. They would be well clothed on going but he had no authority to answer for anything further.[396] A report of the outrageous behaviour of the Independents failed to move the Government; Nepean replied that the destination of the criminals could not be altered.[397] In December Miles, then on the Coast, received through the medium of a newspaper a hint that more convicts were to be sent. His comment on the proposal was an expressed fear that the felons would take possession of the forts and massacre their commanders.[398]

In the following month Miles acknowledged receipt of 13 convicts from the ship *Den Keyser*. So moved was he by their arrival that he entered into a pragmatic consideration of transportation generally. Admitting that a possible motive of the Government was a desire to save life he expressed his conviction that "the grand consideration" seemed to be "to get them out of Europe at all events without even once adverting to the evil consequences that must attend the mode". In other parts of the world they might support themselves; in Africa it was impossible. The Company could use them only as soldiers; the natives had no employment for them. "They are landed as it were naked and diseased on a sandy shore; the more hardy of them will probably plunder for a few days for a living until the climate stops their progress and then, shocking to humanity, loaded with additional diseases incident to this country the poor wretches are to be seen dying upon the rocks or upon the sandy beach under the scorching heat of the sun without the means of support or the least relief afforded them". Only by breaking orders could they employ them as soldiers as their number was carefully prescribed and in any case by doing it they were risking their own lives. As for the women, two of whom (shocking to relate) had been landed, he did not doubt the Europeans would contribute towards their maintenance, "but, good heavens, Gentlemen, only consider, women of our own colour, landed here to be common prostitutes among the blacks. A knowledge of all the dreadful consequences of such a measure prompts me to say that if their lives are forfeited to their country it were humanity rather to let the forfeit be paid. I entreat you, therefore, put a stop to it".[399] But unfortunately for the Committee its position was weakened by its financial dependence upon the Government. Townshend, the Secretary of State, was adamant; the male convicts were scattered among the forts as soldiers; the women disappear from the correspondence. The *Den Keyser* landed certain convicts at Goree also and some of these as we have seen were later transferred to Cape Coast Castle but they included only 17 men.[400]

The convict soldiers received one unsolicited benefit from the Council of the Castle. In December 1782 the Africa Committee forwarded instructions that the convicted felons were to be placed on soldiers' half pay.[401] What inspired this is not clear as the Committee had no intention of shouldering the cost of those troops, for in the preceding year it had directed the Castle officials to keep a careful record of the additional expense produced by the presence of the convicts in order that it might claim the same from the Government.[402] In reply the Castle authorities stated that the convicts were being paid as its soldiers were "for if we reduce their pay to the stipend mentioned in your letter it would be insufficient for white men in this country to support life upon".[403]

In the year 1784 convicts continued to arrive on the Gold Coast. Writing in March the Governor and Council stated that those received lately had been sent to Accra and Wydah. In December of the same year the Company at "the earnest desire of H.M. Government" agreed to accept another 20.[404] In the following June the arrival of 17 of the 20 was announced, accompanied by an urgent appeal that not more than 20 or 30 should be sent annually as a greater number would endanger both the settlement and the officials' lives. With this also went a request that only those possessing useful trades might be sent in the future as among those already received there was not a bricklayer, carpenter, or any tradesman who could be useful to them.[405] Finally, on 7 January 1785, the Committee protested to Lord Sydney that it could not, consistently with safety, receive any more felons into its forts, but so great was the Government's difficulty that it was even forced to persuade the Company in the same year to accept one more convict, named John Miles.[406]

And now for the purposes of this work we may leave the Gold Coast. Both in peace and in war attempts had been made there to solve the gaol problem, and as a small safety valve it might still reduce the pressure on English prisons, but routine had now taken the place of experimentation in West Africa. In a later chapter we shall consider a project to establish an inland African convict settlement of an entirely different kind. Meantime the other shore of the Atlantic had become a scene of attempts to rid British gaols of their surplus felons. To those attempts we now turn our attention.

Engraving by Sachse and Co.

Courtesy National Maritime Museum, London

Bird's eye view of the City of Annapolis, Capitol of the State of Maryland
Annapolis was the landing place of British convicts to Maryland

5

American Experiments, 1783-1785

O NLY A FEW DAYS after the removal of Captain Kenneth McKenzie from the Gold Coast the Peace of Versailles (3 September 1783) restored uninterrupted commercial relations with the Eastern Coast of the North American continent. The way was open therefore to a renewal of the transportation of English convicts to America, provided that persons could be found to undertake the carriage of the convicted felons and that there still remained Americans who were prepared to purchase them. No doubts existed concerning the supply of exportable human labour. Even before the conclusion of peace with the United States the British Government was preparing for an exportation of criminals to the North American mainland. On 3 January 1783 George Rose, a secretary to the Treasury, informed the Undersecretary, Evan Nepean, that their lordships had agreed that it was highly important because of the great number of convicts in Newgate that they should be removed immediately without waiting to settle the terms of transporting them to America.[407] Lord Townshend's determination to despatch criminals to the Gold Coast in spite of the opposition of both the Africa Committee and the Cape Coast Council, and the decision that convict soldiers were not to return to England, are only two among many signs of a discomfort arising from gaol pressure. The prospect of a peace which would narrow the stream of convicts flowing into the land and sea forces made imperative a timely discovery of another outlet.

Before the Revolutionary War the sale of felons in the American colonies had made the problem a comparatively simple one. Cheap labour was still in demand in the same areas and the British Government was prepared to encourage any contractor who would undertake the task of conveying that labour to the Southern States or elsewhere. The effect of a hope of the revival of the trade was revealed in the sentences of the period. Transportation to Africa continued to be a normal punishment but even before the signing of the preliminary articles of peace the sentence "transportation to America" had been restored.

It is possible that Duncan Campbell was approached in the matter, but he had been for several years engaged in superintending the Hulk System which apparently was more remunerative and assuredly more certain than the transportation of felons.[408] It need not surprise us, then, that Campbell played no part in the actual carriage of convicts to America after the declaration of peace. A man, however, was not wanting; George Moore, another London merchant, offered his services and his offer was accepted.[409]

Of the details of his first venture little information remains. From instructions delivered by Lord North to the Treasury we learn that Moore had agreed, with the King's permission, to transport 143 criminals to America.[410] That the collection of the convicts began before the ratification of peace is also confirmed by the fact that Campbell, on 29 April 1783, claimed £886 6s 0d "for the temporary reception of male convicts ordered for transportation to America".[411] By the terms of his agreement Moore was to be paid £500 and although no mention is made of any right to sell the services of the convicts we can safely assume that that was understood.[412]

The date of his ship's departure is uncertain. It is possible that it left the Thames late in August 1783, as on the 12th of that month Campbell was directed to deliver to Moore 56 convicts that were under his charge on the hulks.[413] Six days later these were transferred to the contractor.[414] A new agreement between the Treasury and Campbell encourages the belief that more were transferred, but evidence soon to be presented suggests that some were transferred directly from Newgate to the transporting vessel. The next hint we receive of the undertaking is a notice in the *Gentleman's Magazine* of 1 September 1783 that three convicts had been captured by the police. On being questioned they deposed that they, with others, were taken from Newgate on the 14th of the preceding month and put on board a vessel for transportation to America. These had later overcome the captain and crew and then run the ship ashore on the coast of Sussex, after which some of them escaped in the two long boats.[415]

A few weeks later Philip Stephens, a secretary to the Admiralty, informed Evan Nepean that Admiral Montagu, the Commander of H.M. Ships at Portsmouth, had reported the bringing in of a convict ship by the *Perseverance*.[416] In all this evidence there is no mention of the name of the ship or of the contractor; nevertheless there is little doubt that it all refers to the same undertaking. One thing is certain: a number of Moore's convicts did leave his ship, for in recommending the payment of the promised £500 to Moore North advised the paying of the whole amount in spite of the fact that several of the criminals had "made their escape and come ashore".[417] The number who were retaken is not given. Although Moore expressed his readiness to accept

84

them they were not returned to the ship because, as North declared, such action was not judged to be advisable.[418] On the last day of the year 1783 the *Mercury*, Moore's vessel, arrived in Maryland with a cargo of 70 convicts, all of whom were landed.[419]

One noticeable feature of this transportation was the theoretical responsibility assumed by Duncan Campbell. In advising him of their acceptance of his offer to provide accommodation for those sentenced to America the Lords Commissioners of the Treasury impressed upon him the absolute necessity of his entering into a contract with the clerk of arraigns for the transportation of the felons before they were delivered into his custody. At the same time they declared that they would provide means of sending them to their destination "in order to bear him harmless for not performing the condition of the contract so entered into".[420] This became a regular practice; on 18 October of the same year Nepean informed Christopher Gullet of Exeter, when directing him to forward convicts to the hulks at Woolwich, that Duncan Campbell would be "ready to enter into the usual bonds for conveying them to the places of their destination on that continent".[421] Again, in March of the following year, the Solicitor General told the House that Campbell had contracted to carry 260 felons solely to free the gaols as the convicts could not be delivered to him save under the idea that they were going to be transported.[422]

That the Government considered a more direct plan of transporting is revealed by an estimate of a contract between (Blank) and W.H. for receiving on board a ship in the River Thames convicts from the different gaols and transporting them to a port in North America.[423] The document, which is undated, is enclosed in Duncan Campbell's proposal of 27 December 1782 to provide accommodation for those ordered to be removed to America. By the terms of this estimate W.H. was to provide a ship for the reception of any number of convicts, not exceeding 250, and was to be paid 250 pounds a month and one shilling a head per diem during the period they remained on the river. A ship, properly equipped and victualled, was also to be provided to convey the felons to any port in North America for which the contractor was to be paid 3600 pounds or the equivalent of 18 pounds per head for all transported. After arrival the convicted were to be removed from the vessel within the space of five days or demurrage and subsistence charges of 10 pounds per day and one shilling a head incurred. This estimate may be interpreted in different ways but it suggests that one and the same person was to be responsible for the maintenance of the criminals from the time of their leaving the gaols until their removal from the ship in America. In practice, as we have seen, this system was not adopted: Campbell maintained them on the Thames; Moore transported them.

Moore was prepared to accept a greater responsibility. He proposed to contract for the transportation of convicts over a period of ten years if the Government would give him the right to sell them in any port in North America save Nova Scotia and pay him ten guineas for every convict received into his ships.[424] The uncertainty of their reception in America and "the extraordinary charge incurred in transporting them, evident from their recent conduct" were his reasons for requiring more than was formerly paid. If the Government would be answerable for their acceptance in the United States and for all consequences he would transport them for five guineas a head. This proposal also lacks a date but as it refers to the "recent conduct" of the convicts and reveals an ignorance of the American attitude towards their reception it probably was drawn up after the departure of his first ship, the *Mercury*, and before the receipt of unfavourable information from America. The document does not indicate to whom it was addressed but the natural assumption is that it was meant for the Secretary of State. The manner of its reception is not recorded but there is no reason to believe that the Government ever paid ten guineas a head to any contractor carrying to America.

Moore was given an early opportunity to experiment with a second cargo of human labour. On 24 August 1783, that is before the arrival of his first ship in America, Lord North reminded Campbell of the agreement to provide for convicts ordered to America made only a little more than seven months before.[425] His letter, which is practically a transcript of that sent by George Rose on 3 January 1783, desired Campbell to receive and maintain 200 convicts until means could be found for their removal to America.[426] Two months later Campbell furnished the following list of felons received on board the *Censor* since 18 August 1783:

Lincoln	2 Sept	6	York	17 Sept	6
Winchester	3 Sept	10	Salisbury	20 Sept	18
Winchester	6 Sept	12	Newgate	4 Oct	72
Winchester	12 Sept	13			
			Total		137

On 18 October 1783 Nepean informed Christopher Gullet of Exeter that Campbell had already upwards of 200 convicts under sentence of transportation. Other felons were added; in November another nine were received from Stafford gaol.[427] In January of the following year Lord Sydney directed Campbell to receive another 200 on the same terms as were agreed upon by Mr Rose.[428] Whether this was in antici-

pation of the removal of those already in Campbell's possession or whether it accounts for the overflowing of transportable convicts into the *Justitia*, noticed in an earlier chapter, is not clear. One fact appears certain: an abundant supply of convicts was at hand for Moore's second venture.

His ship in this undertaking was the *Mercury*. Its date of departure is again uncertain but as Campbell was instructed on 26 March 1784 to deliver to George Moore 50 convicts out of the *Censor* and *Justitia* hulks and others were added shortly after, we can surmise that the vessel sailed early in April. A recommendation for payment of five guineas a head to Moore forwarded to the Treasury by Lord Sydney on 12 April 1784 states that the number carried was 185, i.e. 105 from Newgate, 50 from "the *Censor* hulk", 8 from Maidstone, and 22 from Oxford.[429] The rather extraordinary feature of the transaction was the small number taken from the *Censor* hulk, whose convicts were there for the purpose of transportation to America. The explanation probably lies in the greater pressure or fear of infection within the gaols. The fact that not all the convicts came from the hulks would explain the presence of some women among the cargo of the *Mercury* and their appearance on the *Dunkirk* hulk as described earlier.[430]

Disaster came upon the venture almost at its beginning. From the evidence of Charles Keeling, one of the felons on board the *Mercury*, we learn that the prisoners gained their liberty by sawing through their irons on 8 April. Then, after a contest of upwards of an hour, they took possession of the ship and remained in charge until the 13th of the same month when they ran into Torbay. There, after arming themselves with cutlasses and pistols, many of them landed.[431] The commander of the *Helena* sloop, writing on 14 April, declared that 60 reached the shore on the previous evening; another 66 had attempted to do the same on the morning of the 14th but had been prevented from escaping by his boats. They had been detained in Exeter gaol; the remainder were in the *Mercury*, which was being guarded by the *Hope*.[432] Lord Sydney thereupon directed the sending of a list of the names of the escaped with special emphasis upon the ringleaders so that a proper example might be made of them. Only one man, W. Jones, was recommended for pardon by Moore, who stressed the fact that Jones was the only one worthy of kindness as the cruelties of the others had been "very great".[433] Eighty-five were finally lodged in Exeter gaol;[434] the remainder sailed in the *Mercury* to America. Judging by the numbers reported later at Belize the number of those who actually escaped must have been inconsiderable.

Moore's experiences suggest either negligence or cruelty, or both, and yet there is little evidence to support any of these charges. North had decided that "the accident" in the first voyage "did not proceed from any neglect".[435] After the second mutiny Nepean recommended a more diligent attention to the security of the remaining convicts but he voiced no blame.[436] As for their treatment, if Moore's advice was followed it must have been humane, for in his orders were the words, "Be attentive to their health; keep them clean; those that are in want of clothes may be supplied with my slops that are on board. By your example recommend to your officers and crew vigilance and industry".[437]

It is probable that the *Mercury* proceeded to Maryland, the most likely market for saleable convicts at the time. Moore himself is silent concerning the movements of the ship, but it is possible that an attempt was made to dispose of the cargo in Virginia. Wherever it went in the United States the result was the same: the Americans refused to allow the landing of the convicts. Evan Nepean, only in the following year, after informing the 1785 Committee of the House of Commons that the first venture had been successful added, "We tried it a second time but they would not receive them".[438] Sailing south the *Mercury* arrived at Belize, in Honduras, early in July 1784.[439]

Under normal circumstances it is possible that the British settlers in that area would have given the convicts a cool reception but circumstances were anything but normal when the *Mercury* appeared. British logwood cutters had led a precarious existence in the locality for considerably more than a century. The Peace of Paris, in 1763, had conceded to the settlers the right to cut logwood but had "explicitly recognised the settlement as within Spanish territory by ordering the demolition of all fortifications and handing over the settlers to the protection of His Catholic Majesty".[440] At that time the principal centre of the settlement was St George's Cay, an island a few miles east of Belize. On 15 September 1779 this place was surprised by a superior Spanish force; the inhabitants were forcibly removed to Merida in Yucatan and thence to Havana.[441]

To all intents and purposes the settlement ceased to exist until the year 1783. Then the Sixth Article of the Treaty of Versailles restored the right of the settlers to re-establish themselves between the Rivers Hondo and Belize and to cut, carry, and load logwood.[442] Belize became the chief centre of the revived settlement. On 27 May the Governor of Yucatan formally delivered to the British nation the area described in the Sixth Article of the Treaty of Peace. The receipt of this was acknowledged four days later and on 12 June 1783 a public meeting attended by only 12 settlers made provision for the internal peace and security of the inhabitants and their property by passing a number of resolutions.[443] As recorded these bear 21 signatures. The same public meeting appointed Major Richard Hoare, James McAulay, Wm. O'Brien, Richard Armstrong, and Thomas Potts to administer justice to all His Majesty's legal subjects within the settlement.

The dismay produced by the arrival of the *Mercury*'s 86 convicts in the following year can easily be imagined.[444] Writing in December of that year an unnamed half-pay officer declared that the total free British population did not consist of 30 heads of families. The difficulty of absorbing 86 convicts is therefore apparent and even if, as it was subsequently revealed, Moore's agents had no intention of attempting to sell all the felons, their presence alone must have been viewed with misgivings by the recently restored settlers.

Convicts had been bought in the West Indies and in the American Colonies mainly to become units of labour in systems of extensive field cultivation. But within the limits of the Bay Settlement, as the area occupied by the British was called, no settler was allowed either to own or to cultivate land. Nor was this prohibition lightly considered; Spanish officers at intervals inspected the territory inhabited by the logwood cutters and enforced the destruction of even any attempt to cultivate vegetables for private use. In the Convention of London (14 July 1786) His Catholic Majesty, by the Third Article, allowed only the gathering of purely natural and uncultivated produce of the earth. It was not until the year 1789 that the Spanish Government permitted the growing of potatoes, Indian corn, roots, and vegetables for the settlers' own consumption.[445] Thus when the *Mercury* arrived in the Bay Settlement the employment of convicts on local plantations was impossible.

West Indian and American Colonial experience had demonstrated that the introduction of slave labour reduced the demand for convicts. But slave labour had been a recognised part of the settlement's polity for many years before its capture by the Spaniards in 1779. It was in fact the normal form of labour within the area. It might even be argued that under any conditions, slaves would be preferred to convicts because the felling and handling of heavy timber in the Central American climate was work for which many of the convicts were not fitted. Judged by the results of the military examinations that remain, a large proportion of the inmates of British gaols would speedily have died or have become a burden on their masters by doing much work.

It is a well known fact that in such highly organised communities as Maryland and Virginia convict labourers were responsible for much of the crime committed within them. Both those colonies had possessed well established police systems. Whatever police system could have been created by the heads of "under thirty families" must of necessity have been primitive, but in the Bay Settlement the establishment of an effective police was opposed by the Spanish Government.

In 1785 Colonel Despard, after being appointed superintendent of the settlement, decided that it would be useless for him to go to the area until a police and government had been created.[446] Near the close of the year 1785 the settlement was described as an open receptacle for outlaws, felons, and those who fled from justice.[447] In July 1784 the magistrates of the locality must have realised the danger of introducing 86 felons.

The limited area assigned to the settlers and the uncertainty concerning the attitude of the Spanish Government toward the introduction increased the doubt. Major Hoare described it as an effectual step to violate the Definitive Treaty which would provide the Spaniards with a pretext for routing them out of Honduras.[448] He emphasised also the destruction of their own commercial credit, "for who will trust men that live in a country that is to become an asylum of villains?".[449] Robert White, the settlement's London agent, maintained that there was no proper refuge for convicts in the West Indies. He concluded his complaint with the following observation which must have rankled in the mind of the Undersecretary: "We are the only nation on earth who seem not to know how to dispose of our criminals".[450] Thus it is not surprising that the officers of the *Mercury* met with some resistance in their attempt to land convicts in the Bay Settlement.

Despite this opposition we cannot be certain that all the free inhabitants resented the appearance of the convicts. A person describing himself as a half-pay officer, in a letter addressed to Moore, attributed the resistance to "a few designing men without paying the least attention to their own interests who wanted servants"; further, that those who had resisted "were soon made sensible that they had entered into resolves prejudicial to themselves". Their desire now was to purchase them in small numbers and scatter them throughout the settlement and by that means "avoid the risque attending having too many". He expressed the conviction that all the work in Honduras could be performed by whites but believed that for the present the settlement could not receive more than one hundred criminals per annum.[451]

To establish the truth or otherwise of this evidence is naturally difficult. That some of the colonists would have been prepared to accept convict labour is not without the bounds of possibility, but the behaviour of the settlement on this and a later occasion contradicts the view of this half-pay officer, whose desire to conceal his own identity may be construed as an indication that he felt his opinions were not in harmony with those of the leaders of the community. The whole tenor of his letters suggests a desire for self advancement. They, therefore, are not as convincing as Major Hoare's, whose words breathe an actual fear of the consequences to the whole community.

The attitude of the settlers was shown in a public meeting held on 9 August 1784 and attended by four magistrates and 15 other inhabitants.[452] It resolved:

"that the agent, factor, or super cargo for the said convicts shall be required to order that they might be removed from the settlement, at, or before the expiration of the 15 days allowed for her stay".

"That three days shall be allowed for the execution of this order after which no convict shall be suffered to leave the *Mercury* on any pretence whatever. Failure to comply with this order will incur a penalty of £100".

"That the purchase of one or more convicts will make the purchaser liable to a fine of £100 a head for all secured".

The *Mercury* was commanded by Captain Arnott; its supercargo who was responsible for the sale of the convicts was a Mr Whaley. According to Hoare this man landed with British Acts of Parliament and learned arguments, which were dismissed by him with the words that "all the Acts he had had no more effect where he was than were he at Madrid".[453]

The natural question is, what authority had Whaley to sell convicts in the Bay of Honduras? The warrant directing Campbell to deliver 50 convicts to Moore on 26 March 1784 stated that they were to be conveyed to North America. Sydney's letter directing the Treasury to pay Moore mentioned America as their destination. Not much weight need be attached to the omission of the word "North" as Sydney at that time did not anticipate that the felons would be carried to Central America, but writing to Governor Clarke of Jamaica in October 1784 he reported how Admiral Gambier had stated that the convicts lately sent out "without the authority of the government" were likely to be "well received in the Bay of Honduras".[454] It would seem that the information came to him as a surprise, and we may assume therefore that the Baymen spoke with some reason when they questioned Whaley's right to land felons in Honduras, although we can be quite sure that the Secretary of State would have commended the work of Moore's assistants if the experiment had succeeded.

The attitude of the local authorities soon dispelled the hope of a speedy sale. Whaley, therefore, attempted to avoid a certain loss by employing the convicts in cutting logwood. He soon died, but his policy was continued by Daniel Hill, chief mate of the *Mercury*, who assumed his duties. According to his evidence he was allowed to clear ground and erect a house and blacksmith shop at the Haulover. Then, leaving his son in charge there, he took 22 convicts up the Northern River to cut logwood.[455] These operations aroused opposition; Hoare declared they were undertaken without the least respect for the magistracy. A certain Henry Jones also deposed that he considered the presence of the convicts threatened his existence. A warrant was therefore issued for the arrest of Hill and his associate Moses Pastom. The case was tried before three magistrates and a jury of 17 settlers. The jury found for the plaintiff, declared that the defendant had acted contrary to the Resolves signed on 9 August, and reported that a majority of them were of the opinion that Jones had acted as they would have done.[456]

In Hill's absence the convicts on the Northern River were persuaded by promises of liberty to board a vessel. They were then landed with four days' provisions on Key Chapel, "a desert and barren island in the Spanish territory". Whether they were removed is uncertain. The half-pay officer declared that humanity induced the inhabitants to agree that they should be re-embarked "in order to dispose of them as had been consented to" but Hill would not hear of it and Captain Arnott was easily persuaded to hold the ship in readiness to oppose any attempts of the inhabitants to embark them.[457] As far as reliable evidence is concerned these unfortunate men, except for a fleeting reference, soon to be made, at this point fade out of this depressing picture.

Captain Arnott then decided to take a hand in the business. Protracted delay probably explains his activity but the half-pay officer took upon himself the credit for screwing up his courage to the point of action. On 2 October he (Arnott) charged Hill with claiming to act as Moore's agent and asked for a court ruling on the matters in dispute.[458] The court found Hill guilty of acting in defiance of the settlers' Resolutions in attempting to form establishments at the Haulover and Northern River. It was of the opinion that they were prejudicial to the interests of the settlement and considered the one at Northern River "now removed to Key Chapel would very soon be driven to acts of desperation by the calls of hunger and nakedness".[459] It therefore advised Arnott and Hill to collect "the poor starving wretched convicts" that were dispersed throughout the country and to re-embark them. If that were done there was "hardly a man in the country who would not contribute his mite" towards supporting them for the present and transporting them to some other country.

Three days later, according to Hill's account, he himself was seized by Captain Arnott and the crew and imprisoned in the *Mercury* for six weeks while the convicts were distributed among, and employed by, the inhabitants.[460] The half-pay officer, on the other hand, declares that Arnott disposed of what remained as far as possible. The change of attitude within the settlement, if it had changed, might perhaps have been due to humanity or to a realisation of the comparative harmlessness of the felons themselves. Arnott apparently profited by the enterprise as Hill reports that he himself received nothing while Moore recovered only "a trifle" from Arnott who suffered six months' imprisonment after his return.[461] In the following year when Nepean was questioned concerning the whereabouts of the convicts he frankly replied that he supposed most of them were still there.[462]

The results of the two ventures naturally displeased Moore who estimated that his losses exceeded 4500 pounds.[463] To reimburse himself and, as he said, to be of some use to the Government he attempted a third time to transport convicts to the New World. The Government's willingness to permit another experiment is revealed in Lord Sydney's letter to Governor Clarke of Jamaica, written on 5 October 1784. In it he declared that the more he considered the matter the greater difficulty he saw in disposing of criminals in any other places in the possession of His Majesty's subjects. He opined that he would have to send some to Honduras and he instructed Clarke to find out how they would be received by the settlers. Whether the third attempt originated with Sydney or with Moore is not stated but in September 1785 Moore entered into a third contract, this time to transport to Honduras Bay 29 convicts together with a number of negroes and other servants. This time he aimed at securing logwood as well as disposing of his felons.[464]

The difficulties which his lack of authority had occasioned in the previous year caused him to be prepared for any similar resistance. From Evan Nepean he secured a letter to Superintendent Despard informing him that Mr George Moore had, with the Government's approbation, engaged to carry about 30 convicts to the Bay of Honduras and that it was Lord Sydney's desire that he (Despard) would allow them to land and then assist in furthering the project generally.[465] According to Moore's later letter he also received from Nepean a verbal assurance that no obstruction would be offered. He therefore hired the *Fair American*, secured all necessary implements and arrived at the Bay Settlement in December 1785. There, the settlers under threat of violence forbade the landing of the criminals. Their declared authority for this action was a conversation between their agent, Robert White, and Lord Sydney in which the latter had stated that he had no desire to influence the conduct of the settlers in respect of accepting convicts.[466] For about five weeks the ship remained in vain after which the magistrates and settlers enforced the removal of the convicts and of a Jamaican who had purchased some of them. Apparently the convicts were landed on the Mosquito Shore.[467]

The sequel in England was decidedly unpleasant. The ship-owner claimed from Moore demurrage charges of £745 18s 4d. Moore, declaring that his failure had been due to the duplicity of the Secretary of State, claimed nearly £1600 from the Government. He cast upon the Government also the responsibility of removing the convicts from the Mosquito Shore "conformable to the terms of the late convention". With the ins and outs of the dispute we are not seriously concerned. Sydney probably had no intention of engaging in double dealing. His aims, as conveyed to Despard, were expressed as a desire rather than as a command and, unfortunately for Moore, required Despard to assist only as far as was consistent with the interests of the settlement. It is possible, also, that Sydney had said to White that he had no desire to force settlers to accept convicts. That was the Government's attitude towards Nova Scotia at the time,[468] but he might have had in mind the fact that the Bay settlers had accepted Moore's felons in 1784. One supposition, presented earlier, the incident tends to confirm: viz., that convicts were unsatisfactory units of labour on the shores of the Bay of Honduras. The reputation created by those of 1784 certainly produced no clamour for further supplies, a fact which discounts many of the opinions expressed by the half-pay officer.

The results of the post-Revolution experiments in America were therefore no more satisfactory than those which had been obtained from the attempts on the Gold Coast. In a sense they were less satisfactory, for the number of felons disposed of in the New World was certainly less than the total landed on the shores of West Africa. Moreover, convicts were still dribbling into the forts while hope of sending them to America had to be abandoned. A comparison of the mortalities is impossible because of a lack of evidence concerning the fate of those who reached America. One noticeable omission in the reports of the Bay Settlement disputes is reference to deaths among the convicts, although it is clear that the state of many was desperate. What their condition was later is a matter for speculation.

The most important result of these experiments was their reduction of the possible field for transportation. After 1784 the British Government could never expect again to establish a regular trade in convicts with the North American continent; after 1785 Central America was closed to them. Musing on the possibility of reducing the pressure within English gaols in October 1785 Lord Sydney had perceived the Bay of Honduras as the last possible place, occupied by His Majesty's subjects, to which convicted felons might be sent. That hope had vanished after Moore's third venture; to areas beyond those already occupied by British subjects the Secretary of State had therefore to look for later experimentation.[469]

6

African Schemes, 1785-1786

THE ATTEMPTS TO SOLVE the gaol problem already treated in this work were genuine experiments in the sense that they removed convicts from England. Repeated failure then compelled an appeal to other untried possible solutions. These, the gravity and duration of the problem produced in large numbers. The great majority of them never entered the sphere of action; a few received official sanction and passed into the early stages of execution. Of these, only one was carried to completion, viz. the transportation to New South Wales. Experience forbade a continuation of the experimenting in all the other attempts. These intermediate projects concern us now. They lay between the opposite poles of mere intention and realisation and they all were directed towards Africa.

To Lord Sydney, as Secretary of State responsible for the administration of the Home Office, the outlook at the opening of the year 1785 must have been gloomy indeed. Honduras appeared to be the only British field within which to operate, and its settlers were already demonstrating a dislike for convict labourers. The only alternative to providing for their maintenance in England seemed to be the discovery and utilisation of a site that lay outside the Empire. One was speedily discovered; it was Lemaine, an island situated 450 miles up the Gambia River.

Mr John Barnes, a merchant in the African trade, who had lived on the Gambia and Senegal Rivers, proposed the area.[470] His reasons, according to his later statement, had been the distress of the Government and the refusal of the Africa Company to receive convicted felons. His method of suggesting the site is not recorded, but there still remains a detailed although unsigned recommendation of it entitled "Description of the Island of Lemaine and the opinion of some African traders on it as a place for the reception of convicts", and Lord Sydney forwarded this to the Treasury when he gave instructions for the occupation of the island on 9 February 1785.[471] This might have been the medium through which Barnes brought the area under the notice of the Secretary of State, but it is possible that the scheme was projected earlier as in August 1784 Nepean was directed to provide "a map of the River Gambia and any papers" which he might think necessary for the Cabinet meeting of the morrow.[472] To account for Sydney's acceptance of the scheme a brief resume of the "Description" must be given.

According to that document the island was 12 miles long and 1.5 miles wide.[473] Its land was extremely fertile and covered with timber except in those parts which had already been cleared. The adjacent country was well stocked with black cattle, goats, and sheep. The natives were hospitable and inoffensive and would readily cede the area upon receipt of payment of a small annual rent. They could also supply all the necessary rice or corn for seed. A harvest could be expected within four months "and so multiplied" that no further demands from Europe would be necessary. Any amount of tobacco, cotton, indigo, etc. could be produced on the island for the use of the convicts; tropical fruits in great abundance were to be found in the vicinity. There was little prospect of the convicts' escaping as no one would shelter them; an armed vessel stationed below the settlement during the trading season would prevent escape and the capture of merchant ships. When that season was over it should return to the mouth of the river where the health of the crew "would more likely be preserved".

The supplies raised by the convicts themselves would enable a regular succession of British criminals; as they became rich they naturally would become honest and in a few years the settlement would be a considerable advantage to the Mother Country. The island would easily support 4000 people but overcrowding was not likely for a long time because "when felons find we have the power of punishing them they will be more cautious" and consequently fewer in numbers. The cost of conveying and settling 500 convicts would be approximately 10,000 pounds,[474] a sum less than the cost of confining an equal number on the Thames for eight months. One defect was admitted: it was natural to suppose that a great many of the transported would die because of the change of climate. The form of government suggested was one by a chief and council elected by the convicts themselves. To that governing body should be given authority to punish crime and to control the property and provisions supplied for their use.

In addition to this "Description" the Secretary received from Mr John Barnes certain suggestions concerning the proposed guardship. He advocated an annual payment of £4300 to any contractor who would undertake to provide a vessel armed with cannon, swivel guns, blunderbusses and the like and manned by a crew of 60 men, 25 of whom should be African natives. Realising the impossibility of always maintaining a full complement of white men "in a country so unhealthy and so little resorted to by Europeans" he recommended giving the captain authority to fill deficiencies with natives. Should the loss due to mortality, desertion, or other unavoidable causes amount to one-fifth part or more, and continue so for a month or longer, he suggested a deduction of £2 10s per man, per month, until others were embarked to take their places.[475]

Mr Robert Heatley, who possessed much West African experience, offered to command the suggested guardship in return for an annual salary of £700. He proposed to accompany the convicts to the island and, after they had been settled, to withdraw to a more convenient part of the river near or at Yanimarew. He suggested the removal of the vessel, during the rainy season, to the mouth of the river "for the sake of the health of the crew" and because at that time of the year there would be no trade upstream nor would it be possible to approach the island due to the flooding of the river. He considered that the island could be secured for an annual rental of 100 to 150 pounds and that the cost of conveying 150 convicts from the transports, which could not approach within 60 miles of Lemaine, and of supplying them with provisions, bedding, and materials for huts etc. would not exceed 1000 pounds.[476]

Anthony Calvert, another London merchant, also expressed his willingness to contract for the carriage of 150 convicts to a point as near the island in the Gambia River as his ship could go at a rate of eight pounds a head, plus a demurrage charge of five pounds a day to be paid 30 days after arrival, or at a rate of 14 shillings a ton per calendar month "until her return to the port of London".[477]

All this information Lord Sydney forwarded to the Lords Commissioners of the Treasury on 9 February 1785. He also stressed the dangers of escape and infection due to the crowded state of the prisons, declared the Government's intention of placing convicts on Lemaine for the purchase of which a Mr Richard Bradley had set out some weeks before, entreated their lordships to take the matter into their consideration and receive His Majesty's further commands in respect of sending forth 150 convicts with all necessary provisions together with an armed ship, as the most healthy season for the emigration to the coast was advancing rapidly.[478] Three days later, and before the Treasury had replied to his first letter, he forwarded a second announcing His Majesty's intention to increase the number of convicts from 150 to 200 because the Recorder of London and other persons had represented to him that effectual relief could only be secured by the removal of that number.[479]

The Treasury referred the matter to the Navy Board which saw no objection to accepting Mr Calvert's terms, "considering the nature and danger of the service", although they considered them high. It recommended the hiring of Calvert's vessel at 14 shillings per ton per month; as for Barnes's proposals concerning the provision of an armed vessel it thought them very extravagant and it had no doubt that it could get a proper vessel on more reasonable terms.[480]

The law as it had been in 1775 had provided for the transportation of offenders to His Majesty's Plantations and Colonies in America. The American Revolution and the accumulation of convicts within the gaols and hulks had caused the 1779 Committee of Enquiry to recommend the substitution of other places for America. This was accomplished by the Act 19 Geo. III, c.74. Sentences of transportation to Africa then became the rule. Transportation to America was restored in 1783. Within the following two years the resistance of the United States, of British settlers in America, and of the Africa Company practically closed all avenues through which criminals could be removed from England. Thus Mr T.B. Bailey, an acting magistrate of Lancaster, informed the 1785 Committee that offenders had been sentenced to imprisonment in England because of a difficulty in effecting the punishment of transportation.[481] By that date, however, provision had been made for the removal of convicts to other places; the Act 24 Geo. III (2nd session) c.56 authorised the sending of convicted felons to any place appointed by the King in Council. From the passing of that Act the sentence "Transportation overseas" became the usual one, the King in Council later determining the destination of the convicted.

But several of those who were then detained in English prisons had been sentenced to transportation to America. This difficulty was overcome by the same Act which provided that in such cases it should be lawful "for the Court of the King's Bench or the court before which the guilty had been convicted or any other court having like authority, or in vacation, any two Justices of the King's Bench, Common Pleas, or Barons of the Exchequer of the degree of the Coif to order that such shall be transported to any part beyond the seas which shall have been appointed by His Majesty for the transportation of such offenders".

As the *Censor* hulk alone contained over 260 convicts awaiting transportation the number required to settle Lemaine might easily have been taken from that vessel. In actual fact, however, many of those selected to go to the Gambia were taken directly from the gaols, probably as a result of the greater pressure within them. The Recorder of London was directed to furnish a list of the names of 100 criminals in Newgate. His list is an interesting commentary upon the development of English statute law in the years that followed the American revolt.[482] It contains the names of the following offenders:

8   convicts already sentenced to Africa for whom no order was necessary;

2   convicts pardoned on condition of service in West Africa but "having

returned remain under sentence of death and require a new pardon on condition of being sentenced to Africa for life";

30 convicts sentenced to death, respited during His Majesty's pleasure and recommended to pardon on condition of being transported to Africa;

37 convicts sentenced to such places as His Majesty in Council should appoint; for them an order in Council directing them to Africa was necessary;

22 convicts sentenced to be transported to America for whom an order in Council was needed stating that such sentence could not be conveniently executed and ordering the court to transport them to Africa.

In March 1785 the Government realised that a postponement of the plan was inevitable unless the convicts were to be landed on Lemaine during the unhealthy season, which action the Government wished to avoid. Its decision was conveyed to Duncan Campbell together with a request that he should propose accommodation for those already selected until the following September because of the immediate necessity of removing them from their gaols.[483] The result was the creation of a new hulk named the *Ceres*, upon which the proposed settlers were placed to await their transportation.[484] Destiny ruled otherwise for on 16 March 1785 Burke, who apparently had heard a rumour of the plan, directly attacked the Government's maladministration of the transport system generally which he declared was expensive, unfair since it failed to distinguish between serious and trivial offences, and conducive to inhumanity because the Government's power to alter destinations made possible an increase of suffering. He estimated that no less than 100,000 were awaiting removal and he trusted they were not to be sent to Gambia which "though represented as a wholesome place was the capital seat of plague, pestilence, and famine".[485]

On 11 April also Lord Beauchamp brought before the notice of the House a rumour that the Government was contemplating the formation of a convict colony outside the limits of British territory. It appeared to him to be a subject well worthy of inquiry.[486] Burke, who was well prepared for the discussion, supported the proposed inquiry declaring he could not reconcile with justice a mock display of mercy which compelled those whom the law had spared from death to undergo it by being sent to a land where they could not live and death might be singularly horrid. He imagined that the gallows would rid them of their lives more mercifully than the climate and the natives of Africa would. Pitt, by interjecting that Burke was assuming facts without any better authority than report, moved him to the spirited reply that he understood there were 75 felons now on board a ship which, if it sailed before morning, might soon be out of reach of Parliament.[487]

The King by his coronation oath had bound himself to execute judgement in mercy and the Right Hon. Gentleman was the trustee of the King's Oath. Public safety as well as humanity called for an interposition of Parliament. The result was the appointment, on 20 April, of a Committee of the House of Commons to inquire into what had been done to execute the Act 24 Geo. III (2nd session) c.56. Among its members were Lord Beauchamp (chairman), Messrs. Fox, Burke, Ord, Eden, Hussey, Popham, Dundas, Sheridan, Francis, and many others including Lords, Knights of the Shire, and merchants.[488]

This Committee commenced its public inquiry on 26 April, by questioning Thomas Butterworth Bailey, the already-quoted acting magistrate of Lancaster. It continued to examine witnesses for about a fortnight at the end of which time it had collected enough evidence to present a very unfavourable report of Lemaine. This evidence, gathered from 13 expert witnesses and constituting the most authoritative criticism of the Lemaine project, cannot be omitted in any satisfactory treatment of the plan.

Mr Thomas Bailey testified to the great accumulation of offenders that had arisen because of the check in the transportation system. The prisons, he declared, were insufficient to accommodate them; some who were under sentence of transportation had been confined from three to three and a half years. Magistrates were unable to execute the law "since they knew of no place to which convicts could be conveyed".[489] Mr Akerman, the keeper of Newgate, supported this evidence, stressing the fact that his gaol contained about 600 prisoners whereas its inmates five or six years before had totalled approximately half that number. He was convinced that no gaol could reform a criminal. The hulks in his opinion had failed to do it also.

Mr John Barnes, as the proposer of the site, naturally presented a pleasant picture of Lemaine and its neighbourhood. He had passed the island although he admitted he had not been on the Gambia since the year 1757. The natives were the best disposed people in the world; the climate upstream better than at its mouth. He believed that the natives would let sufficient land, that escape would be difficult, that Europeans could cultivate enough for their own sustenance without prejudice to their health, and that convicts, deprived of all means of debauch, would stand a good chance. He admitted the difficulty of preventing boats from passing in the night but pointed out that the island contained no timber from which canoes could be built. He also supposed that the natives would punish those who offended them and if those offenders sheltered among the settlers the natives would punish them too.

Mr Evan Nepean, the Undersecretary, described the Government's

100

intentions. As the Africa Company had refused to take any more convicts those on the *Ceres* hulk were to be sent to Lemaine which, although not definitely accepted, was preferred to every other site. The plan was to land 200 convicts, including women, on the island with provisions to support them until they were able to raise food for themselves. They were to take with them tools, merchandise, grain, a medicine chest etc.. He thought that only a few firearms would be supplied to them since protection would be unnecessary as the natives were inoffensive. After being settled on the island they were to be left to themselves; a guardship would be stationed below the settlement to prevent escape; a person appointed by the convicts themselves would distribute their stores and provisions. He confessed that he did not know whether the same chief owned both sides of the river in the area. No other place was available; America, Honduras, and Nova Scotia had protested against the reception of British criminals; Cape Breton had too few settlers to accept any. The expense during the first year would not be greater than that incurred by the hulks; later it would be less "even if they were all to live".[490]

The evidence of the other witnesses was anything but encouraging. Mr Boone, an army surgeon, declared that fevers prevailed from July to November, fluxes from December to March; at Senegal two-thirds of the King's forces had perished annually; not one of a company of between 50 and 100 soldiers sent up that river had returned. He did not think a European could labour there for a month without the attention of an able surgeon. Mr Call reported that only three out of 300 men sent up the Senegal ever returned. Their tools had been ruined by the climate. Sir George Young believed a ship of war would lose nine-tenths of its crew if it remained on the coast during the rainy season; white men would die in an hour if they attempted to labour; at Albreda only one French woman had survived and she had had five husbands in three years. Commodore Thompson doubted whether two out of a hundred would survive if they had to support themselves; convict women would certainly die on Lemaine.

The fact that the island produced rice was a proof that it was swampy and therefore unhealthy. Mr Henry Sweatman, who had lived on the coast, prophesied that not one would be alive at the end of six months; that persons carried in irons would be quite unfit for labour and therefore starve unless the natives supported them. Mr John Nevan had passed Lemaine as a trader. He had lost six out of 21 employees when he was in the "healthiest part"; white traders living there could hardly crawl. Lemaine was certainly not the place in which Englishmen could labour; it had first to be cleared. Mr Thomas Nesbitt had started up the river but had been told by Captain Heatley that he had lost all his crew in the healthiest season.

As for the natives, Boone believed that they would take all that they could lay their hands on. Sir George Young was convinced that if the settlers went armed they would kill the natives; if not the natives would kill them. If the natives were insulted they would avenge themselves on any white man. Commodore Thompson regarded them all as thieves; men entering the woods would be murdered; undisciplined convicts would make them more barbarous; they would cede the required land and then cut off the settlers afterwards. Sweatman was satisfied that, if injured, they would retaliate on the innocent as well as on the guilty. Nevan declared that they would murder all the whites and seize their goods; when he was there the native chiefs on the opposite sides of the river were at war.

The proposal to establish self-government was equally condemned. Call imagined that if military discipline could save so few lives there was little hope for an uncontrolled mob; they would probably seize a trading ship or provoke the natives to revenge and be extirpated. Sir George Young declared that convicts could not be kept there without government except in irons. Commodore Thompson asserted that England had not sufficient strength on the Gambia to control 150 armed felons. Mr Street, who went out with McKenzie's companies, reported that the convicts had behaved themselves while in the presence of the warships but had later inspired their officers with terror.

Any attempt to prevent escape by means of a guardship was likewise ridiculed. Call predicted that 50 to 60 good subjects would perish each year in taking care of from 200 to 300 criminals. The belief that British trade in the area would be ruined by the introduction of convicts was commonly held. Nevan maintained he would rather trust the natives.

All this information and more was placed before the House of Commons in a Report on 9 May 1785. No comment or recommendation was attached to it; apparently the evidence alone was considered sufficient to condemn the scheme. To assess the blame is not easy. Pitt's interjection in the House was clearly questionable if it was meant to convey the impression that no transportation was intended but he might have been referring to the declared unhealthiness of the site, about which the "Description" said little. It did, however, predict the deaths of many of the first settlers, but many had died in the American transportation and even greater numbers in the hulks; nor can we be sure that Pitt was conversant with all the details of the plan although, as a member of the Treasury Board, he ought to have known the facts. Barnes had emphasised the difficulty of maintaining a full complement of Europeans and Heatley had stressed the need of removing the guardship during the rainy season. Sydney, if he had read the correspondence, must have suspected a serious mortality yet in his correspondence there is no hint of intended cruelty and if he had aimed at simply getting rid of the convicts he could have despatched them before the inquiry without waiting for the return of the healthier season. There was certainly nothing illegal about his action.

The "Description" predicted a flourishing settlement after a preliminary suffering and its facts, according to its writer, had been gathered from members of the Africa Company who had resided in the country and who should therefore have been reliable authorities on the matter. Barnes and Heatley were evidently hoping to advance their own interests but in justice to themselves we should note that they did not suppress all the unpleasant facts. Nepean's reference to the cheapness of the scheme even if all the convicts were to live indicates that the Undersecretary was not entirely ignorant of one of the possible results; but it must not be forgotten that many of the selected convicts had forfeited their lives and that report foretold a heavy mortality within English gaols and their neighbourhood if something were not speedily done to reduce the pressure upon them. Difficulties of this kind may have caused Sydney to concentrate on the general sense of the proposals laid before him and to neglect their unpleasant details but, when all this is admitted, idealists will ever rejoice that the persistence of Beauchamp and the eloquence of Burke produced evidence which prevented an inevitable catastrophe and withheld from British annals a blot which time itself could scarcely erase.

During the taking of this evidence other convicts had been added to those destined for Africa. The Recorder of London, on 28 April 1785, reported that only 78 of those he had selected had been removed from Newgate.[491] On 3 May he forwarded a supplementary list of 22 names of criminals chosen as "most proper to be treated with severity".[492] The Committee's report however discouraged a continuation of the plan. When the determination to desist was reached is not known but an undated and unsigned note among the Home Office papers gives the reason. It reads, "As so much noise has been made and so many objections started to the sending the convicts to the Island of Lemaine on account of its very unhealthy situation it might be advisable to change the place of their destination".[493] Possibly, however, this decision was not arrived at until after the Committee's second report on 28 July of the same year as the note suggests Das Voltas as a substitute for Lemaine and that was the site recommended by the second report.[494]

Meantime the convicts detained on the *Ceres* were required to labour on the Thames, and in West Africa Richard Bradley was obeying his instructions to purchase Lemaine. There he met seven traders resident on the Gambia who wrote to Sydney supporting the proposal and trusting that "so prudent a plan" would not be dropped.[495] This letter seemingly arrived too late to avert the rejection of the Lemaine project; it is possible that it was delivered by Bradley on his return when he reported the purchase of the island and presented his account.[496] This showed that five chiefs, in addition to the local king, were interested in Lemaine; further that their consent to anything desired of them could be secured only by bestowing upon them presents or entertainment. Now it is certain that the convicts would not have possessed the means to entertain these native rulers had they been established on Lemaine. Moreover, the account demonstrates that the chiefs themselves were not in submission to the local king. Consequently the settlers could have expected little protection from their immediate native ruler. Thus the evidence supplied by Richard Bradley only goes to support the view that an attempt to establish a convict settlement on the Gambia would have failed because of the effects of both native oppression and climatic conditions.[497]

On 28 July 1785 the same Committee issued a second report. This was both recapitulatory and constructive. Its historical criticism has already been presented in the treatment of the American transportation.[498] More interesting, at the present moment, is its statement of the determinants of a satisfactory penal settlement. Firstly, its position and climate should be healthy since the Royal pardon implied that the transportation would not expose lives to any imminent danger. A coastal situation was to be preferred to that of an island one for reasons of defence and supply. Unless a distant site were selected, "whence return would be difficult", the purpose of the transportation would be defeated. The outcasts of an old society would never serve as the sole foundation of a new one. Discipline was essential; to establish a colony of convicts with no other government than that which they themselves should create could answer no good or natural purpose as bloodshed and confusion would probably ensue, and the Committee could point to "no spot so distant that its evil effect would not be felt on the trade and navigation of these kingdoms".

Nevertheless the Committee was satisfied that convict labour could be employed to establish settlements for the encouragement of British trade. The enterprising spirit of many of the convicted when under strict control and when far removed from evil associations would incite them to be honest, while the lack of any hope of return would urge them to consider that their own happiness was involved in the prosperity of the new settlement.

The number of felons under sentence of transportation could not be determined as the Committee had received returns of such offenders from the Home Counties only but it supposed the total could not be less than 1500. Every session added to the number; consequently a revival of transportation on a considerable scale was necessary, if that mode were exclusively adopted, to prevent a further increase in the prisons. The expense would be great but perhaps less than that spent on the hulks.

The Committee believed that future public benefit and relief to gaols were closely connected and it hoped therefore that it would not be impossible to fix upon some site whose commercial and political advantages would indemnify the public for its original charges. It viewed with grave concern the probable lessening of respect for authority due to the impossibility of carrying into effect sentences of transportation. It was in complete agreement with the Africa Company in its opposition to the receipt of further convicts. Its views on the Gambia plan had been revealed in its last report but it pointed out that within the African continent lay a vast tract between Portuguese Angola and the Dutch Cape of Good Hope which was neither possessed nor occupied by Europeans. Its soil was fertile and well stocked with flocks and herds, herbs and vines. A rich copper vein lay near the great river of Das Voltas which flowed within the area. Travellers who had traversed portions of it had found the natives hospitable. A fine harbour lay near the mouth of that river into which H.M. Ships could retire during the unhealthy season and which could also form a base for whale fishery as far as the Falkland Islands. Its prevailing winds were favourable for trade with the Rio de la Plata, Brazil, the West Indies, and the Guinea Coast. It would provide a port of call for East India vessels and therefore reduce the advantage possessed by the Dutch and the French. Its settlement could be most easily effected during the interval between 1 August and 15 September.

Convicts could be established within the area at a cost not exceeding 25 pounds a head. Artificers, mechanics, and husbandmen should be chosen for the experiment although a lack of the last-named "would not matter since land in those latitudes requires little skill in cultivation". Many Loyalist American families were prepared to settle there; they could utilise the labour of the convicts. Should it succeed it would provide the means of annually relieving the gaols of England and of diverting the stream of English emigration from the United States to places still subject to the Crown of Great Britain. If the Legislature still persisted in its desire to transport to Africa this alone seemed practicable but the Committee recommended its adoption only "as the commercial and political benefits of a settlement on the South West coast of Africa might be deemed of sufficient consequence to warrant the expense inseparable from such an undertaking, at the same time that it restored energy to the execution of the law and contributed to the interior police of this kingdom". It estimated that the cost would be as follows:

Annual expense of a 40 gun ship	£4,392
Annual expense of a 200 ton tender	1,400
Annual expense of 3 Companies of marines, i.e. 180	6,550
Annual expense of clothing & victuals for 600 convicts, without liquor	4,827
Annual expense of Superintendent and establishment	1,500
	£18,669

But this expenditure would probably decline as food was produced and troops were withdrawn, to £7000 a year.

Freight of 600 convicts including the cost of the two guardships, at £45 a head	£27,000
Tools, etc.	1,000
Seed and stock	1,300
	£29,300

The Government responded promptly. In less than a month from the publication of this report the Admiralty was instructed to despatch one of H.M. Ships on the coast of Africa to the River or Bay of Das Voltas, situated between 28 and 29 degrees south latitude, to survey and secure intelligence concerning the area in order to determine its suitability for a settlement. No offence was to be given to the natives and as success would depend upon the employment of qualified persons their lordships trusted that such additional officers or qualified persons would be employed as would be necessary.[499] The vessel selected for the task was the *Nautilus* sloop; among the "additional persons" who sailed in her was a botanist, Mr P.A. Howe, whose instructions had been drawn up by Sir Joseph Banks.[500] During their absence preparations were continued at home.

The House of Commons maintained its interest in the gaol problem; on 7 March 1786 it ordered returns to be forwarded from all parts of England setting forth the number of persons convicted of any offence and detained since 1 January. Four days later Lord Sydney directed letters to more than 50 areas calling for this information.[501] On 31 March a similar order resulted in the despatch of another large batch of enquiries concerning the number, the offences, and the punishments of felons convicted in the year 1785.[502] The Secretary of State moreover checked the returns as they were received for on 24 June he informed certain sheriffs and the Chairman of the Quarter Sessions for Middlesex that his orders had not yet been executed.[503] Should Das Voltas prove to be a suitable site for the reception of convicts Lord Sydney meant to know where he might lay his hands on them.

Tenders were invited for the transportation of felons to the area. In June Nepean informed Thomas Steele of the Treasury that as Mr Pitt had desired that he should find out the cost of conveying convicts to "Cape Voltas" he had made enquiries. Duncan Campbell had estimated that it could be undertaken for 20 pounds a head if 850 males and 150 females were transported under the escort of a warship but he did not desire to engage in the business. "Messrs. Turnbull Macaulay & Co." and Mr Anthony Calvert had also sent in proposals. These he forwarded together with some observations on the necessity for immediate action, as the *Nautilus* sloop was expected to return within six weeks.[504] Steele referred the tenders to the Navy Board which expressed the opinion that the proposal of "Messrs. Turnbull Macaulay and Gregory" seemed very reasonable but an escort appeared to be highly necessary under any agreement of the kind.[505]

Everything then hinged on the report of the officials sent in the *Nautilus* sloop. Nepean foretold the future aright when he predicted the return of that vessel in about six weeks' time. In August Sydney informed the Treasury that the *Nautilus* sloop had reported that the coast between 15 degrees 50 minutes and 33 degrees was sandy, barren, and unfit for settlement.[506] What seemed to be the last hope of settling any of the occupied continents had therefore to be cast aside; one unoccupied continent remained, and to it the Government now directed serious consideration. In that same letter Sydney reported the Crown's intention of transporting felons to Botany Bay,[507] situated on the coast of New South Wales in a latitude of about 33 degrees South.

There was little that was similar in these two uncompleted experiments. Both aimed at transferring convicts from English gaols to portions of Africa but, whereas in the first scheme only 200 were marked down for removal, in the second it is almost certain that the Government hoped to transport a thousand criminals. Otherwise what reason could Campbell and Calvert have had for basing their estimates on that number? The change was probably due to the facts concerning the gaols set forth in the returns ordered by the House of Commons and to the encouragement given by the House of Commons to the second scheme. The former also aimed at settling an area 450 miles inland, regularly visited by merchants, and lying approximately 13 degrees north of the equator; the latter directed attention to a position on a coast, sandy and practically unknown, and situated in between 28 and

29 degrees south of the equator.

Stranger still was the contrast between the methods of approach. Lemaine would have been settled without any inspection, while the more humanitarian method of an official survey was practised in the second experiment.[508] Secrecy was employed in the Lemaine preparations to such an extent that even members of parliament were compelled to trust to rumour. It would be easy to attribute this to a desire to avoid inquiry into a doubtful enterprise, but secrecy within the Cabinet was a recognised practice at the close of the 18th Century, and governmental measures were often conducted on the same principle; a haze of public uncertainty hung over the preparations for transportation to New South Wales some time later. Das Voltas, on the other hand, was recommended by a Committee of the House of Commons.

The uncertainty under which the Government itself laboured throughout the period is demonstrated by an undated rough draft of an order changing a destination to Africa, found among the Treasury papers. In this draft a space occurs after the words "shall be Africa" and at the side is written, "Here insert what part of Africa". Continued uncertainty often provokes bold action and this, in part, probably explains the determination to adopt so extraordinary a plan as transportation to New South Wales.

7

Unofficial Proposals

THE EXPERIMENTS TO REDUCE the number of convicts in British gaols which have already been discussed were of two kinds: those in which convicted felons were actually conveyed from the British Isles, and those in which the attempts were discarded before the removal of any criminals. One thing they had in common, viz., official support. A greater number of suggested remedies were never accepted by the Government. Some had been presented to Lord Sydney before the issue of the 1785 Committee's Report and had been regarded by him as unworthy of attention.[509] Others, proposed at a later date, met a similar fate. Because of their private origin and their lack of governmental support they are here described as unofficial proposals. Their interest lies not in what they accomplished, for they accomplished nothing, but in the light they shed upon the attitudes of their originators towards the less fortunate of their own period. As data to be used in forming an estimate of the mentality of the 18th Century Englishman they have a real value; as an indication of the almost general interest in the gaol problem they are now presented.

Their presentation is not without its difficulties; a lack of dates prevents a chronological treatment and their diversity opposes the discovery of any idea common to them all and discourages any attempt at reasoned sequence. The method adopted will therefore be geographical rather than historical. Beginning with those schemes whose suggested testing ground was England itself, it will then consider in turn foreign and distant proposals; it will conclude with those which pointed to New South Wales, and so prepare the way for the succeeding chapter.

The first of these suggestions, that of Sir Watkin Lewes,[510] may reasonably be judged to be irrelevant to the subject of transportation as it made no provision for the removal of convicts from Great Britain but, as a suggested alternative method of reducing the overcrowding within British gaols, it certainly is germane to any study of the disposal of convicts and is consequently included. He offered to enter into a contract with the Government to feed, clothe, and employ any number of convicts up to 600 men and 30 women in the making of rope and other cordage. He suggested that the Government should hand over to him the Woolwich Rope Yard as a place of both labour and confinement. To secure individual isolation as much as possible he proposed to prohibit all unauthorised visiting and to erect within the Yard at government expense 600 cells at a cost of 10 pounds a piece. His suggested establishment included a Governor, two lieutenants, a chaplain, surgeon, master rope maker, commissary, purser, steward, miller, brewer, two matrons, and a large number of assistants making a total of over 50. Peace and order were to be preserved by a marine guard of 44 supplied by the Government, which also was to be responsible for the maintenance of a hospital. The male convicts would be employed at making rope and cordage which would be sold to the Navy[511] at ten guineas a ton over the market price of hemp, thus making a saving of about five pounds a ton.

Diligence was to be encouraged by the adoption of piece work and a payment of from two to four tickets a day, each having an ideal value of one penny, which could be used to purchase strong beer, cheese, check shirts, and other desirable articles. The riotous and refractory were to be tamed by rolling the ground with rollers proportionate to their strength, the boatswain meantime flogging the dilatory. Other troublesome folk would raise water by a capstan pump, beat hemp, or be placed in a tub fitted with a pump "so that they must either pump or drown". Whipping was to be reserved for serious offences only; when inflicted it was to be ordered by a magistrate and performed in the presence of a surgeon. The women were to be employed in washing, mending, and making linen for the men, from whom they were to be kept entirely separate.

The food ration, the convicts' uniform, even the method of keeping the convicts clean were carefully explained; thus those enjoying sheets, a luxury allowed to the diligently docile only, were to have them washed every two months, and a Captain Swobber, with the aid of sundry assistants, was to see that the convicts combed their hair night and morning. Even the clergyman's duties were prescribed, for the subjects of his discourses were to be "the moral duties of Christians and the necessity of submitting to civil law and appointed governors . . . leaving all abstract points of Divinity and logical distinctions, definitions, etc. of prelates and schoolmen". In return for his services in employing 600 convicts the proposer desired the Government to advance to himself 6000 pounds which he would repay at a rate of 250 pounds every three months. He supposed that his method would save the public at least 10,000 pounds a year.

On 1 May 1786 a Mr John Donaldson proposed to employ "convicts, vagrants, and other idle and disorderly people whether old, young, and of either sex" in the North Sea herring industry.[512] The suggestion was based upon the proposed establishment of a great fishing company entered into "under the patronage of the Royal Boroughs of Scotland" in the year 1720. Donaldson held their books and was the only person alive who knew the causes of the discontinuation of that project. In return for the right to continue the experiment with convicts and to have a share in the profits for a certain number of years, he would explain the plan of which he had the original contract "with all its signatures". If put into practice soon he believed there would be "few robberies etc. about London and other places next winter".

Perhaps the most extraordinary of all these proposals was that which suggested the perpetual retention of convicts in mines 50 to 100 fathoms underground because Holy Writ had declared that the Deity had ordained eternal darkness as a just punishment for sinners.[513] On the principle that the sun was not intended to shine on both the just and the unjust the writer advocated the exclusion of convicts "from the common bounties of nature" and their imprisonment "where the vicissitudes of day and night are not known and where they will sigh in perpetual darkness and the whole length of their slavery will be one mournful alternative of insensibility and labour". The futility of sending offenders abroad where they might enjoy liberty and a climate possibly more attractive than that of England impressed him; terror alone could reform the convicted: "see the consequences of the rack abroad". Mining was almost equal to death; it would demand a minimum number of keepers, provide time for the convicts to reflect and in all probability make necessity a virtue. Those who were turbulent or refractory might be cured by a reduction of their victuals or by confinement in a condemned pit. Escape could easily be made utterly impossible; by simply pulling up the ropes the confined would be as safe as if "they had already crossed the River Styx".

Nor would he accept the view that mining was unhealthy; its freedom from scorching sun and winter winds promoted health; near Crackow was a mine in which upwards of a thousand lived, some of whom had never seen the sun for years. To encourage industry he proposed to pay the convicts one half of the normal wage, which could be used in supporting their families or be allowed to accumulate for their use when released. The opposition of the miners could be overcome by offering to them as a bounty to leave their occupation the money "now" spent in transportation. If they returned they should be liable to punishment; their children could "follow the sea" and in that way become an advantage in time of war.

To remove suspected objections he suggested that the scheme might be attempted in Cape Breton Island which an attached newspaper

111

cutting declared contained coal and salt mines, for "salt mines would be just as effective as coal mines". As for the women, they should be kept in penitential houses and employed in making clothes for the Army and Navy, their pay also accumulating for their use when set at liberty. The plan he believed would save the public at least 50,000 pounds a year besides bringing to the Government all the present owners' profits. Internal evidence shows that this plan was prepared in 1786. It bears no signature but its closing paragraph proclaims that the writer had some years before suggested the sale of convicts to the Algerine pirates. Now William Eden (Lord Auckland) had suggested that scheme. Thus, apart from its inhumanity, the most astounding feature of this "darkness cure" is the fact that it was probably mooted by a man who at the time was reputed to be one of England's foremost writers on matters economic and legal, for it is difficult to imagine any scheme that could have provoked more economic and legal disputing.[514]

Eden's earlier proposals were included in his work, "A Discourse on Banishment", written probably in or about the year 1784.[515] Utility was again the foundation of his argument. Comparing the Russian and the English systems of transportation he came to the conclusion that the former was superior since it provided that those whose misconduct had caused them to lose any claim to indulgence should be compelled to labour in mines in the places of better citizens. The English method produced the opposite effect: its banishment was beneficial to the criminal and injurious to the community for it deprived the kingdom of a subject while it transferred him to a new country as fertile, as happy, as civilised, and in general as healthy as that which he had offended. In the writer's opinion there was reason to believe that the method had actually encouraged crime. To redress that he suggested the strict employment of a limited number of convicted felons in the dockyards, stannaries, salt mines, and public buildings of the kingdom. The more enormous offenders might be sent to Tunis, Algiers, and other Mahometan parts for the redemption of Christian slaves; others might be compelled to dangerous expeditions or be sent to establish new colonies, factories, and settlements on the coast of Africa, and on small islands, for the benefit of navigation.[516]

The Algerine pirates were not the only foreign power that appeared in proposals to dispose of English convicts; on 17 October 1785 the Dutch ambassador in London (de Lynden) addressed to Lord Sydney a letter declaring that the 300 English criminals[517] promised by the Secretary of State were awaited in the ports of Helvoet and the Texel.[518] The proposal, which he declared he had referred to the consideration of the Companies of the East and West Indies as well as to the College of the Admiralty of the Republic, had been accepted on 4 September last. He complained that the Secretary of State was not fulfilling his promise and he suspected that he was considering some other method of disposing of the convicts. Now whether Sydney ever promised definitely to present 300 convicts to the Dutch is not certain as no written evidence is available[519] but de Lynden's lack of restraint in distributing sarcasm in his complaint gives the impression that he believed himself duped, and if it were true that the Dutch vessels were awaiting the arrival of the criminals the offer must have been taken seriously.

That the Secretary of State had been considering something of the kind is demonstrated by a letter addressed to Sydney by Lord Howe four days earlier; in it Howe stated that "if the conditions required by Mr. de Lynden to be sure of retaining the convicts in the service of the States until the term of their transportation expires had been confined to the term of their passage to any of the Dutch settlements abroad" he would most heartily concur in the proposal as he knew of no other so effective expedient to deter them and others of similar inclination. But if it meant that Great Britain could reclaim such convicts neither on land nor sea, he feared that the Dutch would use the plan to frustrate England's right of search for British sailors in Dutch ships "by refusing to surrender every British seaman they may seduce into their service under some colourable plea that they also were convicts, which British naval commanders might not be able to disprove".[520]

As an indication of the extent to which rumour or fancy could impose upon the credulity of even a man of business we might refer to the offer of Mr J. Margetson. In writing to Nepean on 15 July 1785 he stated that he understood that the Government intended to purchase "a large ship for the use of convicts to lay on the coast of Africa".[521] He declared that he had in his possession the "French 64, *Actionaire*", a vessel of about 1400 tons burthen which he supposed would be a complete ship for the purpose. He was prepared to sell it and he desired to know to whom he should make the tender. Margetson could not have supposed that a vessel of the size of the *Actionaire* would serve the purpose of a guardship on the River Gambia. It is clear that he supposed that the Government was considering a plan of establishing a hulk on the African coast. A more fantastic method of disposing of convicts could hardly be conceived.

About the same time a Colonel Dalrymple proposed a settlement on the Caffree coast of South Africa.[522] He emphasised the presence in the area of large herds of cattle, of an abundance of sea cows and elephants and of a climate and soil that would enable the growth of vines and vegetables. Dalrymple made no reference to the introduction of convicts into his suggested settlement but in view of the fact that the

113

Government was at the time seeking a site suitable for colonisation by convicts in South Africa the proposal is interesting.

A considered scheme for transporting offenders to Madagascar was put forward by a Captain Blankett in November 1786 after the return of the *Nautilus* sloop from Das Voltas.[523] The plan was not uninvited as it is introduced by a statement declaring that it was forwarded at the wish of the Undersecretary (Evan Nepean). Blankett recommended the purchase of a convenient site from the natives. The convicts should be confined within the purchased area only; escape should be discouraged by the offer of rewards to those natives who should return such as ran away. Women could be admitted "as freely as should be judged necessary". Male convicts who had completed their sentences or had been reformed could be recruited for the Company's service in India. Among its advantages were the establishment of a port of call on the India route and the encouragement of a British trade in timber, slaves, rice, and gums in return for manufactures. He believed it would prove itself of more value than the most sanguine expectation had yet imagined.

Tristan da Cunha was proposed as a site of a convict settlement by Alexander Dalrymple in September 1786,[524] ostensibly because of the failure of the hulk system and the danger of keeping an "alarming number of convicts" in England, but probably because of a rumour of impending occupation of Norfolk Island or New South Wales by the Government. He suggested that the felons should be sent early in order that they might enjoy the "height of the summer . . . to prepare for the winter". The situation of the island was such that it could easily be supplied with provisions at little or no expense by the southern whalers from the Cape of Good Hope or England. The abundance of sea lions and penguins on the island would make a supply of salt provisions unnecessary. Bread alone would be needed until the settlers had raised potatoes. The convicts could be left entirely to themselves without firearms and with only such small boats as could not go to sea. Escape would be impossible; thus the cost of guards and government would be avoided.

He admitted that all forms of disposing of convicts which allowed them to be their own masters "destroyed in part the effect of the punishment", but on Tristan da Cunha the prospect of comfort was so small without the utmost exertion of industry that it would probably bring most of them to a due sense of their folly, particularly if they were left to the rigour of their own government or brought to that sense of the benefits of regulated society which anarchy would produce. Very turbulent offenders might be transferred to other neighbouring islands, to Gough's Island or, with the permission of the East India

Company, to the Islands of St Paul and Amsterdam which, like Tristan da Cunha, were too remote for the convicts to escape or do any mischief, two necessary attributes of any satisfactory penal settlement.

The concluding suggestions pointed to the Pacific Ocean. In March 1784, during the debate in the House of Commons on the employment of convicts awaiting transportation on the hulks, Mr Hussey declared he could not understand why those who had been delivered to Mr Campbell had not been transported.[525] He was sure nothing short of transportation could effectively overcome the evils of the land. He advised the Government to send its convicts "to an island and to give every man a woman". "There was an island. It was New Zealand".

Probably the most grandiose scheme presented to the Government was that of Colonel Call.[526] The furtherance of British trade was his aim. To accomplish that he had suggested to Lord North in 1779 an expedition to the South Seas to assist the peoples of Chile and Peru against their governments. It might even be wise to offer Gibraltar for Porto Rico. In any case His Majesty's Government might consider some establishment on the coast of New South Wales, New Zealand, New Caledonia, and some other islands nearer the Line.[527] The first appearance of the Cape of Good Hope had been disappointing but it now produced a superfluity. It was reasonable to suppose that New Holland possessed what other countries in similar latitudes did. New South Wales and New Zealand might form the principal settlements; the other two could be their auxiliaries.

He enumerated probable objections to his proposal but maintained that a site should be selected for British subjects who wished to emigrate. Then there was a moral point; it concerned the disposal of convicts which of late had not only been expensive but had been conducted in a manner "disgraceful to the humanity of our character". Instead of being removed from the society they had violated they had been formed into distinct societies for more complete instruction in crime.[528] He proposed, therefore, to transport them to some distant situation where all temptation to a renewal of their former crimes would be wanting and necessity indicate a different conduct. The Navy, the Army, and the East India Company had reformed some atrocious criminals; he believed the same could be accomplished by sending any number of convicts of both sexes with seed, animals, etc. to New Zealand or New South Wales. At first they might quarrel but mutual convenience and the desire for security would unite them into social bonds, and some form of government would then arise though none were given to them. Then, the distance of the proposed settlements would be an advantage to the Mother Country. Distant colonies could not be constantly asking for and drawing supplies from England. Their remoteness would promote navigation and discourage a declaration of independence. He prophesied as a result of an adoption of his scheme a "commerce equal to any quarter of the globe".

Other plans were suggested but examples sufficient to demonstrate the aims of the chapter have been presented. No comment is necessary; the proposals themselves reveal the characteristics of those who advanced them. With possibly one exception the common object of ridding England of undesirables inspired them; the common fate of rejection befell them all.

8

Preparations for New South Wales[529]

THE UNFAVOURABLE REPORT of the nature of the soil in the neighbourhood of Das Voltas ended convict colonial experimentation in
southern Africa. From its inception the Government seems to have entertained some doubts of whether the attempt would be successful;
during the absence of the *Nautilus* sloop Evan Nepean informed
Thomas Steele that "it seemed to him that Mr. Pitt's intention was, if
Voltas was not suitable, that some other spot should be fixed upon to
the southward of the line and as that was his determination it might
not be improper to contract for C. Voltas under certain conditions that
if the spot were changed the ships might be hired at so much a
month".[530] The failure of the attempt, therefore, placed no real check
upon the preparations that had been begun; they were continued but in
a new direction.

Eighteenth Century ministers have on occasion been charged with
negligence and ignorance in the administration of their departments.
Lord Sydney can be acquitted of both; his personal interest in the prisoners was shown some months later in a complaint addressed to the
Lord Mayor of London concerning the dilatory method of reporting
convicts sentenced to death whereby "45 unhappy persons were in the
condemned cells and another session upon the point of beginning".[531]
The gaol returns, ordered by the House of Commons,[532] had placed
him in possession of the facts concerning the numbers awaiting transportation. Then a rumour that the Government intended to remove
convicts to New South Wales inspired the numerous sheriffs and
Clerks of the Peace to renew their complaints of overcrowding with
even greater emphasis. A detailed description of English gaol conditions based upon their reports would fill a long chapter; a few facts
alone will suffice to explain the activity of the Government.

In Newgate were about double the number that it had contained
five or six years before. Southwark gaol was burdened by 140 prisoners
and the most alarming consequences were feared if the military guard,
which had been removed, was not restored. Maidstone gaol contained
103 immediately after gaol delivery and it was almost impossible to

escape infection as its crowded condition forbade proper airing and cleaning. Leeds Castle reported 43 inmates under sentence of transportation alone. Norwich detained in addition to other prisoners 29 who were under sentence of death. They had been reprieved but were awaiting transportation. From Suffolk came an appeal to remove 22 convicts. The insecurity of its gaol had caused the authorities to order the building of a new one. Lancaster gaol was so crowded that it was only with the utmost exertion that the prisoners could be kept "free from putridity". The Chairman and Justices of Dorset described their gaol as so exceedingly crowded that "the health of the prisoners was much to be feared". From a number of prisons came the information that convicted felons had been awaiting transportation for three years; in Ipswich some had been detained four or five years. Seven "desperate fellows" had nearly got out of the strongest room in Reading gaol; some of the inmates of Hereford prison had escaped in spite of the utmost vigilance.

The gaoler of Lancaster Castle expressed the opinion that it never was the magistrates' intention, when they sentenced men to transportation, that they should linger for the principal part of their terms in loathsome gaols upon a scanty pittance, to the injury of their health, morals, and everything that was dear to them.[533] The report of the Surrey gaoler, covering the years 1783-1786, must have been a depressing reminder of past failure. It contained 52 names of offenders, 6 of whom had been ordered to America, 3 to Africa, 22 to beyond the seas, 9 to such places as His Majesty in Council should appoint, while the remaining 12 had been sentenced to death and were awaiting transportation.[534]

These facts and many more equally unpleasant ones were received by Lord Sydney. They were accompanied by a number of complaints concerning the hulks. From Pembrokeshire came the hope that criminals would be "sent to a further distance than the hulks";[535] the High Sheriff and Grand Jury in the Assizes at Bodmin begged that His Majesty would be pleased to consider measures to remove them out of the kingdom.[536] The Lord Mayor of London, some months before, had recommended a reorganisation of the police system of the metropolis, special laws against receivers of stolen goods, the employment of friendless boys on guardships or by the East India Company, a registration of Jews, and a speedy transportation of offenders from the gaols.[537]

Botany Bay had been among the first of the suggested sites suitable for convict settlement. As a witness in the 1779 inquiry, Sir Joseph Banks had described it as a place from which it would be difficult to escape and within which convicts could maintain themselves after the first year with little or no assistance from the Mother Country.[538] Its climate, he believed, was similar to that of Toulouse in southern France. It lacked beasts of prey and he estimated that its native population did not exceed 50 souls. Fish abounded, the grass was luxuriant and would, he believed, cause oxen and sheep to thrive. It was well supplied with water; there was an abundance of timber. If at the beginning 200 or 300 convicts were established there with a year's supply of provisions and all necessary implements he anticipated "an advantageous return". Banks's opinion was not one to be considered lightly but at that time the seriousness of the gaol problem did not warrant an undertaking of such magnitude.

Four years later James Maria Matra brought forward a proposal for the establishment of a settlement in New South Wales to provide an asylum for American Loyalist refugees and to encourage British trade.[539] He stressed the suitability of its climate for the production of "the goods of Europe and of both the Indies" and predicted that a few settlers established there might within a few years cause a revolution in the whole system of European commerce by cultivating spice, sugar cane, tea, coffee, silks, tobacco, indigo, and other commodities. By this means also and for an expenditure of less than 3000 pounds, not including the cost of the vessels and "many of the tools" which could be drawn from the Ordnance Stores, a favourable trade with China might be established as well as a fur trade with the Aleutian Islands and a trade in wool with Japan and Korea. Strategically the plan was attractive since, in the event of war, the commerce of both Holland and Spain could be easily intercepted from New South Wales.[540]

Matra claimed that the scheme offered further advantages: a continuous supply of naval masts which returning ships could bring from New Zealand, and a diverting of British emigration from the United States of America to a British settlement. He proposed the sending of a single ship to discover and allot a suitable district for occupation or, if the Government were disposed to extend the plan, the despatch of two ships with two companies of marines "acquainted with husbandry and manufactures" and about 20 artificers to found a settlement. Cattle, sheep, goats, and other provisions could be bought at the Cape of Good Hope, and cotton seed, plantains, and grape vines obtained from Savaii or any of the Molucca Islands which were "near New South Wales". One of the vessels might be usefully employed in securing a few families and "as many women as may serve for the women left behind" from New Caledonia, Otaheite, or neighbouring islands.

What consideration this proposal received at the hands of the North-Fox Government is not revealed, but since that administration fell in December 1783 it could have had little opportunity to discuss the plan. In the succeeding ministry the Younger Pitt was Prime Minister and Lord Sydney was Secretary of State for the Home Department. The latter discussed the New South Wales project with Matra and suggested the use of convicts as settlers, which caused Matra to declare that in the Secretary's proposal good policy and humanity were united.[541] No attempt, however, was then made to transport convicts to New South Wales; for the time being the Government directed its gaze across the Atlantic.

In January 1785 the Attorney General, Richard Pepper Arden, forwarded to Lord Sydney yet another proposal for settling the coast of New South Wales.[542] This was the work of Sir George Young, whose experience in the Army and Navy had caused him to traverse much of the world. He emphasised the importance of New South Wales in Pacific trade because of its comparative proximity to South America, China, the East Indies, and the Spice Islands and because of its commercial and productive potentialities due to its various climates. He made special reference to the New Zealand flax plant which could be cultivated in New South Wales and would, he believed, oust all other materials in the manufacture of cordage and canvas.

Like Matra, Arden suggested the establishment of American Loyalists in his proposed settlement, which also could receive convicts and thus revive punishment by transportation.[543] In addition to these, other settlers might be secured from the Friendly Islands and China. His estimate of the cost, viz. less than 3000 pounds, was the same as Matra's. He recommended the sending of a 40-gun ship with only half her lower deck guns, a 600-ton store ship and a small vessel of about 100 tons, carrying 110 marines in addition to their crews. Fifty felons could be transported with the first expedition; in following years two ships might each convey a number not exceeding 70. These vessels, on their homeward passage, could lade the wares of the East India Company; thus the transportation could be effected economically.

Three months after the presentation of Sir George Young's proposals the House of Commons appointed its Committee of 1785 to consider the proposed settlement of Lemaine and effectual means of transporting felons from England.[544] As a witness before that Committee Sir George condemned the Gambia project but he does not seem to have suggested any settlement in New South Wales nor did the Committee apparently question him concerning its colonisation.

Matra, on the other hand, was examined and declared that he believed that 500 convicts might with safety be taken to Botany Bay provided the necessary guardships accompanied them.[545] Among his other beliefs were the possibility of establishing additional convict settlements on the coast of New South Wales, because of its great extent, and the certainty of inducing any number of native women to leave their island homes and live with European men in the new settlements. He thought it would be imprudent to experiment with more than 500 felons in the first instance. He recommended despatching them in July and offered to undertake the administration of such a settlement "as a regular colony or as a convict colony", not as a contractor but as an officer under the Government. He would be prepared to administer a convict colony only if he were provided with a force of 200 marines and a guardship. His earlier estimated cost of 3000 pounds he now explained covered only the expense of providing tools, seeds, stock, the suggested 200 marines and 20 artificers; it was entirely independent of the convicts, the cost of whose carriage and landing he had not calculated.

Sir Joseph Banks was again questioned and repeated his favourable account of the Botany Bay area. He did not think the natives would obstruct the settlement of 500 men on that coast and when questioned concerning the possibility of securing native women replied that he had no doubt that they could be obtained at no other expense than the cost of bringing them.[546]

In spite of these favourable reports the Committee recommended transportation to Das Voltas. New South Wales apparently came in for some serious consideration as its members instructed their Chairman "to form such a report as he conceived they might be warranted to make relative to the coast of New South Wales or the west coast of Africa between the latitudes of 28 and 30 degrees south".[547] Unfortunately for Matra and Young, Lord Howe adversely criticised the New South Wales project by stating that "the length of the navigation, subject to all the retardments of an India voyage", did not encourage him to hope for a return of the many advantages in commerce and war contemplated by Matra.[548]

An attempt, however, was made to discover the cost of transporting felons to that area; Mr C.T. Coggan, clerk of the shipping at India House, stated under examination that the cost of conveying recruits to India had averaged £25 2s 5d a head.[549] Duncan Campbell estimated that the carriage of convicts on a voyage of probably six months' duration without any kind of trade could not be undertaken for less than 40 pounds a man if only 200 were carried. Three hundred might be transported at the rate of 30 pounds a head.[550] But for half that sum the Committee believed felons could be conveyed to Das Voltas; Botany Bay was a great way off in 1785. It is not surprising therefore that South Africa was recommended.

The unsatisfactory report on the nature of the soil at Das Voltas directed attention to New South Wales. Its coast had been visited by such well known men as Captain James Cook and Sir Joseph Banks, each of whom had left a description of the area. Cook's Journal, although not altogether flattering, had been interpreted by some, at least, in a way that proved the place possessed a satisfactory harbour and was a suitable site for settlement. Banks had championed the area since the year 1779; as a noted botanist his views were worthy of attention particularly as his financial independence was an earnest of his pecuniary disinterestedness. It is possible, however, that the Government had no real desire to look too curiously into the merits and demerits of the proposed site. Repeated failure on occasion encourages risk. Something certainly had to be done and Pitt had decided to establish a settlement south of the Line, even if Das Voltas failed, before the return of the *Nautilus* sloop.[551]

The stated reasons for the New South Wales experiment are to be found in the Instructions forwarded to the Commissioners of the Treasury on 18 August 1786.[552] They read as follows:

> The several gaols and places for the confinement of felons in this kingdom being in so crowded a state, that the greatest danger is to be apprehended, not only from their escape but from infectious distemper which may hourly be expected to break out amongst them, His Majesty, desirous of preventing by every possible means the ill consequences which might happen from either of these causes has been pleased to signify to me His Royal Commands that measures should immediately be pursued for sending out of this kingdom such of the convicts as are under sentence or order of transportation.

Then after a reference to the unfavourable report of the officers of the *Nautilus* sloop in respect of southern Africa the Instructions continue:

> His Majesty has thought it advisable to fix upon Botany Bay, which according to the accounts given by the late Capt. Cook, as well as the representation of persons who accompanied him during his last voyage[553] who have been consulted upon the subject is looked upon as a place likely to answer the above purposes.

The urge of the gaol difficulty is shown also in the "Heads of a Plan",[554] a document probably composed within the Home Office but one which reflected the views of Matra and of Young. It described the proposed transportation as a "remedy for the evils likely to result from the late alarming and numerous increase of felons in this country and more particularly in the metropolis" and declared that the expenditure attaching to the proposal would be "too trivial to be a consideration with the Government, at least, in comparison with the great object to be obtained by it, especially now the evil is increased to such an alarming degree from the inadequacy of all other expedients that have been hitherto tried or suggested".

Other possible advantages were also mentioned by the "Heads of a Plan". The "fertility and salubrity" of the soil and climate of the proposed settlement would enable the cultivation of the New Zealand flax plant which would be of great consequence to Britain as a naval power in the manufacture of canvas and cables. Its fibre, moreover, would provide the means of producing the finest linens. Most of the commodities of Asia could probably be cultivated within the area, which in a few years would render recourse to neighbouring powers unnecessary. Finally, the trees of New Zealand which grew close to the water's edge and which were superior to anything hitherto known would offer any quantity of masts and ship-timbers for the use of the fleet in India.

To reduce the pressure on English gaols was undoubtedly the immediate aim of the New South Wales experiment. It was the motive stressed by contemporary unofficial critics. Thus in the House of Lords the Earl of Rochford voiced the satisfaction of the members on learning that means had been proposed to remove the inconvenience arising from the crowded state of the gaols.[555] In the Commons Viscount Compton declared that transportation was the only remedy for an evil which required immediate redress.[556] The author of the "Narrative of the late expedition to Botany Bay" stated that the keeping of large numbers of convicts at home had been found inconvenient as well as dangerous to the quietness of civil society,[557] and Captain Hunter in his Journal described the intention of the Government as a means "to remove the inconvenience which the country suffered from the gaols' being so exceedingly crowded with criminals".[558] William Eden viewed Botany Bay as "a settlement for the purpose of exonerating this country of its obnoxious members"[559] while Captain Arthur Phillip who led the first expedition to New South Wales wrote, "the cause of the determination to send convicts was, as is well known, the necessary cessation of their removal to America and the inconvenience experienced in the other modes of destination adopted after that period".[560]

But the future, as well as the present, came within the range of these writers' criticism also. The author of the "Narrative of the late expedition" thought that perhaps the distant idea of replacing lost colonies was one of the reasons for selecting Botany Bay. Eden believed that the "present colonisation . . . might for ages to come incite the industry and extend the navigation of this country". He never contemplated a settlement of convicts only for he declared the Government would never be at a loss for colonists, as England always possessed "a considerable number of loose hands ever ready to embrace any such expedition, who, although they carried few symptoms of industry about them at home, strangely enough often became remarkably diligent on changing their soil". Phillip bade farewell to Nepean in the following terms: "At a future period when this country feels the advantages that are to be drawn from our intended settlement you will enjoy a satisfaction that will, I am sure, make you ample amends",[561] a statement hardly applicable to a penal colony only.

The "Heads of a Plan" reveals official opinion. As an interdepartmental summary of aims and means it cannot be accused of presenting idealistic advantages to placate a dissatisfied public and yet in addition to stressing the necessity for immediate prison relief it set forth aims both imperial and commercial. Moreover, to assume that the Government desired a permanent penal settlement is almost as unreasonable as the belief that it intended to establish a hulk on the African coast. No House of Commons would have tolerated so great an expenditure without the prospect of some financial return, and few believed that convicts alone could found a colony. What men foresaw, though dimly, was a restoration of the American system. That model was always in their minds. Before the expedition sailed Nepean was corresponding with Messrs William Sparrow and J. Singleton[562] about the possibilities of working New Zealand flax, and long before the fall of the Younger Pitt his Government was arranging for the despatch of private settlers to New South Wales.

The proposal provoked less comment than might have been expected from so extraordinary a decision. One critic contended that no place could be more improper as it would be impossible firstly to convey convicts to New South Wales at a moderate expense and secondly to keep them alive after arrival, save by a miracle, since the area was perhaps the most barren in the southern hemisphere.[563] Another, adopting the pen-name H.D., quoted the substance of Cook's Journal to demonstrate that the settlement could scarcely be effected without the shedding of blood.[564] In reply to this a third critic, who assumed the title T.W., declared that it was nobler to die in battle within a colony than perish by the halter at home.[565] He believed that delinquents were being bountifully provided for and if they were to experience hardships it was what they deserved. The American Loyalists were encountering them already and they certainly were not transgressors of the law. He looked forward to the day when "under the care of a generous and forgiving nation" the colony would flourish and become respectable. The writer of the Narrative of the late expedition took a similar line. He considered that the convicts, if reasonable, would realise their advantageous circumstances, for they travelled at the country's expense and began a new life instead of being hanged, which would be the fate of nine-tenths of them if they stayed at home.

The task of arranging the expedition was, as we have already stated, entrusted to the Treasury on 18 August 1786.[566] Eight days later the Treasury transferred much of the work to the Commissioners of the Navy (or Navy Board) with a recommendation that it would be advisable to give notice that it "was prepared to receive proposals for the passage and the victualling during the same, and for a stock of provisions to be landed equal to two years' consumption at the rate of 1000 rations a day".[567] Three days later the Board directed that notice be given in the usual papers that it would be prepared on Tuesday 12 September to treat for about 1500 tons of shipping, by the ton, to carry persons and provisions to Botany Bay.[568]

The rumour of this intended settlement had produced a tender for the carriage of convicts a few days earlier. On 21 August Messrs Turnbull Macaulay and Gregory offered to convey them and provide for them on the way at a rate of 28 guineas a head.[569] This proposal was not accepted; the successful tender was that of William Richards Jnr, a ship broker, who entered into his contract on 12 September 1786.[570]

Past experience had demonstrated that transportation could be performed more economically by making it a part of ordinary commercial activity. Thus Campbell had stated before the 1785 Committee that the carriage of cargo on his American transport vessels had reduced the cost of transporting the convicts from 12 pounds to between 5 and 6 pounds a head.[571] Sir George Young, in proposing New South Wales as a site for settlement, had suggested that the convicts could be carried in ships of the East India Company. This idea evidently impressed the Government for it laid before the Company the economy that would be effected by convict ships' carrying tea on their homeward journey.[572] The Company expressed its willingness to accept the arrangement provided the Government employed suitable ships. Its reason is clear: this method would free it from the expense of covering the cost of the outward voyage.

On these conditions Messrs Richards and Fernie, on 25 September 1786, tendered five ships which had been surveyed and approved by the officers of the East India Company — the *Brothers*, *Britannia*, *Friendship*, *Scarborough*, and *Lady Penrhyn* — as vessels which would be suitable for the carriage of tea from China on the return voyage, and the *Britannia*, *Columbus*, and *George* for the voyage to Botany Bay and back alone.[573] About a fortnight later the Navy Board directed the Deptford Officer to survey, measure, and report on the *Scarborough*, *Lady Penrhyn*, *Britannia*, *Alexander* (in lieu of the *Friendship*), *Golden Grove* (in lieu of the *Three Brothers*), and the *Borrowdale* (in lieu of the *Young William*).[574] Four days later Richards tendered the *Friendship* and *Fishburn* to complete the contract.[575] By these means the following ships were selected for the voyage: *Alexander*, *Scarborough*, *Charlotte*, *Friendship*, and *Lady*

Penrhyn to carry convicts, and the *Fishburn, Golden Grove,* and *Borrowdale* to be store ships.[576] That the Government was not prepared to accept any offered vessel is proved by its refusal to consider the use of an Archangel ship which had been surveyed by the Company and declared very suitable for the China trade.[577]

The state of the gaols alone was a sufficient reason for a speedy preparation of the fleet. It was reinforced by the agreement with the East India Company which provided that the ships were to be discharged from government service if they reached China by 1 January 1788. Otherwise they were to remain in the pay of the Government until their return to Deptford.[578] What time the authorities allowed for the passage of the fleet from New South Wales to China is not stated but three months from the date of its arrival in Botany Bay would probably not have been excessive. Calculating on that basis the ships would have to arrive at that port not later than 1 October 1787, that is, a little more than eleven months after the date of the agreement mentioned. The voyage to Botany Bay was estimated to occupy six months; thus the Government had at its disposal only a few months in which to fit and provision a fleet which was to establish a settlement almost at the antipodes.

The fitting of the fleet was a serious business. The "Heads of a Plan" directed that two vessels were to escort the convicts to Botany Bay, one "a ship of war of a proper class with a part of her guns mounted", the other a tender of about 200 tons.[579] Instructions to this effect were forwarded to the Admiralty who selected the store ship *Berwick* and commanded the Navy Board to equip her for the intended service with all possible dispatch and at the same time provide another vessel of about 200 tons to act as a tender.[580] After rejecting the *Eclipse, Rattlesnake,* and *Grantham* packet the Board finally suggested the *Supply,* a brig of about 175 tons burden, which suggestion the Admiralty accepted.[581] The tender retained its name; that of the *Berwick* was changed; in October 1786 the Admiralty gave orders that she was to be registered on the list of the Royal Navy as a sixth rate "by the name of the *Sirius*".[582]

The conversion of the transports from ships of commerce to prison vessels naturally involved a considerable alteration and strengthening of those parts within which the convicts were to be secured. As early as 1 November the officers of the Deptford Yard recommended "work by job" on the fitting of bulkheads etc. "on board the *Lady Penrhyn, Britannia, Charlotte, Alexander,* and *Scarborough*".[583] In the same month the Deptford officers were ordered to fit the convict ships with such strong hatch bars between decks and over the gratings of the upper decks and such strong locks as Captain Teer should desire.[584] Barricades, occasionally mentioned in the records of the American transportation, apparently were not erected on these vessels for, on 7 December, Captain Teer informed the Navy Board that the two larger ships (*Alexander* and *Scarborough*) had quarter decks nearly three feet above the main decks which he thought sufficient with the marine guards to prevent any danger. The other two ships (*Charlotte* and *Friendship*) carried so few convicts in proportion to the marines and ships' companies that there did not appear to be any occasion for barricades. The main and fore hatchways, however, had been secured by strong bars which could be taken off in a minute.[585]

A little more than a week later the officer commanding the marines on the *Alexander* complained that the hatchway of that ship might easily be broken open. He proposed the addition of two more bars with six strong bolts secured by rivets and locks. Should the convicts riot or prove disobedient there were no loopholes through which the marines could fire upon them. Orders were consequently given to set these faults right.[586] A few weeks later a complaint was received from the marine officers of the *Charlotte* declaring that serious consequences were to be feared should an insurrection occur on that vessel.[587] The officers on the *Friendship* then desired that the alterations which had been made in the *Charlotte* should be effected in their ship. The necessary orders were issued a few days later.[588]

The difficulty of preparing the transport ships was very much increased by changes introduced into the scheme after the issue of the original orders. In its instructions of 26 August 1786 the Treasury had directed the Navy Board to provide a proper number of vessels for the conveyance of 680 male and 70 female convicts, one of which ships was to be fitted up for the accommodation of all the convict women "so as to keep them separate from the men".[589] As a result the *Lady Penrhyn* was fitted up to carry all the women convicts and in addition 36 marines including four officers. Then Teer was suddenly informed that 150 women were to be transported to New South Wales. As many as could be carried in the *Lady Penrhyn* were to be placed on board that vessel; the remainder were to be distributed among the other ships.[590] His disgust can be realised from a description of the trouble he had taken in allotting space in the *Lady Penrhyn*; the women convicts were assigned the area before the after part of the main hatchway where there was a strong bulkhead "fit for men"; from that to the middle of the main hatchway was filled with provisions; then a slight bulkhead kept the marines from the provisions; then cabins were arranged for 32 men, and between them and the seamen was a grating bulkhead to allow air to pass and keep them separate.[591]

The care expended on the *Lady Penrhyn* was certainly not greater than that spent on the other ships; there is good reason to believe that it was less since the authorities had little fear of a dangerous insurrection among the women. It illustrates, however, the attention that was paid to the fitting of the vessels and sheds some light upon the attitude of the Government towards the convicts themselves.

In the transportation to the American colonies the responsibility for the preservation of discipline had rested upon the contractor and his officers. The influence of that system appeared in Lord Sydney's instructions of 18 August 1786 in the words, "If the persons who may contract for the passage of the convicts should be desirous of obtaining military assistance for their greater security they may be accommodated with a part of the marines".[592] In fact, however, the duty of preserving order on the voyage was transferred to the warships and the companies of marines who sailed with the convicts, and no evidence exists to show that the contractor (William Richards) controlled or directed them in any way; the most reasonable supposition is that he accepted with pleasure the assumption of responsibility by other people.

The naval and marine force that proceeded to New South Wales was not chosen solely to preserve discipline on the voyage; a much smaller force could have done that; it was but incidental to the duty of establishing a new British settlement and it is probable that in their selection that fact received first consideration. Arthur Phillip's appointment as captain of the *Sirius* and governor of the colony aroused the wonder of Lord Howe who, as First Lord of the Admiralty, informed Sydney that he certainly would not have selected him for a service of so complicated a nature.[593] He was chosen probably because he was well known to the Undersecretary and possibly because he had for a time engaged in farming, an occupation upon which the new settlement would depend for at least several years.[594] Among the other notable naval officers appointed for the undertaking were Captain John Hunter, second captain of the *Sirius*,[595] and Philip Gidley King, Second Lieutenant on the same ship (each of whom later became a governor of New South Wales), Henry Lidgbird Ball, commander of the *Supply* tender, and Lieutenant John Shortland, agent for transports going to the colony. According to the directions issued for the provisioning of the two Royal Navy ships their complements were 160 and 55 respectively.[596]

In addition to these a considerable marine force proceeded to New South Wales, not only to protect the settlement against possible native attacks but also to preserve order within it. The "Heads of a Plan" proposed an establishment of two companies of marines but the Secretary of State's instructions raised this number to three companies or "to about 180".[597] The orders which actually called the force into being were despatched to the Commanding Officers of Portsmouth and Plymouth on 8 October 1786. They provided for a total of four companies each of 12 commissioned and non-commissioned officers and 40 privates.[598] The volunteer system was recommended and adopted. Each of the ports mentioned provided 80 privates together with the necessary proportion of non commissioned officers. The Government was almost embarrassed by the number of applications for service which it received from commissioned officers; long after the required number had been accepted, tenders continued to flow in; their number almost suggests that little hardship and few terrors were anticipated within the distant settlement. The force was placed under the command of Major Robert Ross; less than a week from its departure, its distribution among the seven ships (or sick, ashore) was as follows:[599]

	Siri.	Alex.	Scar.	Char.	Frie.	Prin.	Lady P.	Sick	Total
Major	1	-	-	-	-	-	-	-	1
Captain	-	-	1	-	-	-	1	-	2
Capt-Lt	-	-	-	1	1	-	-	-	2
1st Lieut	-	2	2	2	-	2	1	-	9
2nd Lieut	-	-	-	-	2	-	1	-	3
Adjutant	1	-	-	-	-	-	-	-	1
Q'master	1	-	-	-	-	-	-	-	1
Sergeant	1	2	2	2	2	3	-	-	12
Corporal	-	2	2	2	3	2	-	1	12
Drummer	3	1	1	1	1	1	-	-	8
Private	7	22	26	34	36	23	3	9	160

The provisioning of so large a body of men and women, both for the voyage and for two years after arrival, was a serious undertaking. The original intention, as stated in the Treasury's recommendations to the Navy Board,[600] was to entrust the provisioning of the marines on their outward journey to the Victualling Department and to provide for the convicts during their passage, and for the whole settlement during the two years mentioned, through the medium of a contractor. The disappearance of Richards's contract leaves some doubt as to the method actually adopted but such evidence as remains suggests that the original plan was rejected in favour of one which placed upon Richards the entire responsibility. Thus after the decision to increase the number of marines it was to him that the Navy Board turned to supply the necessary additional provisions "agreeable to his contract of the 12th September, 1786".[601]

The amount of food that was to be supplied to the expedition was calculated by determining an individual daily ration and multiplying it by the number of daily rations and the number of days to be provided for. In determining the daily ration no distinction was drawn between the marines and the convicts except in respect of alcoholic liquors, which the Government decided should not be supplied to the convicts. Apart from the allowance of spirits, the standard adopted was that of the troops serving in the West Indies. Thus the Treasury ordered the supplying of the following weekly ration to the marines and male convicts after their arrival in New South Wales:[602]

7 pounds of bread or 7 pounds of flour
7 pounds of beef or 4 pounds of pork
3 pints of pease
6 ounces of butter
1 pound of flour or one-half pound of rice.

The weekly allowance for the voyage was only two-thirds of this amount on the ground that that was the rule observed in victualling soldiers when on the sea and because, as Sir Charles Middleton said, conditions on board ship would not admit of much exercise and consequently a two-thirds allowance would be more advantageous than a full one.[603] The ration provided for the marines during their passage to Botany Bay was therefore in some respects less than the amount stated. It was as follows:[604]

		SUN	MON	TUE	WED	THU	FRI	SAT	TOTAL
Bread	(lb)	1	1	1	1	1	1	1	7
Beef	(lb)	–	–	2	–	–	–	2	4
Pork	(lb)	1	–	–	–	1	–	–	2
Pease	(pt)	$\frac{1}{2}$	–	–	$\frac{1}{2}$	$\frac{1}{2}$	$\frac{1}{2}$	–	2
Oatmeal	(pt)	–	1	–	1	–	1	–	3
Rum	(pt)	$\frac{1}{2}$	$\frac{1}{2}$	$\frac{1}{2}$	$\frac{1}{2}$	$\frac{1}{2}$	$\frac{1}{2}$	$\frac{1}{2}$	$3\frac{1}{2}$
Butter	(oz)	–	2	–	2	–	2	–	6
Cheese	(oz)	–	$\frac{1}{4}$	–	$\frac{1}{4}$	–	$\frac{1}{4}$	–	$\frac{3}{4}$
Vinegar	(pt)	–	–	–	–	–	–	$\frac{1}{2}$	$\frac{1}{2}$

Since, as we have already noticed, no distinction was drawn between the convicts and their guards in respect of their rationing we may assume that the convicts enjoyed a similar or equal weekly allowance, omitting of course the $3\frac{1}{2}$ pints of rum.

The women convicts' ration, according to the Treasury's instructions, was to be two-thirds of that supplied to the men.[605] The generosity of this allowance is demonstrated by comparing it with the normal ration issued to the wives of soldiers and marines, which was only one-half of that received by their husbands. Its liberality almost raises doubts but, as Phillip himself reported from Sydney[606] that the convict women were being given two-thirds of the men's ration, we must suppose that they were more favoured than the wives of the marines who accompanied them, for *they* were assigned only half a male ration. The benefit was extended to the children of the convicts, as in each class children were granted half a mother's allowance.

The presence of children on the transports raised an unexpected problem. The original instructions had made no reference to children and had therefore omitted to order any provisions for their maintenance. According to custom, however, the wives of some of the marines were allowed to accompany their husbands, and some of them took children with them. A few of the convict women also were mothers of young children, and these infants were permitted to go to New South Wales too. A return for 10 June 1787 shows that, at that date, 17 marine and 13 convict children were on board the different transports,[607] but three of the latter class had died since embarkation; the total number embarked must therefore have been 33. In April 1787 Richards reported that the children were barely subsisting on portions that they received from their mothers' allowance.[608] About a week later Major Ross described how he had found a marine, his wife, and two children existing on a ration and a half,[609] but more than a month before, he had reported the lack of any arrangement for victualling the marine children and had stated that the American practice had been to allow children a quarter ration.[610] The delay apparently occurred in the Undersecretary's office as Nepean had been immediately informed of the situation.

The later complaints of Richards and Ross seem, on the other hand, to have produced an almost immediate response because on 20 April the Navy Board informed the Agent for Transports (Lieutenant Shortland) that the contractor had been instructed to supply the marines' wives with half a ration of each species and the children with a quarter ration, "spirits excepted".[611] The need of the convict children was not so great for it is clear that the majority of them were very young. But they were not overlooked; before the departure of the fleet Lord Sydney himself expressed the belief that they were entitled to a small portion of provisions and ordered that it should be supplied to them.[612]

The determination to deprive the convicts of any kind of alcoholic drink, save as medicine, was maintained until the date of departure. Captain Phillip, in writing to Nepean in March 1787, declared that they were allowed nothing more than water. The daily ration for the marines while at sea included half a pint of rum but no provision was made for supplying them with any spirituous liquor after arrival in the colony. The natural inference that this was due to official negligence is contradicted by a note of 2 November stating that "the exception of the allowance of spirits was to extend to the marines as well as to the convicts after their landing in the settlement".[613]

In view of the fact that rum became almost normal currency in the colony only a few years after its establishment this intention to create a "dry" area is particularly interesting. It aroused considerable alarm among the marines, who resorted to the time-honoured remedy of petitioning to have their grievances righted. They asserted that they had been promised the usual victuals; they thought that a moderate distribution of spirits was indispensably requisite for the preservation of life; that without it they could not be expected to survive. Their complaints received the support of both Ross and Phillip who prophesied disagreeable consequences unless the men were given what they normally expected to enjoy.[614] Moral advantage therefore gave way to practical necessity and Phillip was informed that Lord Sydney would recommend the purchase of a three years' supply of wine and spirits at some port of call on the way to New South Wales "to remove every possible cause of dissatisfaction".[615]

But before any transportation could be directed towards the proposed site of settlement certain legal formalities had to be considered. None of the convicts on the hulks had been ordered to go to Botany Bay; some had been sentenced to America, others to Africa, several to both continents. As already explained in an earlier chapter the Act 24 Geo. III (second session) c.56 provided for this difficulty.[616] There followed consequently a series of Orders, beginning on 6 December 1786, which directed all the convicts concerned to the eastern coast of New South Wales or some adjacent island or islands. Some were composite in character and covered offenders already sentenced to different places. For example one of 6 December dealt with 104 ordered to Africa and 50 sentenced to America;[617] another of the same date referred to 327 offenders ordered to be transported beyond the seas.[618] The fact that some of these Orders are signed by two judges is an indication that the courts were in vacation at the time.[619] For more than four months these Orders continued to be issued. The great majority of those affected were sentenced to serve in the new settlement for seven years, a much smaller number for fourteen years or life; very occasionally a sentence of five years was included.

Another curious remnant of the past which had to be revised was the transferring of George Moore's rights to William Richards Jnr. Many of Moore's convicts who had never reached America were still confined in England. By law, however, he still retained the right to dispose of their labour. On 2 April 1787 he assigned his rights over 51 male and 7 female convicts to his nephew Thomas Quayle, who transferred his privileges and responsibilities to Richards on 10 June 1787.[620] Thus those who might have reached Honduras finally arrived in New South Wales.

Another hindrance to transportation to Botany Bay was the East India Company's monopoly of right to sail between the Cape of Good

Hope and Cape Horn. To obtain the necessary licence the Navy Board directed its secretary to send to India House a list of the ships going to New South Wales, together with a request that its Court of Directors would grant the required permission.[621]

Then according to custom it was necessary for Richards to enter into bonds and sign contracts for the effectual transportation of the felons to the new settlement. These unfortunately have disappeared but the evidence that they existed cannot be denied. On 13 December 1786 Nepean informed several Clerks of the Peace that the commander of the *Alexander*, bound for Botany Bay, as well as the contractor, Mr William Richards Jnr, would be ready to enter into the usual bonds for the removal of certain convicts on the hulks "on Friday morning at 9 o'clock".[622] Four days before, he had reminded Sir Charles Middleton that it would be necessary for owners, as well as masters and mates, to enter into bonds.[623] On 1 January 1787, also, he requested Mr Thomas Shelton, who drew up transportation contracts for the Government, to prepare the necessary bonds and contracts for certain offenders on the hulks, while in April of the same year Richards reported to Nepean that Shelton had sent the bonds and contracts for eight women and three men.[624] Thus although the disappearance of these agreements prevents a clear exposition of the contractor's responsibilities there is sufficient evidence to establish the fact that the system adopted in 1786-1788 was in principle, at least, the same as that practised more than 50 years before, when Jonathan Forward entered into bonds and affixed his signature to contracts for the conveyance of convicts to America, above those of the captains in his employ.

Meantime the Navy Board had attacked the task of fitting the fleet with commendable energy. On 18 October 1786 when it reported the acceptance of the necessary shipping it was hopeful that the transports would be able to proceed to Gravesend in a month's time furnished with provisions and water sufficient for the whole voyage.[625] This estimate proved to be too optimistic; a second letter, dated 5 September, informed the Treasury that the Board believed that the shipping could be "got ready" within six weeks.[626]

In the course of the preparations an important change was made in the respective numerical strengths of the male and female convicts going to New South Wales. The Treasury's instructions of 18 August 1786 prove that the original intention was to despatch 750 convicts to the proposed settlement, of whom only 70 were to be women. This disparity between the sexes was to be reduced by the introduction of 200 native women from the Friendly or other Islands for the stated reason that "without a sufficient proportion of that sex it is well known that it would be impossible to preserve the settlement from gross irregularities and disorders".[627] The supposed moral advantages which were to be expected from the importation of these island women seem quickly to have declined in value. The reason for the change of mind is not recorded but it is probable that a discovery that several women would remain in English gaols after the departure of the fleet suggested an increase in the number of women that might be sent. At any rate the Government decided to transport 150 convict women and, since the ships could accommodate only 750, to reduce the number of males to 600.[628] This decision caused the Secretary of State to depart, but not without protest, from his original intention of sending all the women in one ship; 102 were now allotted to the *Lady Penrhyn* and the remainder divided between the *Charlotte* and the *Friendship*.

A few days later Lord Sydney informed the Treasury that he had learned that some of the marines could not be accommodated on either the *Sirius* or the transports; further that there were about 30 women in Newgate who had recently received sentences of transportation and "as it would upon many accounts be advisable to increase the number of women" he thought it right to recommend the taking up of an additional vessel to receive these women and the marines mentioned.[629] The *Prince of Wales* was therefore hired on the condition that she should follow the fleet if not ready at their time of sailing. She was tendered by Richards on 27 December 1786 and accepted on the following terms: 12 shillings per ton per month until the date of her discharge in China if it were possible for her to arrive there in time to pick up a cargo; otherwise to be discharged in England in return for a payment of 10 shillings per month for the whole voyage.[630] The terms on which the other transport ships were chartered were probably similar if not identical.

Little difficulty was experienced in securing the proposed number of male convicts for the *Alexander*, which was allotted the duty of transporting felons from the hulks on the Thames. The returns of the *Justitia*, *Censor*, and *Ceres* show that during the quarter ending January 1787 they contained no less than 799 prisoners, the great majority of whom were awaiting transportation.[631] The method of selecting them is not recorded; they were reported on by Campbell and probably chosen on his recommendation. There is no evidence to support the statement made at a later date by Captain Tench (of the marines) that they were selected because of their trades. Phillip's complaint after arrival in the colony was that so few of them possessed useful trades.

Before these convicts were placed on the *Alexander* a guard had been supplied. It consisted of 30 private marines together with the necessary NCOs and two subalterns who were drafted from Portsmouth and reached Woolwich on 5 December 1786.[632] On 3 January

1787 the warrant authorising the transfer of the convicts from Campbell to Richards and Captain Sinclair was issued to Richards.[633] According to the hulk returns 185 convicts were delivered to Captain Sinclair on 6 January in the following manner: 52 came from the *Justitia*, 31 from the *Censor*, and 102 from the *Ceres*.[634] On 15 January the remaining convicts were received.[635]

The *Lady Penrhyn* was chosen to receive the women convicts from the various gaols of London; they came on board in smaller groups. The log of that vessel tells that 56 women were received from Newgate on 6 January 1787; subsequent entries show that by 31 January only 90 women and four children had been placed on board. The available supply of women was indeed limited. To secure the proposed number orders had been forwarded to the various gaol authorities during the preceding three months directing the gaolers to forward returns of all women awaiting transportation and commanding them to send the women themselves to London or Plymouth.[636] In spite of these precautions it would seem that the total number (102) assigned to the *Lady Penrhyn* was not secured while the ship lay in the Thames. Some were certainly accepted while she remained on the Mother Bank awaiting the departure of the fleet.[637]

Towards the end of January the *Alexander* and the *Lady Penrhyn* dropped down the river. The days spent in the higher reaches of the Thames had not lacked incident. The male convicts had demonstrated that they could remove their irons; their disorderly behaviour and the proximity of the shore had alarmed the captain sufficiently to cause him to order the ship's boats to be rowed round the vessel to prevent escape.[638] On 29 January the *Sirius* also descended the river and commanded the transports to follow her.[639] The *Supply* tender joined them at the Nore. The *Sirius*, *Supply*, and *Alexander* sailed to Spithead in a very leisurely fashion; they reached the Mother Bank on 22 February where they found the *Scarborough*, the three store ships, and the *Lady Penrhyn* which had arrived 12 days earlier. The *Friendship* and the *Charlotte*, according to directions, had proceeded to Plymouth to pick up the *Dunkirk*'s convicts.[640] On 15 and 16 March they joined the convoy on the Mother Bank. Meantime the *Prince of Wales*, although hired so much later than the other vessels, had left the Thames and arrived at Spithead on 23 February 1787.[641]

The preparations for the voyage were marred by a serious outbreak of sickness on the *Alexander*. In the second week of January, i.e. while the ship was still in the river, Lieutenant John Johnstone of the marines on that vessel reported that four of her convicts had such fluxes and were in such a condition that the surgeon declared them to be totally unfit to proceed to sea and liable to infect others.[642] On the same day Captain Phillip forwarded a long complaint to Nepean stating that among the convicts were several who could not help themselves, that no surgeon's instruments had been placed on any of the transports, that the 184 already on board the *Alexander* filled that ship, and that it was not safe to allow them on deck while the ship remained so close to land. He hoped that the *Alexander* and *Lady Penrhyn* would be permitted to sail immediately to Spithead where the convicts could be given greater liberty and before any more convicts were received because "the most fatal consequences may be expected if the full number is kept on board any length of time before sailing".[643]

The health of the intended settlers had received attention from the outset. Phillip, on 18 August 1786, had informed the Treasury that a supply of surgical instruments, medicines, and necessaries for the sick would be needed and as soon as an estimate could be formed it would be forwarded to their Lordships. On 24 October 1786 the Treasury ordered the Navy Board to provide and ship a two years' supply of medicines for the use of those going to New South Wales.[644] On the following day the Board directed the "Apothecary Company" to prepare a list of medicines equal to that allowed to a second-rate man of war with a complement of 750 men for two years and to ship the same according to Captain Teer's directions. At the same time it asked the Company whether it could supply "a suitable set of instruments".[645] On 14 November, however, a list of surgical instruments prepared by the Surgeon General and the Chief Surgeon of the intended settlement was forwarded to the Treasury; this list was substituted for that ordered on 24 October 1786.[646]

On 7 February 1787 the Chief Surgeon of the settlement (John White) complained to Phillip that neither the marines nor the convicts had been provided with necessaries in case of sickness. The complaint received almost immediate attention as on the same day the Navy Board was instructed to do "what may be proper".[647] Five days later the Commissioner at Portsmouth was directed to cause such a quantity to be put on board as should be a proper proportion for the number of convicts and marines on each vessel during the passage.[648]

On 19 February 1787 also the Treasury was informed by Lieutenant Shortland, agent for transports, and William Balmain, assistant surgeon on the *Alexander*, that the probable cause of the sickness was a lack of fresh food. They recommended that this, instead of salt provisions, should be supplied to the emigrants while the ships remained in England.[649] Again the response was prompt; three days later the contractor was instructed to supply such fresh meat as Lieutenant Shortland should require.

Shortland interpreted his instructions in such a way as to supply both sick and well with fresh provisions. This soon provoked a reproof from the Board which declared that only the sick were to receive the privilege.[650] This decision produced a rousing complaint from Captain Phillip who, after reporting that one in six of the marines were in hospital, put forward a defence against any future charges of incompetence that might be directed against himself. He stressed again the evil consequences that were to be expected from overcrowding small vessels and from sending them to sea without a supply of flour when no antiscorbutics had been provided. In short, he complained that the garrison and convicts were being sent to the extremity of the Globe as they would be sent to America, a six weeks' passage. He was prepared to meet difficulties but he had one fear: that it would later be said that the officer in charge should have known that he probably would lose half his garrison and convicts.[651]

A few days later Phillip reported to Nepean that only the sick were being supplied with fresh meat; he also recommended that the *Friendship* should be turned into a hospital ship and that invalids should be granted an allowance of wine. The evils he foresaw might still be redressed but if neglected the seamen might soon desert the ships to avoid the gaol distemper, or the expedition might be refused entrance into a foreign port. He renewed his request to supply all the convicts with fresh meat while they remained at Portsmouth and the sick with a little wine; he asked that the allowance of bread might be increased, as 16 pounds for 42 days was very little; he also requested the removal of the *Alexander*'s convicts in order that that ship might be "smoked".[652]

All the desired objects were secured; Richards was instructed to victual all the marines and convicts on the terms already fixed upon for the sick, who also were to be provided with wine at the surgeon's discretion; one ton weight of essence of malt (an antiscorbutic) was to be distributed among the ships carrying marines and convicts; the *Alexander*'s convicts were placed on board a lighter while that transport was scrubbed, whitewashed, and smoked;[653] the Portsmouth Yard Officers were instructed to inspect the vessel and to recommend such improvements as they could suggest, and Phillip was advised that he could convert one of the transports into a hospital ship but only under urgent necessity.[654] This, however, he did not do.

The sickness among the convicts on the *Alexander* naturally caused Phillip to take measures to prevent a recurrence during the voyage. At his request, supported by Shortland, the contractor's right to substitute half a pound of rice for a pound of flour was cancelled and Phillip was authorised to take on board in the course of the voyage such quantities of wine as the Commissioners of the Treasury should declare to be necessary, as well as any fresh provisions which it might be requisite to

procure for the use of the marines and convicts.[655] The general effect of
these instructions was to place in the Governor's hands the means of
combating sickness by entrusting him with discretionary power.

The clothing of 750 convicts called for some thought, particularly
as the Government decided to equip them with a two years' supply of
wearing apparel. Estimates of the necessary garments were forwarded
to the Treasury with the instructions of 18 August 1786 and after consideration the following clothing was allotted to the male convicts for
a single year:[656]

Jackets	2 @ 4s 6d	9s 0d
Woollen drawers	4 @ 2s	8s 0d
Hats	1 @ 2s 6d	2s 6d
Shirts	3 @ 3s	9s 0d
Stockings, worsted	4 @ 1s	4s 0d
Frocks	3 @ 2s 3d	6s 9d
Trousers	3 @ 2s 3d	6s 9d
Shoes	3 @ 4s 6d	13s 6d
	Total	£2 19s 6d

The women's garments were not enumerated in the estimates but by
calculation they can be obtained from the orders given to the various
contractors who supplied them. They show that the annual allowance
to the women convicts was :[657]

White shifts	4	Petticoats, serge	1
Jackets, grey	1	Handkerchiefs	3
Jackets, white	1	Caps	2
Jackets, check	2	Hats	1
Jackets, woollen	1	Stockings, pairs	4
Petticoats, canvas	2	Shoes, pairs	3
Petticoats, linsey woolsey	2		

The estimates assumed that the cost of women's clothing would equal
that of the men. The general tenor of the instructions encourages the
belief that the Government assumed that the convicts would wear their
own or their gaol clothes during the voyage, while the two years' supply would be retained for use in the settlement. If this were so it soon
had cause to alter its opinion. Before leaving the River, Shortland was
instructed to issue to the convicts such slops as Captain Phillip should
order. The condition of the women at the time of their arrival in the
transports aroused the indignation of both these officers. Phillip
declared that "the situation in which the magistrates sent the women
on board the *Lady Penrhyn* stamped them with infamy"; being "almost
naked and so very filthy . . . nothing but clothing them could have prevented them from perishing". He recommended that both the convicts

and their clothing should be washed before embarking on the transports.[658] Shortland also on his own responsibility supplied new clothing to the women convicts on board the *Charlotte* and *Friendship*,[659] but in spite of the activity of these officers, a considerable portion of the feminine apparel was left behind when the expedition sailed.

This was not the only omission; before arrival at Teneriffe the lack of any musket balls, paper to make cartridges, and tools to keep the marines' arms in repair was discovered.[660] Still later, the lack of any records concerning the convicts' crimes and sentences, and of superintendents to control the convicts, caused considerable trouble.[661] These omissions, as well as the sickness experienced before departure, may have encouraged the belief that the preparations were hasty and the Government not entirely free from charges of negligence and inhumanity in their treatment of the convicts themselves. A brief inquiry into the matter will therefore not be amiss.

A consideration of the official attitude towards the women's clothing establishes the fact that it was sympathetic. Phillip's and Shortland's complaints were not directed against the Government, and the records prove that the latter adopted their suggestions. Hearing that the women required more clothing the Navy Board, on 11 May, forwarded the provided list of needed articles to Portsmouth together with an enquiry concerning the possibility of purchasing them in that port.[662] Phillip, whose zeal to obey orders caused him to declare that he would sail with the first favourable wind after his arrival in Portsmouth, departed on 13 May, before the clothing had been placed on board.[663] Thus the governmental officials can hardly be charged with negligence in the matter.

As far as the sentence lists are concerned we may confidently discard any supposed intention or desire on the part of the Government to repatriate the convicts. One of the finest attributes of New South Wales was its distance from England and the difficulties this would put in the way of return. The Government exported criminals but it neither guaranteed nor attempted to restore them to their native land. Alexander Dalrymple, at the time, questioned the right of ministers to transport convicts "to a country whence they could not at their own option return at the termination of their sentences".[664] The need of any record which would have given the convicted a legal freedom at the close of their period of servitude does not seem to have occurred seriously to anyone until the last moment. Phillip, on 8 May, informed Nepean that he had not received the characters of the convicts. Shelton, who prepared the necessary bonds and contracts, could have drawn up a list but the need of one does not seem to have impressed him. He may have prepared one; unfortunately his detailed account of legal expenses is missing. What is noticeable is the lack of concern which greeted Phillip's announcement. The Government evidently was not seriously disappointed because of the omission, nor did it send the list in the next ship that proceeded to the colony.

The Gilbertian situation of a force of marines proceeding to a strange land without ammunition implies a serious neglect on somebody's part. Ross had reported the lack and had been informed that the necessary ammunition would be supplied by Lieutenant-General Smith of Portsmouth. The same day a letter was addressed to Smith directing him to provide the needed amount.[665] Ross, probably, was the person most directly concerned, but nobody seems to have been blamed; no one apparently anticipated a protracted shooting of convicts. Fortunately that error could be righted at Rio de Janeiro.

The lack of superintendents was a result of a misconception concerning the future duties of the marines. Phillip evidently believed that they would assume the role of superintendents, but the marine officers naturally resented any attempt to convert them into convict drivers. They were prepared to defend the settlement, although apparently there was practically no need for defence, but they would not assume the status of convict superintendents save when they employed the convicted for their own benefit. Ultimately Phillip therefore had no alternative to placing convicts in charge of convicts.[666]

The sickness on the *Alexander* was certainly unfortunate. Phillip's return at Teneriffe records the death of 21 convicts on that vessel between the first embarkation (6 January) and 10 June 1787. Surgeon White's report at the same place and the Victualling Lists establish the death of six since the departure from the Mother Bank; thus 15 perished on the *Alexander* before leaving England while the only recorded death on all the other transports during that period was that of Ann Wright on board the *Lady Penrhyn*.[667] Now, it will be clear that if the mortality had been caused by any negligence in selecting the diet for the expedition or in the quality of the food supplied, the deaths would have been more widely distributed. No suspicion of negligence, however, need be entertained as the usual precautions to oppose fraud such as the retention of samples were certainly adopted. Moreover, Captain Tench, in describing the voyage, stated that the provisions were good and of much superior quality to those usually supplied by contractors.[668] Further, they were issued under the inspection of Lieutenant Shortland and the marine officers by the contractor's agent, Zacariah Clark, who himself sailed with the fleet. Sir Charles Middleton could speak with authority in such matters and he, in describing the daily ration, stated that it might be termed abundance when compared with the bread and water which he took for granted was the normal prison allowance.[669]

Any valid criticism of the Government's treatment of these convicted felons must take one fact into account: official custom demands that a minimum practicable estimate must form the basis of any operation. To condemn Pitt or Sydney because Phillip or Shortland were compelled to ask for additional supplies is to display an ignorance of common practice. The strain that the organising of the fleet involved is revealed in the correspondence of the officials concerned.[670] Moreover, those who arranged the conditions of the voyage were not gaol officials; their ideas of comfort etc. had been formed in providing for the naval forces of the country and they maintained that standard. Phillip certainly deserves credit for adding to the comfort of the voyagers for it was mainly on his suggestion that the expedition was supplied with such additional necessaries as sour krout, essence of malt, portable soup, and oatmeal. But the Government's response to those suggestions is a proof of its humanity.

Any charge that the whole undertaking was hastily planned is refuted by the facts for, after the ships had been fitted and provisioned, they remained at anchor for six months during which time improvements were proposed and effected. Contemporary opinion occasionally accused the Government of over-kindness. William Eden hinted that the punishment assigned to the convicts was milder than their crimes merited, that it was no deterrent to evil-doing; and it is true that certain prisoners did petition to be transported.[671] Captain Teer, whose business was the equipping of the expedition, in December 1786 expressed the opinion that the "accommodation and provisions" of the vessels proceeding to New South Wales "were better than any set of transports" he had "ever had any directions in".[672] He did not write to impress the public; his letter was a part of the usual routine of his office. We may assume, therefore, that he wrote with conviction and that his conviction reflected the aims and the activities of the Government and its officials.

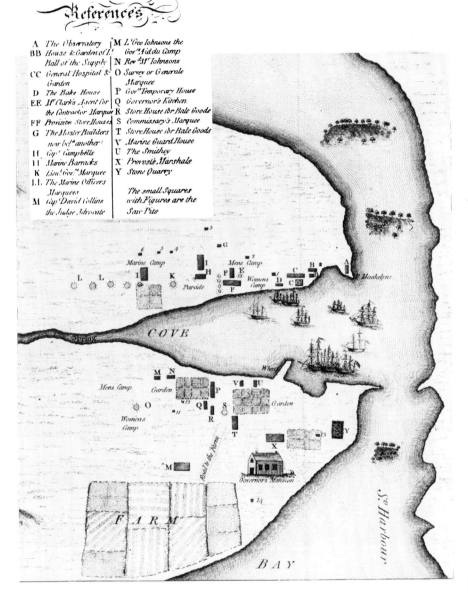

Attributed to Francis Fowkes   Courtesy National Library of Australia, Rex Nan Kivell collection.

Map of the convict settlement at Sydney, New South Wales, 16 April 1788

9

The Voyage to New South Wales

I N SPITE OF the expressed desire of the Secretary of State for an early start the fleet did not leave England until nearly three months after the arrival of the *Sirius* on the Mother Bank. The delay, as we have already seen, was not altogether detrimental to the interests of those who were departing but it compelled a reconsideration of the agreement with the East India Company. In February 1787 a Company Court of Directors authorised the retention of the *Lady Penrhyn* in China until the following season, provided she were prevented from reaching that country within the prescribed period and provided no additional expense fell on the Company.[673] Two months later, also, the same authority directed that the owners of the ships chartered for China from Botany Bay should be excused from the obligation of arriving in China by 15 January 1788.[674]

The causes of the delay, which are not very material to the transportation, must be inferred as no record of them remains. The legal requirements connected with the bonds and contracts, which must in many cases have been sent to distant parts of the country, probably lengthened the period of preparation; late in April 1787 William Richards reported the signing of contracts for women on the *Lady Penrhyn*. Constitutional arrangements certainly were not completed until almost the date of departure. On 11 May Phillip acknowledged receipt of his warrant to appoint Courts Martial.[675] The decision to transport an additional number of women cannot, in itself, be regarded as a source of delay as the Secretary of State, in announcing it, explicitly stated that their ship would follow the convoy if necessary,[676] a circumstance which did not arise.

Not all the transports carried convicts to the Mother Bank; those of the *Scarborough* and *Prince of Wales* were shipped there. The majority of these felons came from London and Middlesex, being conveyed to Portsmouth in waggons. Others, however, had been convicted in such widely separated places as Essex, Kent, Lincoln, Dorset, and Cornwall.

On the evening of Friday 11 May 1787 the ships had completed their provisioning and watering. At one o'clock on the following afternoon the *Sirius* signalled departure, weighed anchor, and stood towards the east. The other warships, *Supply* and *Hyaena*, the latter of which had been ordered to accompany the expedition until it was one hundred leagues distant from the Channel, obeyed the command; but as some of the merchant seamen refused to move their ships the attempt proved abortive.[677] The following morning, Sunday 13 May, at 4 o'clock the attempt was repeated and on this occasion succeeded, the 12 ships passing through the Needles into the Channel. Eight days later the *Hyaena* left the convoy and returned to Plymouth as the ships were then "nearly 100 leagues clear of the channel". She carried to Nepean a letter which demonstrates Phillip's uneasiness while the ships remained in English waters. "The clearing the channel", he wrote, "is one great point gained and with which I look on all our difficultys as ended".[678]

That Phillip should have been uneasy in his mind is not surprising; the merchant sailors had demonstrated their independence on the Mother Bank, and the warships had revealed their comparative helplessness by failing to compel them to sail. A sudden mutiny, engineered under cover of darkness, might have caused the desertion of a vessel and if, by some unexpected means, the convicts had gained possession and headed for a neighbouring shore, the naval force could not easily have checked its progress. To dismast a fleeing vessel would have forced it to desert the convoy; to sink it would have involved the Government in a financial dispute with the owner and countered the intention of establishing the convicts in New South Wales. Boarding might have been adopted, but 200 desperate convicts could have offered a serious resistance.

To determine the exact number of convicts that left England is a problem that has troubled more than one reader of contemporary evidence. In Phillip's "Voyage to Botany Bay" alone three different estimates are given.[679] One of the safest means of approach is probably through the Victualling List. This shows that 559 male and 192 female adult convicts arrived at Santa Cruz on 3 June 1787, making a total of 751.[680] On the following day Surgeon White reported the following deaths since the voyage began (13 May):[681]

Alexander	5
Charlotte	1
Friendship	1
Lady Penrhyn	1
Total	8

Phillip, in an enclosure showing the general state of the garrison, on 10 June mentioned 24 deaths since the taking of the convicts on board the ships, viz. 21 on the *Alexander* and three children.[682] These children may be assumed to be those recorded by White as dying on the *Charlotte*, *Friendship*, and *Lady Penrhyn*. Thus five adults must be added to the number given above, making a total of 756 at the time of leaving the Mother Bank. Then, since 13 "convict" children were also alive on arrival at Santa Cruz, the number that left England must have been 16.[683]

On 3 June, as already stated, the fleet arrived at Santa Cruz in Teneriffe. Although eight persons of the convict class had died since leaving England the general health of all on board had improved. For seven days, while the ships remained in that port, the marines and convicts enjoyed a diet of fresh provisions. Early on the morning of 10 June the fleet sailed with the intention of calling at Port Praya, in the Cape Verde Islands, to secure vegetables.[684] On approaching its harbour, however, unfavourable winds and a strong current caused Phillip to change his mind; the ships sailed on, crossed the Line on 5 July, and anchored in the harbour of Rio de Janeiro on the evening of 6 August 1787.[685] Seven more convicts and one "marine" child had died but Phillip was able to report that the ships under his command were "remarkably healthy".[686]

For nearly a month the fleet remained at Rio. The ships were repaired, 115 pipes of rum purchased for the marines and 15 pipes of wine for the hospital, 10,000 rounds of ammunition were secured from the local arsenal, and specimens of fruits and plants likely to thrive in New South Wales, "particularly the coffee, cotton, indigo, and cochineal", collected for the new settlement. Fresh provisions were issued daily to marines and convicts alike.[687] On 4 September the fleet sailed for the Cape of Good Hope with the intention of making only a short stay in that port. It arrived on 13 October 1787 having lost one convict, who fell overboard, and with 93 others on the sick list. Phillip therefore requested to be allowed to purchase fresh provisions. Only after a delay of ten days was the desired permission secured.[688] Then for nearly three weeks those who were free busied themselves in buying provisions for the remainder of the voyage and in collecting livestock and plants for their new home. During all this period the convicts and their guards enjoyed fresh food. Finally on 12 November the ships sailed for Botany Bay.

Thirteen days later Phillip (the fleet being then 80 leagues eastward of the Cape) left the *Sirius* and went on board the *Supply* tender. At the same time he directed Lieutenant Shortland to take command of the three ships *Alexander*, *Scarborough*, and *Friendship* with orders to proceed to Botany Bay as expeditiously as possible. The *Sirius*, with the slower transports and store ships, was placed under the control of Captain John Hunter, second Captain of the *Sirius*. After these orders had been carried out the *Supply* tender, which was the fastest sailer of the fleet, set forth alone with the intention of exploring the site of the intended colony before the arrival of the other ships of the expedition.[689] She arrived off Botany Bay on 15 January 1788 but was prevented from entering by rough weather until 18 January. Next day the three ships under Shortland's command appeared; the *Sirius* and her consorts sailed in on 20 January.

Phillip had evidently over-estimated the sailing qualities of the *Supply*; the few recorded references to that brig suggest that she was built for speed rather than seaworthiness. In a light breeze she could outsail any other vessel in the convoy, but in rough weather she laboured heavily and shipped water freely. Unfortunately the normal swell of the Southern Ocean was broken by heavy squalls and intense cold. Lieutenant King's statement that "the seas made fair breaches over her and many of them wetted the head of the foresail"[690] explain the failure of the *Supply* tender in that ocean race. The greater beam of the heavier vessels gave them an advantage which the *Supply* lacked.

Phillip had begun his exploration of the neighbourhood before the arrival of the last ships. In company with Hunter he continued his searching on the 20th but, as Hunter's Journal narrates, found no spot very inviting for the purpose.[691] Major Ross probably offered little encouragement as his written accounts of the area suggest unbroken depression and a belief that the only alternatives facing the settlers were death or removal. Consequently on 21 January Phillip, Hunter, the two masters of the men of war, and a party of marines set off in three boats to explore Port Jackson, which Cook in his description of the area supposed might be a satisfactory harbour. Two days later the party returned with the news that they had discovered one of the finest harbours in the world as well as "country greatly superior in every respect to that of Botany Bay". By the evening of 26 January all the ships lay at anchor in Port Jackson; the inlet which Phillip chose as the site of the new settlement he named Sydney Cove.

A few of the convicts had been landed at Botany Bay to cut grass for the livestock that had survived the voyage and to clear the ground preparatory to the establishment of a settlement. These attempts were not continued after the superiority of Port Jackson had been demonstrated; the whole body of settlers moved round to Sydney Cove and later ships sailed directly to Port Jackson, omitting to call at Botany Bay. By 28 January all the marines and the male convicts were on shore. The women, who were detained on board until some shelter had been provided for them, left the ships at the end of the first week of February. The three "China ships" — *Charlotte, Scarborough,* and *Lady Penrhyn* — were discharged on 24 and 25 March and left Port

Jackson on 5, 6, and 8 May 1788 taking with them, we imagine, the Governor's declaration of the landing of their convicts. The *Alexander, Prince of Wales, Friendship*, and *Borrowdale* sailed under the command of Lieutenant Shortland on 12 July; the remaining two vessels, the *Fishburn* and *Golden Grove*, were retained for longer periods, the former because she carried the three years' supply of rum, the latter because she was employed in conveying 21 men and 11 women convicts to Norfolk Island, where a subordinate settlement was established under the command of Phillip Gidley King, Second Lieutenant of the *Sirius*.[692]

The general health of the ships' companies had been maintained during the passage from the Cape of Good Hope. On 20 December Surgeon White records the appearance of scurvy and dysentery which, however, he was "pretty well able to keep under" by the use of essence of malt and wine. Thus both Phillip and Ross asserted that the convicts were healthy when landed in New South Wales, but death had not been avoided, as the following figures prove:[693]

DIED BETWEEN EMBARKATION AND LANDING

	CONVICTS	MARINES	
Men	36	1	
Women	4	1	
Children	5	1	
	45	3	TOTAL: 48

By deducting from this convict total the 15 who died before departure (omitting Ann Wright's case) and the 15 who perished at sea before reaching the Cape of Good Hope we arrive at the fact that another 15 were removed by death during the last stage of the journey. The *Alexander*, meantime, had maintained her unenviable early record. Returns from Teneriffe and Rio provide the following data:[694]

CONVICTS DIED SINCE DEPARTURE

	TENERIFFE	RIO
Charlotte	1	2
Alexander	5	10
Friendship	1	1
Lady Penrhyn	1	1
Prince of Wales	-	1
	8	15

This recorded mortality alone is not a true index of the sickness that was experienced on the voyage as many of the sick recovered, a fact revealed by the following table:

147

SICKNESS ON THE VOYAGE TO NEW SOUTH WALES

	TENERIFFE	RIO	CAPE
Convicts	74	65	93
Marines	7	16	20

Phillip's interest in the health of the convicts displayed during the preparations for the voyage was further demonstrated by his rationing of food at the various ports of call on the way. The following table illustrates this:[695]

DAILY RATIONS

1. At Santa Cruz	BREAD (lb)	BEEF (lb)	WINE (pt)	BUTTER (oz)
Marines — Men	1	1	1	4 on 2 days
— Women	$\frac{1}{2}$	$\frac{1}{2}$	$\frac{1}{2}$	2 on 2 days
— Children	$\frac{1}{4}$	$\frac{1}{4}$	-	1 on 2 days
Convicts — Men	$\frac{3}{4}$	$\frac{3}{4}$	-	3 on 2 days
— Women	$\frac{3}{4}$	$\frac{3}{4}$	-	3 on 2 days
— Children	$\frac{1}{4}$	$\frac{1}{4}$	-	1 on 2 days

2. At Rio de Janeiro	RICE	BEEF	RUM	
Marines — Men	1	$1\frac{1}{4}$	$\frac{1}{2}$	
— Women	1	$1\frac{1}{4}$	$\frac{1}{4}$	
— Children	1	$\frac{3}{4}$	-	
Convicts — Men	1	$1\frac{1}{4}$	-	
— Women	1	$1\frac{1}{4}$	-	
— Children	1	$\frac{3}{4}$	-	

3. At The Cape	BREAD	BEEF*	WINE	BUTTER
Marines — Men	$1\frac{1}{2}$	1	1	9 per week
— Women	$1\frac{1}{2}$	1	$\frac{1}{2}$	5 per week
— Children	$1\frac{1}{2}$	$\frac{3}{4}$	-	3 per week
Convicts — Men	$1\frac{1}{2}$	1	-	-
— Women	$1\frac{1}{2}$	1	-	-
— Children	$1\frac{1}{2}$	$\frac{3}{4}$	-	-

* Or Mutton

These figures illustrate a break with tradition; custom required that women and children should respectively receive one-half and one-quarter of the allowance granted to men, a practice observed in the victualling of the marine families at Santa Cruz. But at each succeeding port marine men and women were treated alike as far as the two stable elements of their diet were concerned. Sex had no effect on the daily ration of the convicts either, and, ironically enough, at Santa Cruz the convict women and children were granted a more liberal allowance than the wives and children of marines. The progressive increase in the convict ration is another noticeable result of Phillip's care; at the Cape of Good Hope their children received six times as much bread and three times as much meat as had been allowed at Santa Cruz. Thousands of English children whose parents had never come within the clutches of the law probably lived on less, and such a diet would have brought comfort to the adult inmates of many an English gaol. The cautious will naturally question the tables in an attempt to discover discrepancies between figures and facts but there is no evidence to show that smaller amounts were issued; the various journals that remain all encourage the belief that the convicts were generously treated.

Overcrowding and the wearing of irons had been important causes of the mortality in the American transportation. Charges of overcrowding were occasionally uttered during the preparation for this voyage. Thus Sir Charles Middleton declared in December 1786 that more women could not be put on board as already they had an allowance of only one and a half tons space each.[696] Phillip also asserted that the *Alexander* could carry no more male convicts after she had shipped 184, but that vessel left England with 197 convicts.[697] However, the best answer to these charges is the Government's chartering of an additional vessel and Middleton's statement that one and a half tons were allowed to each convict as that was the regular allowance granted to marines in the Navy. Irons certainly were worn by the men while the ships lay on the Mother Bank but they were removed the day the *Hyaena* left the fleet;[698] Hunter, usually a reliable witness, traced the almost immediate outbreak of a supposed mutiny on the *Scarborough* to Phillip's humanity in removing the irons. And in writing from Rio the commander of the expedition attributed the healthy state of the prisoners to the permission which allowed all of them on deck during the day and many of them during the night.[699]

Medical attention also contributed towards the healthiness of the ships' companies. The "Heads of a Plan" had suggested that each ship should carry at least two surgeon's mates. This generous proposal was not adopted; the following surgeons were allotted to the marines and convicts:[700]

Surgeon General	John White	*Charlotte*
Assistant	William Balmain	*Alexander*
Assistant	D. Considen	*Scarborough*
Assistant	J.T. Altree	*Lady Penrhyn*
Assistant	T. Arndell	*Friendship*

In addition to these the *Lady Penrhyn* carried a surgeon to watch over the health of its crew. This man, Arthur Bowes, in the course of the voyage was appointed surgeon of the *Lady Penrhyn* in the place of the Assistant Surgeon Arndell who was found to be "very unequal to the task". That these medical officers worked effectively is proved by the results. On the voyage proper, i.e. from 13 May 1787 to 26 January 1788, only about three percent of the marines and convicts died in spite of the fact that all the latter had never left the ships for eight months while those of the *Alexander* and *Lady Penrhyn* had been on board for more than a year.[701] The average loss on a late American voyage had been ten percent, and its duration had been estimated to be approximately two months.[702] At every port of call White inspected all the ships; even at sea, when the weather permitted, he travelled from ship to ship observing the health of his charges.

Little attention was paid to the spiritual welfare of the convicts during the voyage. At the request of Wilberforce and his friends a chaplain, the Rev. Richard Johnson, B.A., was appointed to the new settlement, but as he sailed in the *Golden Grove*, which carried no convicts, he had little opportunity to engage in pastoral work save when in port. Then, according to Collins, he performed divine service on two transports every Sunday.[703]

Discipline obviously occupied an important place in the routine of a transportation voyage. Phillip, before departure, had noted down that he hoped to make the convicts "sensible of their situation" and to assure them that their happiness or misery "was in their own hands". At the same time he recorded his doubt concerning the deterrent effect of capital punishment. Only two crimes (murder and sodomy) merited death in his opinion and he even suggested that convicts guilty of them should be given to the natives of New Zealand to be eaten.[704] After considering these views the reader would hardly be surprised if the ships' logs were found to teem with floggings and brutality, but the surprising thing about them is the infrequency of such entries. The *Sirius*'s log records that two of the *Scarborough* convicts were flogged for attempting mutiny on 21 May 1787. That of the *Prince of Wales* tells that two were put in irons on 7 July 1787, but Surgeon White reports that Thomas Brown who received twelve lashes for insolence after leaving Rio was the first on the *Charlotte* that had been punished.[705] In fact a study of the logs makes it clear that more sailors were flogged than convicts. Naturally the suspicion arises that convict floggings were not recorded, but in addition to the logs there are the private journals of several voyagers and they do not describe such brutality.

A little thought will explain the omission of such entries. On the authority of Captain Tench we know that the convicts were assured that any misbehaviour would be met by instant death, and we have already noticed that the ships were fitted to make possible the deliberate shooting of offenders. Surgeon White also states that hardly ten minutes ever elapsed without some officer "going down among them".[706] Under such conditions the futility of insurrection was apparent.

Phillip's proposal to transfer some evil-doers to New Zealand cannibals lays him open to a charge of inhumanity but his conduct at sea dispels any possibility of sustaining the charge. His treatment of the convicts suggests benevolence rather than brutality. Not least among the satisfactory features of the transportation was the presence of a disciplinary body strong enough to enable such a commander to give rein to his natural inclination.

That little serious trouble was experienced is therefore not surprising. While in the River the convicts had demonstrated that they could shake off their irons, and both there and on the Mother Bank, boats were at times rowed around the ships to prevent escape, although no attempt to escape is recorded. Eight days after leaving Spithead two convicts on the *Scarborough* were given two dozen lashes each for attempted mutiny.[707] Phillip evidently did not take the matter seriously as he stated that he would not mention it since he supposed it would be described in letters from the *Scarborough*. At Santa Cruz one of the convicts escaped; he was recaptured and put in irons but, as White records, "he so wrought on the governor's humanity as to procure a release from his confinement". At Rio it was discovered that in the course of the voyage a convict named Thomas Barnett had manufactured spurious quarter dollars out of pewter spoons and marines' buttons and buckles.[708] Between Rio and the Cape some sailors conspired with certain convicts on the *Alexander* to set them free by providing them with "iron crows and other utensils".[709] For this offence the "principals" of the convicts were stapled to the deck while the sailors were transferred to the *Sirius*. On two occasions, also, those on the *Alexander* were charged with stealing ship's stores.

In the matter of misbehaviour, therefore, the voyage can hardly be described as eventful.[710] The officers' opinions of the convicts do not present them as abandoned and dangerous outlaws; Phillip began by assuming that they were "compleat villains" but at Santa Cruz he wrote, "In general the convicts have behaved well". Southwell declared they were more tractable than might have been expected,[711] while Tench affirmed that he would be doing them an injustice if he did not bear witness to their sobriety and decency.[712] The change is not surprising; English gaols at the time were not provided with those amenities which enable men to preserve an appearance of respectability. It was therefore understandable that those who saw convicts for the first time regarded them as a disreputable and villainous lot. But the overwhelming discipline during the voyage compelled sustained obedience, and the convicts' docility caused the critics to revise their first opinions.

The immediate effect of the New South Wales experiment was the removal of more than 770 convicts from the prisons of England. The advantage went further than the immediate present as the possibility of a return of even a minority of them was exceedingly remote. An important step had therefore been taken in solving the problem which had harassed the Government for so many years. Never since the American period had there been such an exodus from English gaols. Viewed from that angle the New South Wales experiment had undoubtedly succeeded. However, the Gold Coast and Honduras had each received many convicts also, and failure there had been occasioned by the Government's inability to continue the carriage of felons to them. Thus the real, or final, success of New South Wales had still to be demonstrated.

10

Transportation 1789-1793

THE EXPEDITION OF 1787 and 1788 was organised to overcome an immediate difficulty but from its commencement the Government hoped that it was but the beginning of a system that would provide a more than temporary solution of the gaol problem. Thus it is not surprising that Phillip's instructions should have contained directions to encourage the formation of a reserve of provisions "for a further number of convicts which you may expect will shortly follow".[713] The transitory effect of the expedition was soon emphasised by a complaint from the Sheriffs of London that Newgate contained 750 convicts and that the women's quarters were particularly overcrowded.[714] Under these circumstances Lord Sydney recommended that 200 of the female convicts should be placed immediately on board a vessel for transportation. His doubts concerning the success of the New South Wales experiment are then revealed by his suggestion that they should remain at Spithead "until it could be determined to what place it might be eligible to send them".[715]

The Treasury, in transmitting these orders, named North America as an alternative to New South Wales; a few weeks later Nova Scotia was bracketed with Botany Bay as the two possible destinations of the embarked women. Not until after the receipt of news of the success of the first expedition did the Government, on 24 April 1789, order the women to be conveyed to Port Jackson.[716] From that date, for the remainder of our period, New South Wales and Norfolk Island were the officially recognised abiding places of English convicts transported from their mother country. Transportation after 1788 commonly implied removal to one of these two places, as demonstrated in the table of convict voyages on p.154.[717]

A lack of records prevents an exact statement of the number of felons carried by these vessels. The difficulty was realised as early as 1798 when a Select Committee, set up to inquire into the transportation system, reported that it was impossible "to ascertain the precise number of convicts belonging to each year".[718] Some contemporary figures, however, are available and from these the following totals have

SHIP	DEPARTED	FROM	ARRIVED PORT JACKSON
Lady Juliana	29 Jul 1789	England	3 Jun 1790
HMS *Guardian*	20 Sep 1789	England	Wrecked 23 Dec 1789
Second Fleet			
Neptune	19 Jan 1790	England	28 Jun 1790
Scarborough	19 Jan 1790	England	28 Jun 1790
Surprise	19 Jan 1790	England	26 Jun 1790
Third Fleet			
Mary Ann	21 Feb 1791 to	England	9 Jul 1791
Matilda	27 Mar 1791	England	1 Aug 1791
Atlantic	27 Mar 1791	England	20 Aug 1791
Salamander	27 Mar 1791	England	21 Aug 1791
William & Ann	27 Mar 1791	England	28 Aug 1791
Queen	27 Mar 1791	England	26 Sep 1791
Active	27 Mar 1791	England	26 Sep 1791
Albemarle	27 Mar 1791	England	13 Oct 1791
Britannia	27 Mar 1791	England	14 Oct 1791
Adm. Barrington	27 Mar 1791	England	16 Oct 1791
HMS *Gorgon*	15 Mar 1791	England	21 Sep 1791
Pitt	17 Jul 1791	England	14 Feb 1792
Kitty	1 Mar 1792	England	18 Nov 1792
Royal Admiral	30 May 1792	England	7 Oct 1792
Bellona	8 Aug 1792	England	16 Jan 1793
Boddingtons	15 Feb 1792	Cork	7 Aug 1793
Sugar Cane	13 Apr 1792	Cork	17 Aug 1793

been culled[719] (see p.155). Some children were carried after the *Lady Juliana* voyage; those in that ship are shown to illustrate births at sea.

The contract system was continued in the five years that followed the arrival of the First Fleet in New South Wales. William Richards Jnr, whose success in Phillip's voyage had been demonstrated, also transported the women who sailed in the *Lady Juliana*; but the Navy Board's practice of advertising for tenders and accepting the most reasonable offer introduced new contractors into the transportation system. The successful tenderers for the conveyance of the convicts removed by the Second and Third Fleets were Messrs Camden, Calvert, and King.[720] The mortality connected with these voyages then caused the Secretary of State to welcome a suggestion, made by Phillip, that the transportation might be conducted more economically by ships of the East India Company.[721] That Company, on being approached, undertook to do the work; the voyage of the *Royal Admiral.* was the result.[722]

SHIPS	TONS		NUMBER DEPARTED	NUMBER ARRIVED	DEATHS	ESCAPES
Lady Juliana	401	F	230	225	5	0
		Ch	5	10	2	0
HMS *Guardian*	?	M	25	19	6	0
Second Fleet	1640	M	928	672	256	0
		F	78	67	11	0
		Tot	1006	739	267	0
Third Fleet	4007	M	1859	1665	194	0
		F	172	168	4	0
		Tot	2031	1833	198	0
HMS *Gorgon*	?	M	30	30	0	0
Pitt	800	M	352	319	21	12
		F	59	49	9	1
		Tot	411	368	30	13
Kitty	?	M	10	2	0	8
		F	30	27	3	0
		Tot	40	29	3	8
Royal Admiral	?	M	300	289	10	1
		F	49	46	3	0
		Tot	349	335	13	1
Bellona	450	F	17	17	0	0
Boddingtons	350	M	125	124	1	0
		F	20	20	0	0
		Tot	145	144	1	0
Sugar Cane	370	M	109	109	0	0
		F	50	50	0	0
		Tot	159	159	0	0
GRAND TOTALS:		M	3738	3229	488	21
		F	705	669	35	1
		Tot	4443	3898	523	22

So satisfied was the Secretary with the new arrangement that he informed Phillip that he intended for the future to transport both convicts and settlement stores by the same method. A fortnight later, however, the East India Company declined to continue the system because of difficulties that had arisen due to the Act 22 Geo. III, which disqualified contractors from sitting and voting as members of the House of Commons.[723] The Board therefore resumed the private contract system. William Richards Jnr supplied both the *Boddingtons* and the *Sugar Cane*, the last two ships of our period.[724]

Other suggestions were made to link the transportation with commercial enterprises. In October 1790 a Mr Sam Enderby submitted a proposal by a Mr St Barbe to combine the transportation with a South-

SHIPS	CONTRACTOR	CONDITIONS
Lady Juliana	Wm Richards Jnr	9s 6d a ton per month until six weeks after discharge. Provisions while at sea, 6d a head per adult, $2\frac{1}{2}$d per child; while in England, 9d a head per adult, $2\frac{1}{2}$d per child. 1s 3d a head per day for fresh provisions while in foreign ports, the 6d being deducted. 40s a head for clothing. 7s a day for a surgeon.[731]
Second Fleet	Geo. Whitlock	£17 7s 6d a head.[732]
Third Fleet	Messrs Camden, Calvert & King	£19 10s a head.[733]
Royal Admiral	East India Co.	£20 a head.[734]
Boddingtons & Sugar Cane	Wm Richards Jnr	£17 a head for all embarked and an additional five pounds a head for all landed alive.[735]

ern whale fishery[725] but no result is recorded. In April 1792 a person named Edmund Hill volunteered to undertake the transportation of 1000 convicts and to pay the Government 10 shillings a head for them on the condition of obtaining permission to load his ships with saltpetre at Calcutta on the return voyage.[726] Another named George Macaulay volunteered to convey articles to the new settlement at 40 shillings a ton provided he were allowed to load sugar and cotton in a private capacity on his homeward voyage.[727] These last two proposals were vetoed by the East India Company, which resented any abridgement of its monopoly rights.

Nevertheless the Company was prepared to charter ships proceeding to the settlement and it was a common practice throughout the five years under survey for convict ships to proceed from Sydney Cove to China, and thence to England in the service of the East India Company. So regular was this that when the Navy Board selected ships it requested that the Company officer would survey them also.[728]

Some alterations were introduced, however, into the contract system. Early contracts were entered into by the Navy Board, but the last recorded in this chapter was concluded by the Board's Agent, James Bowen, who was responsible for the fitting and provisioning of the transport vessels.[729] No reasons are given; possibly the Board believed that a more direct responsibility would encourage diligence. Regularity also was aimed at; thus in February 1791 Grenville, then Secretary of State, informed Phillip that in future the Government intended to send out two embarkations a year. More important was the adoption of a system of payment by results. After the extraordinary mortality in the Second Fleet had been made known Dundas, the Secretary of State, suggested to the Treasury that contractors should be paid for the number of convicts landed in the colony and not for the number embarked.[730] The Treasury pointed out that on those terms no tenders might be received and it recommended instead a specific sum for all taken on board and an additional sum for each convict landed at the place of destination. This principle was adopted in the *Boddingtons-Sugar Cane* contract which stated that Richards would receive an additional five pounds for each convict landed alive at Port Jackson. The table on p.156 sets forth the facts concerning the important contracts of the period.

One of the most striking facts revealed by the table on page 155 is the extraordinary mortality on the ships *Neptune*, *Scarborough*, and *Surprise*, which made up the Second Fleet. On that voyage 26.5 percent of the total number of convicts that left England perished before reaching Sydney Cove. As the figures show, this was exceptional; the common death rate was considerably lower. The following table gives the mortality percentage for different periods.

VOYAGE		NO. AT DEPARTURE	DEATHS	% DIED
All voyages	Male	3738	488	13.0
	Female	705	35	4.9
	Total	4443	523	11.8
All voyages less Second Fleet	Male & Female	3437	261	7.5
Wm Richards's voyages	Male & Female	534	6	1.1

Death is a result of definite causes; factors in this case would include the convicts' condition on embarkation, their food, clothing, medical attention, and the discipline they endured. Of their condition at the time of boarding the ships little is recorded. Occasionally a reference appears as that of 17 July 1791, in which Major Grose reported smallpox on the transport *Pitt* before her departure,[736] and another telling of the removal of a woman convict from the *Kitty* because of infection by venereal disease.[737] But as medical inspection prior to leaving the gaols was made compulsory in the first voyage we may assume that it was continued in later operations. Moreover the removal of the female convict from the *Kitty* is proof that the Government was prepared to retain the infected in England rather than send them in ships to injure others. Scurvy was the principal cause of death during these voyages and it usually developed after the ships had left England.

Sufficient evidence remains to establish the fact that prisoners on transport ships were not herded together in one large room as those on the hulks were. According to modern standards the cabins provided seem almost absurdly inadequate; two on the *Pitt*, which measured 79 x 94 inches and 163 x 100 inches, were assigned to 10 and 27 women respectively. Nevertheless some improvement was effected during the period. In 1786 Sir Charles Middleton had complained that some of the women were allowed no more than one and a half tons of space each. In the preparation of the Second Fleet, two tons a head was demanded, apparently without any additional space for the soldiers carried;[738] but the *Boddingtons* contract required two tons for each person on board.[739]

During these five years the Government regularly required the attendance of a surgeon on each convict ship. William Richards's agreement concerning the *Lady Juliana* convicts provided that during the time the women remained on board he was to be paid seven shillings a day to cover the cost of supplying a surgeon.[740] Whitlock's contract stipulated that a surgeon was to be carried on every ship. The condition was not relaxed even when store ships transported only a few convicts; the *Kitty* and the *Bellona* each bore a surgeon. Nor was the East India Company's ship exempted, for on the *Royal Admiral*, Richard Alley acted as surgeon to the convicts which that vessel transported.

An improvement in both the amount and the variety of the daily food ration occurred during the same period. The following table compares the daily food ration of the Second Fleet in 1789 with that provided by Richards in 1792:

SEVEN DAY RATION FOR A MESS OF SIX CONVICTS

		MEN 1789	MEN 1792	WOMEN 1789	WOMEN 1792
Bread	lb	16	20	20	20
Flour	lb	12	12	12	12
Beef	lb	14	16	7	7*
Pork	lb	8	6	6	6
Peas	pt	12	12	12	12
Butter	lb	1½	1½	1½	1½
Rice	lb	2	2	2	2
Tea	lb	–	–	¼	¼
Sugar	lb	–	–	3	3
Suet	lb	–	1½	–	1½
"Plumbs"	lb	–	3	–	3

* Women received stock fish in lieu of beef one day a week.

In addition to the men's ration, Richards was required to supply two stock fish and three oatmeal breakfasts a week. In none of these voyages however were the convicts treated as well while in port as they had been by Phillip, who supplied them with fresh provisions every day during their stay. Whitlock's contract required him to give each convict fresh provisions to the value of nine pence a head two days a week, while in Richards's of 1792 the number of days was increased to four at Rio and at other ports which the superintendent-surgeon might think fit to enter.

This period also witnessed an increase in the amount of clothing supplied to the convicts. This is evidenced by the following table:

CLOTHING ACCORDING TO THE CONTRACTS

	SECOND FLEET 1789	RICHARDS 1792
MEN		
Outside jacket	1	1
Waistcoat	1	1
Hat	1	1
Cap	1	1
Shirt	2	3
Stockings, pr	2	3
Trousers	2	2
Shoes, pr	2	2
Drawers	2	2
Bag to hold above	1	1
WOMEN		
Striped jacket	1	1
Striped petticoat	1	1
Stays, pr	1	1
Hat	1	1
Flannel petticoat	2	2
Shift	2	3
Stockings, pr	2	3
Shoes, pr	2	2
Handkerchief	2	2
Bag to hold above	1	1

Each of these lists mentions items not supplied in 1787-88. It will be observed that the 1792 list is the more generous of the two. The improvement can be traced to the East India Company which, in setting forth its tender for the *Royal Admiral*, offered to give each male one shirt and each female one shift and one pair of stockings in addition to the articles formerly supplied, because it was of the opinion that they had not been sufficient.[741]

A greater attention to cleanliness and to the prevention of disease is noticeable as the period advances. The contractors for the Second Fleet were required to supply oil of tar, essence of malt, barley, spice, oatmeal, sugar, etc. in the proportions the surgeons thought necessary, together with wine for the sick at the rate of one hogshead for every 200 convicts. Each mess of six convicts was also to receive two pounds of soap a month, a commodity not mentioned in the first voyage except in references to borrowing it from the marines.[742] In Richards's contract of 1792 the amounts are more definitely stated. He undertook to supply the following articles for every 200 convicts:

> 5 cwt barley, 2 cwt oatmeal, 2 cwt sugar, 2 cwt essence of malt, 100 gallons oil of tar, 200 gallons vinegar, 1 hogshead wine; spices and other necessaries in the proportions the surgeon might think proper and two pounds of soap a month for each mess of six convicts.

To effect its orders the Government continued the plan of sending naval agents with the ships. Thomas Edgar sailed in the *Lady Juliana* on the recommendation of Lord Sydney himself "in order that proper attention [might] be paid to the convicts".[743] The orders of Lieutenant Shapcote, naval agent of the Second Fleet, illustrate the duties of these officers. He was commanded to see that the women were kept separate from the men and "were not abused", to make his way to Port Jackson, touching only where it might be necessary, to visit the other ships as frequently as possible and have them aired and washed, to see that the convicts were kept clean and provided with as much air as was consistent with safety, to enforce the shifting and washing of clothes as well as the separation of the healthy from the sick, who were to be supplied with wine, and finally to compel the giving of justice to all according to the contract. The Third Fleet sailed in three divisions superintended by Lieutenants Samuel Blow, Richard Bowen, and Robert Parry Young.[744] Richard Nairne was agent on the *Pitt*,[745] and Daniel Woodriff on the *Kitty*.[746]

One grave defect applied to the system of naval agents: the ships on which the agent did not sail frequently separated from the convoy and reached the settlement alone. To overcome this fault a policy of appointing superintendent-surgeons to every transport vessel was adopted. The method had been suggested during the fitting of the *Lady Juliana*. Then the Navy Board had submitted "whether it might not answer the purpose" to send a navy surgeon instead of a lieutenant.[747] The plan was rejected at the time but after the sailing of the *Kitty*, superintendent-surgeons sailed in every ship.[748] These were given authority similar to that possessed by the naval agents; thus shipmasters were directed to obey their orders if the health of the convicts caused them to desire entry into any ports on the way; they were particularly commanded to see that a proper proportion of medicines and necessaries was placed on board, that it was properly distributed, and that the contractor fulfilled his agreement in respect of the daily ration.

The behaviour of the convicts during these voyages naturally varied with time and place but the emphasis placed upon the few uprisings that occurred is proof enough that little serious trouble was experienced. The master of the *Lady Juliana*, when requested to report on the number of probable births during his on-coming voyage, replied "there is twenty-one [women] with child already and there is every reason to think that there will be thirty more as every man in the ship has one";[749] but nine months later, when the ship lay at the Cape, its surgeon reported only seven births, so we may assume that the master's evidence was exaggerated. The fact that women convicts were free to walk the decks might have made intercourse with the sailors possible. Captain Trail declared that in the Second Fleet the ship's company frequently broke into the women's quarters on the *Neptune* and had many times "taken the women out . . . and lodged them where they could converse with the male convicts".[750] No one, however, can doubt the Government's intention. It complimented Phillip upon his success in keeping apart the two sexes and the first command to the agent of the *Neptune* was an order to see that the women were kept separate from the men and not abused.

The male convicts on the *Guardian* played an active part in saving that vessel after its encounter with an iceberg. Lieutenant Riou, its commanding officer, commended their behaviour both before and after the accident and upon his recommendation they were pardoned. Lieutenant Shapcote, the agent in the Second Fleet, apparently knew the ways of convicts for he soon discovered and removed between 70 and 100 knives and a great number of chests "with large iron clasps at the corners".[751] That however did not prevent a plan to seize the *Scarborough*. He therefore went aboard that vessel, "punished several who would not confess" and confined five of the ringleaders for Phillip's decision. The other ships he described as "peaceable". The *Albemarle* experienced a real mutiny; while the principal part of the watch were in the rigging certain convicts shed their irons, knocked down the sentinels, took their arms and raced for the helm. A blunderbuss restored order; two of the ringleaders were summarily hanged from the yard arm, others flogged, while two sailors who had organised the rising were imprisoned in Madeira.[752]

When sickness disabled a majority of the crew of the *Pitt*, convicts were freed to work that ship into port. According to Major Grose of the New South Wales Corps they "behaved with great regularity" but seven deserted at Rio and five others followed their example at the Cape.[753] In the latter port the *Royal Admiral* also lost one convict, while from the *Kitty* eight escaped before she had left British waters.[754] But if all those who played a part in these escapades be numbered their total is almost negligible when compared with the number that left England. The explanation probably lay in the presence of overwhelming force.

The practice of carrying troops on convict ships was continued during the period 1789-93. It was rendered possible by the determination of the Government to substitute the New South Wales Corps for the original marines, who had quarrelled with Phillip almost from the beginning. The new corps was despatched in divisions which sailed on transports in and after the year 1790. There is no evidence however to prove that the Government intended to continue the method. In fact it is almost certain that it expected the East India Company to assume the responsibility for guarding its own ship when it arranged the transportation by the *Royal Admiral*. William Richards suspected this at the time and wrote to Nepean stating that he was prepared to carry convicts to New South Wales for 23 pounds for all embarked and 26 pounds for all landed if they went unaccompanied by soldiers but he would reduce his rates to 17 and 23 pounds a head if the Government would supply a military force to guard the convicts.[755] The owners of the *Royal Admiral* evidently believed that soldiers would be supplied, and at their request one NCO and 19 privates were shipped on that vessel.[756] The practice was continued in the case of the *Boddingtons* and *Sugar Cane*; the presence of the guards explains the cheap rates charged by Richards in that undertaking.[757]

A brief consideration of the facts already presented will probably convince the reader of the Government's continued interest in the health and general comfort of the convicts while on their way to New South Wales. To emphasise this, two examples of its willingness to accept improvements may be cited; the women convicts of the *Lady Juliana* complained that they were receiving too much beef and requested that sugar and tea might be substituted for a portion of it; the suggestion was approved by both the ship's surgeon and Richards, the contractor; the latter brought it before the notice of Evan Nepean and as a result, women convicts for the remainder of the period received tea and sugar as a regular part of their ration.[758] The practice of providing soap began during the preparation of the *Lady Juliana* voyage also. The proposal probably originated among the women convicts; Richards evidently sympathised with the idea as he suggested to Nepean the advisability of supplying it, adding the words that he would provide it immediately "as the poor wretches are much in need of it".[759] From that time soap also became a regular part of the ships' "necessaries". And yet it was during this period that a single expedition lost by death no fewer than 267 convicts out of 1006 who sailed from England.[760] In the light of these facts, which apply to the Second Fleet, a little inquiry seems necessary into the Government's attitude at the time.

A Mr Thomas Evans seemingly appointed himself champion of the sufferers. He laid the blame at the contractors' door by declaring that their shipping had been 257 tons short of the required amount and that the master of the *Neptune* (Donald Trail) had already, by his inhumanity, caused 200 seamen to desert that ship before she reached Portsmouth.[761] The Navy Board disposed of these charges by proving that the ships had loaded 2215 tons of tea on their homeward voyage and were therefore capable of conveying 1006 convicts, that the ships themselves had been surveyed by the Company's officer as well as their own, and that the desertion, if it could be established, was not due to Trail's treatment as he had not been master at the time.[762] Evans's charges must therefore be dismissed.

Parliament nevertheless took the matter up; Sir Charles Bunbury, in the House of Commons, moved for an inquiry. The Secretary, Dundas, replied that "he had taken every measure proper to an investigation" and that he was prepared to lay the whole result before the House. He spoke truthfully; several weeks before Sir Charles Bunbury's motion, after he had learned the facts, he wrote to Phillip stating that "the distress in which the convicts arrived in the *Neptune*, *Scarborough*, and *Surprise* would be a subject of the strictest enquiry in order to punish those responsible for such a shocking calamity".[763] The Undersecretary, John King (Nepean was on leave at the time), also declared that several affidavits were taken after the arrival of the *Neptune* in England with a view to prosecuting those who had caused the suffering.[764] That of Trail remains; it was laid before the House.[765]

In it the master of the *Neptune* swore that the convicts were ironed under the inspection of the agent, Lieutenant Shapcote, that those of good character and the indisposed were not compelled to wear irons, that female convicts had the range of both the quarter and poop decks, that the males were allowed on deck 50 to 60 at a time and relieved every two hours, that the boys and the sick were permitted to come on deck at any time, that while in the tropics the number of convicts who slept on deck exceeded that of the marines and sailors who guarded them, and that wind sails and open ports had been used to keep the rooms cool. He admitted that the convicts had had just reason to complain about a little irregularity in their meals during the heavy gales encountered between the Cape and Port Jackson but it had been unavoidable, that "some splashes did get in" during heavy weather, due not to defects in the ship but to the indolence of the carpenter, but he declared that he had supplied the convicts with vegetables that he had shipped for his own use, and given them vinegar "to wash their mouths" after leaving the Cape; further, that the water consumed by the sick was always boiled.

He denied the rumour that the convicts had purposely failed to report the death of their fellows in order to secure the rations of the deceased. The surgeon had visited the sick daily, and convicts in adjoining cabins who could not share any advantage would certainly have complained of "dead bodies among them". As for the cleanliness of the ship, the orlop deck had been scraped and swabbed daily and sprinkled with oil of tar or vinegar twice a week and was "as free from nastiness or bad smells as any ship that ever carried convicts". Lack of evidence concerning Trail's character makes it difficult to estimate the worth of his evidence but it is interesting to note that Phillip avowed that "no specific charge was ever brought against him [Trail] here".[766] Lieutenant Shapcote, in his letters, found no fault with him, and Captain Horatio Nelson, in a signed "character", stated that Trail had served under him with skill and alacrity and was worthy of protection and encouragement.[767]

Phillip traced part of the evil to long confinement for which the agent and master were jointly responsible. Shapcote unfortunately died seven weeks before the arrival of the fleet at Port Jackson but, if Trail's evidence has any value, the convicts enjoyed much more freedom after the agent's death. Certainly many convicts had died before that event; Shapcote himself had reported 68 deaths (45 being on the *Neptune*) and moreover he had added that 64 were in the last stage of scurvy, while 39 others were in the first stage, before the ships left False Bay. Consequently we may assume that the mortality was not due to the death of the agent.[768]

Some really damning charges were made by Captain Hill of the New South Wales Corps. He asserted that the ship on which he sailed (the *Surprise*) had been quite unfit for its work, that she had shipped so much water that the convicts were considerably above their waists in it, that at such times they had been shut down and that no attempt had been made "to purify below decks" after the gales had abated. He further complained that the convicts' irons had been inhuman in so much that any movement was made only at the risk of breaking a limb, that the sick had had no necessaries, that rations had been withheld by the "low-lifed, barbarous masters" who, he feared, would not be honest enough to make a just return of the dates of the deaths of the convicts as it would reveal their desire to kill them off quickly so as to profit by the saving of their rations.[769]

Now this is quite contrary to the evidence of the *Neptune*'s steward, who swore that the contract ration had been distributed under the direction of Lieutenant Shapcote and that both Shapcote and Trail had commanded him never to deliver bad or indifferent provisions.[770] Moreover it disagrees with Trail's evidence and with the orders given to Trail by the contractors, who directed him to victual convicts and soldiers "conformable to the contract".[771] It is unfortunate for Hill that his complaint should state that 370 of the male convicts were already dead, in other words that nearly 120 male convicts perished within a month of landing. The Rev. Richard Johnson, however, who wrote six weeks after the arrival of the fleet, reported the death of only 84.[772]

Even if all of them had been males there would still have been a serious discrepancy. Then, if such flagrant abuses existed, why were they not reported by Hill's superior officer, Captain N. Nepean? The Navy Board pointed out that he had made no charges against the responsible officers and as the brother of Evan Nepean (the Undersecretary, responsible for transportation) we might assume that he would have been among the first to inform the Government's officials. Another circumstance that reduces the value of Hill's evidence is the low death rate on the *Surprise* which was, in reality, the healthiest ship of the three.[773]

He who after a consideration of these statements can to his own satisfaction assess the blame for the suffering on these vessels may count himself lucky. All agreed that the closing of the hatches, which was often unavoidable, was an important cause of the mortality, but there the agreement ended. The ratio between the number of convicts and the alleged tonnage of the ships at the time of hiring, viz. 1006:1640, was certainly higher than that of later voyages. The fleet left and arrived in winter, a circumstance which would encourage the convicts to remain below decks. It also avoided Teneriffe and Rio de Janeiro and therefore removed from the convicts the possibility of having fresh food in those ports. This may have been a result of the new plan, which discouraged delays on the way by paying the contractors so much a head, but they certainly had not broken their agreement as it did not require them to call at those ports. Nevertheless the omission was disastrous and might have been partly avoided if Shapcote had been a man of greater personality.[774] The time spent in reaching the Cape was almost exactly the same as that spent by Phillip in reaching Rio de Janeiro but a part of Phillip's time had been occupied in building up the health of his convicts in Teneriffe, while the Second Fleet missed that opportunity.

If the blame rests on anyone it rests on Shapcote, whose discretionary power was sufficient to compel the masters to put in to Santa Cruz. He surely had reason to suspect an approaching increase in mortality as 11 had died before the voyage commenced. It can be said to his credit that he ordered fresh provisions to be supplied to the convicts every day at the Cape, but by that time 68 had died. The suspicion lingers that if Phillip had controlled the expedition the results would have been less fatal. Nor need we suppose that the Government would have censured some additional expenditure; Sir Joseph Banks writing a little later stated, "Government is always ready to allow the necessary expense but not always able to find out proper people to take charge of the ships",[775] and the evidence at our disposal supports Banks's opinion; for the inquiry revealed what we have already discovered: that the

Government's responsible officers entered into a contract and took all the usual precautions to see that it was literally fulfilled; further, that on receipt of the news from Port Jackson the Secretary of State immediately ordered an inquiry. No one, not even Evans, seriously charged the Government with inhumanity. The voyage was also in a sense experimental as it was the first Australian venture conducted by these contractors.

The treatment of the convicts on the *Queen*, one of the ships of the Third Fleet, caused another inquiry. It is interesting because it reveals that the convicts knew what they were supposed to receive and were able to complain effectively when less was distributed. Their complaint was inquired into by four Justices of the Peace appointed for the purpose by Phillip. They found that the four-pound and two-pound weights which had been used to measure the convicts' food were respectively six and three ounces short of the correct weight and that consequently the convicts had not received their intended ration.[776] But this case was extraordinary, for only after the departure of the *Queen* to pick up her Irish convicts did the Navy Board receive a very "unfavourable account" of Lieutenant Blow, whom it had appointed naval agent for the voyage. It hastily despatched Lieutenant Nairne to supersede him, but before Nairne's arrival in Ireland, Blow had left. This is sufficient to explain the negligence on the *Queen*. The Secretary, Dundas, showed his interest in the case by informing Phillip that he highly approved of the examination and would, when the persons returned home, take care that justice was done.[777]

To dispel the belief that death and brutality were the normal attributes of convict voyages we might remind ourselves that in all the voyages of the period, excepting that of the Second Fleet, the average death rate was 7.5 percent, i.e. 2.5 percent less than was experienced on the much shorter American voyages.[778] But even this success pales before that of William Richards Jnr who, in this same period, despatched to New South Wales three ships carrying 534 convicts of whom only six died, giving a mortality rate of 1.1 percent. Critics may trace this success to special causes but the fact remains that at this early date in the southern transportation he set a standard for the future which must almost have aroused despair within succeeding contractors.

The disparity between the two sexes in New South Wales encouraged the Government to offer to convey women who were not criminals to the settlement. The proposal possibly originated with the convicts themselves; at all events in December 1789 the Navy Board informed Lieutenant Shapcote that it thought it a very humane act to allow such convicts as had wives to take them with them, and four days later it conveyed to him Grenville's desire that he could tell the convicts that they might take their wives.[779] In this decision the Government had no desire to avoid maintaining the wives in question, for it assumed the responsibility not only for transporting them but for maintaining them after arrival. The offer was accepted, for in the Second Fleet alone, seven wives and fifteen children sailed to the new colony.[780] The privilege was extended also to those who had already been transported; thus two convicts on Norfolk Island asked that their wives and children might be sent to them. The petition was supported by Phillip on the ground of good behaviour.[781] The result was an order to give a passage to the persons concerned "if they desired to go". Grenville's permission went further as it authorised "even women that cohabited" with male convicts to proceed to New South Wales at the expense of the Government. Very few if any seem to have availed themselves of this offer.[782]

One important result of the establishment of Sydney Cove and the American troubles that preceded it was the amalgamation of the English and Irish transportation systems. By the Act 25 Geo. III, c.46, Scottish criminals became liable to transportation to places appointed by the King in Council. The Scottish system had therefore combined with the English prior to the sailing of the First Fleet, but it would seem that no Scot was transported to New South Wales before the year 1791. Then, according to Shelton's accounts, 20 sailed in the *Pitt*; in the following year seven more were carried by the *Royal Admiral*. Irish transportation had been conducted by the Irish Government. The closing of American ports to convicts, which had embarrassed the English Government, raised a similar problem within Ireland.

As late as the year 1789, the Irish Government attempted to land convicts in Newfoundland but the attempt failed;[783] they had been placed on board the *Elizabeth and Clare* and sent to England, where their arrival produced a correspondence between the responsible officials of the two governments. This ended in an agreement entrusting the transportation from both countries to the British Government because, as the Dublin Castle letter stated, "His Excellency [the Lieutenant Governor] was convinced" that by that method "the most effectual means for the advantage of the public and the good treatment of the convicts would be secured".[784] The consequence was that English contractors conveyed convicted felons from Ireland. The *Queen*, one of the ships of the Third Fleet, the *Kitty*, the *Boddingtons*, and the *Sugar Cane* all carried Irish convicts to Sydney Cove. But one fact continued to distinguish the two systems: the drawing up of the bonds and contracts for the removal of Irish offenders was not undertaken by Shelton. In that respect the two transportations remained distinct.

The legal work entailed by the removal of felons was considerable.

167

It can best be illustrated by a selection of the items included in Shelton's accounts. Before the convicts who had been sentenced by any court were removed, this man of law procured and perused the documents relating to those concerned in order to prepare a contract and bond. He then drew up the contract which required the contractor to transport the convicts and procure testimonials that they had been landed and "should not be suffered to return". This was followed by the drawing of a bond from the contractor and his sureties to perform the contract. After that he paid the necessary stamp and paper duties, attended the execution of the contract and bond, and prepared a warrant for the delivery of the convicts to the contractor. Each of these duties introduced an item into the account presented to the Treasury, and as this procedure was repeated for every court concerned in the particular transportation it re-appeared many times. In the account for the Second Fleet it recurred 107 times; the account for the Third Fleet raised it to 132.[785] These and other legal procedures make up the accounts presented to the Government; for the Second and Third Fleets they cover 48 and 62 pages respectively.

11

New South Wales, 1788-1793

I N ONE IMPORTANT RESPECT the transportation to New South Wales differed from that to America; in the American system the Government's responsibility normally extended no further than the British Isles; the removal, sale, and subsequent treatment of the convicts were entrusted to others who conducted their parts of the punishment without ministerial intervention.

The great distance separating Port Jackson from the Mother Country and the lack of purchasers in its neighbourhood prevented a continuation of that system. Thus the Government was compelled not only to pay the cost of the carriage of British felons to the new settlement but also to provide for their support, employment, and good behaviour during their periods of enforced absence. In a very real sense, then, their transportation continued after their arrival in New South Wales and can therefore with propriety be discussed in any treatment of this subject.

As already stated the first settlers were landed on the shores of Sydney Cove in January 1788. Their number at that time, regardless of the crews of the two warships, exceeded one thousand, but that total was soon reduced by death and the establishment of a secondary settlement on Norfolk Island, to which Philip Gidley King, Second Lieutenant of the *Sirius*, sailed on 14 February. He was accompanied by a petty officer, a surgeon's mate, two marines, two men who understood the cultivation of flax, and nine men and six women convicts. The arrival of the later transports, as well as births within the colony, caused a fairly rapid increase of population, as proved by the figures on page 170, taken from the victualling lists.[786]

As no accommodation had been provided for the settlers before they landed at Sydney Cove, their first duty was the erection of weather-proof buildings to shelter the sick and the provisions upon whose preservation their existence depended. In May 1788 Phillip reported that he was employing certain of the ships' carpenters to assist the convicts in the building of a hospital and store houses. Meantime his own canvas house was neither wind nor water-proof and we

VICTUALLING LISTS

		27 DEC 1790	18 NOV 1791	8 DEC 1792
PORT JACKSON	Men	1474	2342	2400
	Women	419	399	496
	Children	93	140	176
NORFOLK IS.	Men	286	778	738
	Women	103	285	268
	Children	38	109	130
TOTALS	Men	1760	3120	3138
	Women	522	684	764
	Children	131	249	306

may suppose that those of the marines and convicts were no better. But in spite of this inconvenience and the Governor's desire to provide dwellings for the settlers the work of construction continued for a long time. Six months after the arrival of the fleet, 70 to 100 convicts were still constantly employed in providing accommodation for "the battalion". By that date, however, two store houses and a hospital had been completed and the Governor and Lieutenant Governor had each begun a small house; the convicts were distributed on both sides of the Cove in huts "which had been built for their immediate shelter".[787]

By February 1790 all the officers were in good huts and their men in barracks, an achievement which, in Phillip's opinion, seemingly exceeded general expectation for he wrote at the time, "I believe there is not an individual from the governor to the private soldier whose situation is not more eligible at this time than he had any reason to expect it could be in the course of the three years' station".[788] His own house of six rooms he supposed would stand for a great number of years as it, in common with others then building, was constructed of brick and stone. But he could not hold out the same hope for the dwellings erected on arrival as they had been of a temporary character and "would have to be begun all over again in three or four years' time".

In 1790 the extension of the occupied area to Rose Hill, at the head of the harbour, provided an opportunity for the laying out of a definitely planned convict settlement. Huts, designed to shelter ten felons, were built 100 feet apart so as to form a street one mile long and 200 feet broad. In them, according to the Governor's plan, the convicts were to live until the extension of free settlement caused their removal to cultivate more distant lands.

The slow rate of progress in the housing of the settlers was due to a variety of causes. The convicts themselves showed little inclination to work strenuously and the lack of appointed free superintendents during the first few years of the colony's existence gave them numerous opportunities to shirk tasks assigned to them. The timber of the area also proved to be very unsatisfactory for building purposes. Major Ross complained that it frequently happened that a number of trees had to be felled before one was met that could be converted to any use. Another officer declared that gum trees were "scarce worth cutting down". The failure to discover any limestone also limited the height of brick or stone walls as clay had to be used to bind the materials together. On Norfolk Island this hindrance was overcome by converting coral into lime. Phillip's suggested remedy, as far as the mainland was concerned, was the ballasting of outward ships with English limestone, a method that was consequently adopted.

But the most serious cause of delay was the lack of experienced tradesmen. In his first despatch to England the Governor lamented the discovery of only 12 carpenters among the convicts; thus to hasten operations he was compelled to secure the services of as many others as could be procured from the ships then in harbour. This want continued throughout the whole of Phillip's term of office; in 1791 he complained that a convict whom he wished to retain as a master carpenter had been received on board the *Admiral Barrington* for a return passage to England. In that year the two settlements had only one master carpenter and one master brick layer. Finally, in May 1792, the Undersecretary, John King, informed him that an agreement had been entered into with a master carpenter, William Peat, who would sail in the *Royal Admiral*,[789]but his arrival in the colony was reported in the same letter as that which acknowledged Phillip's receipt of permission to return to England.

Meantime the lack of capable tradesmen and of efficient superintendents to direct building operations had prevented the employment of large numbers of convicts in productive works. As late as October 1792 Phillip reported to the Secretary of State that the numbers engaged on the public buildings, in procuring materials for the same, and in other equally indispensable occupations left no more than 450 for agriculture.[790] The military and civil establishments, the women, and the children also formed a "dead weight" on those who had to render the colony independent in respect of the necessaries of life. A similar report came from Norfolk Island; of the 303 convicts available to carry on all the public works of that settlement 145 were employed as sawyers, carpenters, quarrymen, lime burners, and the like.[791]

Other forms of labour also reduced the numbers of possible convict cultivators. The absence of free settlers compelled their employment in all the branches of work associated with civilised existence.

Thus a Norfolk Island return for September 1792 shows that 101 of its criminal inhabitants were engaged as servants to officers and as overseers, watchmen, cooks, barbers, tailors, shoemakers, and surveyors' assistants. On the mainland the same condition of things existed.

The privilege of employing convict labour was one claimed by the marine officers probably from the foundation of the settlement. In May 1788 Phillip, when seeking instructions concerning their request, admitted that the existing situation of those officers entitled them to some unfree labour as otherwise it would be impossible for them to cultivate enough land to support the animals they had brought with them. The indulgence was allowed; 38 convicts were engaged on officers' farms in 1790, but the officers themselves seem to have gained little by the experiment as two years later Phillip reported that they had not raised sufficient to support their "little stock".[792] He had found, moreover, that the practice was attended with "unavoidable inconveniences" due to the "convicts' being left so much to themselves" and "their mixing with the soldiers". He recommended a discontinuance of the plan after the removal of the marine corps and the granting an allowance of corn to their successors. But as late as October 1792 Phillip still complained that 51 convicts were in the employ of the Major Commandant and officers of the New South Wales Corps, which displaced the marines in that year, while others in like proportion had been assigned to the officers on Norfolk Island.[793]

Another fact militating against the desired self-sufficiency that would result from cultivation was the physical unfitness of many of the convicts for laborious work. In his first letter, of 15 May 1788, Phillip reported that although they had been healthy at the time of their arrival, scurvy had since rendered nearly 200 of them unfit for work. Two months later he informed Lord Sydney that more than 50 were incapable of labour of any kind because of old age or incurable disorders.[794] In July 1790 the surgeon's report disclosed that upwards of 100 would always be a burden on the community; among the females one had lost the use of her limbs for more than three years while two of the men were perfect idiots.[795] At the time of that report 450 were sick. The reason is clear: in the previous month the ships of the disastrous Second Fleet, by landing their convicts in Sydney Cove, had increased the number under medical attention from less than 50 to 488. In his depression the Governor even suspected that the healthy and artificer class of felons were being retained in England while the disordered and helpless were being deliberately sent to New South Wales. Such a practice, he declared, although it might for the present ease English parishes, would certainly cause the colony to remain a burden on the Mother Country for many years.[796]

The landing of the convicts from the Third Fleet was also followed by a heavy mortality: in less than seven months 288 died. That was not the only evil effect, for a majority of the survivors still remained "in the same debilitated state in which they had landed".[797] This however was not the normal experience of the colony. Writing before the close of the year 1788 Phillip told how all save the old and incurable were very healthy. In 1790 he reported that out of 1030 who had arrived in the course of 21 months, "many of whom were worn out by old age, the scurvy, and various disorders", only 72 had died and 26 of them had been the victims of long standing diseases which "it was more than probable would have carried them off much sooner in England". Even the sufferers from the Second Fleet recuperated rapidly.[798]

Phillip attributed these recoveries in no small measure to the climate of New South Wales which he believed was as fine and healthy as that of any part of the world. Even Captain Hill, who carefully catalogued the faults of the settlement and the sufferings of those who were compelled to reside within it, admitted that he found it impossible to convey "a just idea of the beautiful heavenly clime" of the area.[799] This advantage was furthered by such limited aid as circumstances would permit. No hint of deliberate inattention to the wants of the sufferers exists; as already pointed out, one of the first buildings to be erected was a hospital; it was "clear of the town and its situation healthy". Another was later built on Norfolk Island.

A report by Surgeon White that "necessaries" were needed caused Phillip to order a six months' supply of hospital stores from the Cape of Good Hope when the *Sirius* sailed for more grain and provisions in October 1788.[800] His action received the support of the Home Authorities, whose correspondence proves that they were responsive to the Governor's requests and the urge of humanity. On receiving Phillip's report they directed the Lords of the Admiralty to provide a warship for the purpose of conveying to the colony, among other things, a supply of medicines for the use of the convicts. As the *Lady Juliana* was then preparing to sail they gave orders that that vessel should carry an additional quantity equal to one-quarter of the amount already ordered.[801] The wreck of the *Guardian* unfortunately delayed the receipt of needed "necessaries" but the Government's intention can hardly be questioned. As in all departments of the colony's administration, distance increased the Governor's difficulties. Complaints or requests could scarcely expect to produce speedy redress when a single voyage occupied approximately six months.

The Government's realisation that convicts would probably need attention at the time of their arrival is demonstrated by Grenville's instructions to Phillip which directed him to disembark them at Sydney before sending them to Norfolk Island, "as from the length of the passage and the nature of their food" there was every reason to expect that many of them would be reduced to so debilitated a state as to require immediate relief.[802] Later also, when Phillip declared that the increase of numbers in the colony had made it necessary for him to appoint Thomas Jamison of the *Sirius* Assistant Surgeon, another Secretary of State raised no objection.

The most common complaints experienced in the settlements were scurvy and debility. The cause of the former is exposed in Surgeon White's appeal for hospital stores, which he declared were more urgently needed in New South Wales than perhaps in any other quarter of the globe because of "their constantly living on salt provisions without any possibility of change". Writing two and a half years after the establishment of the colony Captain Hill disclosed that between 2000 and 3000 souls still continued to live on salt rations sent from England. Phillip, in December 1791, wrote that although it wanted but one month of four years since he first landed, all the public livestock he had ever received was not more than would have been needed for one good farm.[803] Practically no relief was experienced in the following year; thus, during the whole of Phillip's regime in a very real sense fresh animal meat was an almost unknown article of diet. On Norfolk Island the slaughtering of thousands of "puffins" provided for a short time a change in the daily menu but in that settlement also livestock — except pigs, which were increasing in 1792 — were for all practical purposes non-existent.

Debility was a result of both scarcity and lack of variety in the food. The weekly ration prescribed by the Treasury in 1787 had been as follows:

> 7 pounds of bread or flour, 7 pounds of beef or 4 pounds of pork (both salted), 3 pounds of peas, 6 ounces of butter, and one pound of flour or a half pound of rice,

but this proved impracticable. The fleet had hardly left England before it was realised that the butter would not keep. In March 1791 Phillip reported a total lack of butter, and ten months later accepted a suggestion by John King, the Undersecretary, that oil should be supplied in place of it as experience had proved that butter could not be preserved in New South Wales. In March 1792, a year after he had complained of a total want of peas, he declared that no supply of peas or butter had been received since the colony was established. The want of peas he particularly deplored as peas were indispensable "for people who lived the whole year round on salt provisions".[804] In their place he had supplied some rice, "but it was rice which was too bad to have been issued but in a case of necessity".

About the same time a shortage of flour was met by the issue of some Indian corn grown in the settlement. Vegetables, which appear to have been plentiful after the Rose Hill extension, a limited supply of poultry, and fish which were often scarce, increased the variety of the daily fare. But the failure to raise local supplies of essential foods and the long intervals between the arrivals of ships produced an insufficiency of meat and flour which compelled both settlements to live on short rations for a greater part of the period.

In February 1790 Phillip reported that he had put all landsmen on a two-thirds ration since the preceding November. In April this was reduced to less than a half. In July, when the boats were successful in fishing, ten pounds of fish were served in lieu of two pounds of pork (all the beef having been expended many months before)[805] and the weekly ration was completed by the addition of two and a half pounds of flour, 1 pint of rice, and 1 pint of peas. As late as October 1792 Phillip declared that the arrival of the *Atlantic* and *Britannia* had put it in his power to increase the existing ration, which even then remained "far from satisfactory because of the nature of some articles and a deficiency of others". The lot of those on Norfolk Island was similar; a return of the regular weekly ration for the year 1790 gives the following amounts:[806]

DATE	FLOUR	RICE	PORK
April to May	4 lb	2 lb	2½ lb
May to July	3 lb	1 lb	1½ lb beef or 17 oz pork
July to August	3 lb	1 lb	0

In December 1791 the male ration of those on the island was reduced by one-third, "the women and children remaining as before". More than ten months later Lieutenant Governor King attributed delays in developing the settlement to a reduced ration.[807]

In addition to producing a noticeable debility in many of the convict class this compulsory reduction of the food allowance had two serious results: it encouraged robbery and opposed serious manual labour. The records, however, do not suggest that the debility suffered by the convicts was due only to shortage of food. There is ample evidence to prove that marines and convicts received the same allowance. Phillip's instructions directed him to issue a common ration to both classes. In July 1788 Major Ross complained that in the quantities of provisions served to himself, the officers and men of the detachment, and the convicts there was no difference.[808] More than four years later Phillip stated that the ration issued from the public store to the soldiers was the same as that which he saw daily at his own table. Major Grose, in the same month, declared that a captain of a company and a convict

transported for life divided and shared alike whatever was served.[809]
But this treatment does not seem to have produced serious sickness
within the civil and military departments of the settlements.

Phillip certainly petitioned for a return to England on account of ill
health, and Lieutenants Maxwell and William Collins were allowed to
return for a similar reason; in 1789 also Captain Shea died, but in not
one of these cases was the ration blamed for the disorder in question.
The lack of reports concerning sickness among the marines suggests
that they were healthy. The natural conclusion is that the debilitated
were persons whose constitutions were normally weak or had been
weakened by irregular living or the experiences of the voyage and were
therefore in need of greater nourishment than the food allowance
could supply.

Nevertheless it is only reasonable to suppose that continuous heavy
manual labour could hardly have been performed by men fed as the
settlers were, and it is to Phillip's credit that he admitted that fact; but
that a shortage of food was not the only cause of idleness is shown by
his statement to Grenville that experience had taught him how difficult
it was to make men industrious who had passed their lives in habits of
vice or indolence. In some cases he had found it impossible; neither
kindness nor severity had had any effect.

The stock of provisions within the settlements determined the
ration. The contract for the first expedition provided for a two years'
supply, which was landed as soon as accommodation had been provided to receive it. But not all of this was distributed among the settlers; defective packing and bad stowage damaged a considerable quantity of the rice and flour on the outward passage while rats destroyed
more than 12,000 pounds weight of the same articles during the first
two years of the settlements. In his first letter to the Secretary of State
Phillip emphasised the need of a regular supply of provisions "for four
or five years". Lord Sydney showed his sympathy by directing the contractor of the *Lady Juliana* convicts to place what provisions he could on
that vessel and by ordering the Admiralty to fit out a warship to carry
the remainder of the necessary stores. The vessel selected, the *Guardian*, was a large one according to the standards of the time and she went
heavily laden, but her collision with an iceberg prevented her arrival in
Sydney Cove. Fortunately for the colony the efforts of her crew and
convicts succeeded in bringing her to the Cape where her commander,
Lieutenant Riou, found that the greater part of her salt provisions and
about 200 casks of flour were still fit for use, but the goods that had
been stowed under the lower deck, including flour, rice, sugar, medicines, and clothing were completely destroyed.

Succeeding vessels conveyed what was saved to the colony[810] within which, in the meantime, the ration had been prudently reduced. Transports also normally carried provisions in excess of the requirements of the voyage but, as the numbers of the colonists increased, this practice yielded a diminishing benefit; a year's supply of food for a cargo of 300 convicts obviously lasted only a few weeks when shared among 3000 settlers. Store ships had therefore to be sent; the *Justinian* reached Sydney Cove in June 1790; she was followed by HMS *Gorgon*, the *Kitty*, and the *Bellona*, each of which also carried a few convicts,[811] but the uncertainty of their arrival and the possible consequences of their destruction disturbed the Governor's peace of mind and caused him on occasion to act independently.

Had tradesmen been available he would have despatched the *Sirius* for supplies shortly after his arrival but the compulsory employment of her carpenters prevented such action. In October 1788, however, that vessel sailed to the Cape and secured seed wheat, barley, and four months' supply of flour. Her destruction off Norfolk Island in March 1790 produced almost a panic in both settlements; Ross immediately reduced the ration,[812] placed the island under martial law, and ordered all to turn gardeners for their own support. In Sydney, according to Surgeon White, Phillip called together the officers and arranged a reduced ration "on which they could eke out a miserable existence for seven months".[813]

The *Supply* was also despatched to Batavia with orders to procure six months' provisions for the colonists in addition to what she could herself convey.[814] The reason is clear: no ship, after the First Fleet, reached Sydney Cove before June 1790. In 1791, also because of another shortage, the *Atlantic*, one of the ships of the Third Fleet, was taken into the Government's service by Phillip and sent to Calcutta for flour and peas. A fear that she had miscarried caused him in 1792 to enter into an agreement with the commander of the *Pitt*, which was proceeding to India, to secure provisions if he found that an accident had befallen the *Atlantic*.

Despite these various efforts the state of the settlements was at times precarious; when the *Sirius* went down, the Sydney colonists had only a three months' supply of salt meat after the ration had been reduced to two pounds a week. Before the *Gorgon*'s appearance the settlers lacked peas, butter, and spirits, while the flour which they had secured from Batavia was one-sixth bran and the rice bad. Before the *Atlantic* was hired and after the *Gorgon*'s arrival the settlement had only "5 months' flour, 12 days' peas, and 23 days' oatmeal".[815] Norfolk Island was hardly more fortunate; the returns of that settlement show the state of provisions there as follows:[816]

	FLOUR	BEEF	PORK	PEAS	OATMEAL
			WEEKS ON FULL RATION		
11 Feb 1791	28	28	42	0	0
18 Nov 1791	16.5	9	38.5	0	0
8 Dec 1792	25	5.75	25	39	0

Surgeon White in describing the sending of the *Supply* to Batavia declared she was sailing in the hope that the Dutch might be able to send food in time to save them. He ended his statement with the words, "Should any accident happen to her, Lord have mercy on us". He was probably exaggerating; the trials of the colony seem to have developed within him a certain pessimism which contrasted with the optimism of Phillip, revealed in his writing to Nepean, "Dismal accounts will, I make no doubt, be sent to England, but we shall not starve".

Such conditions were not anticipated when the colony was projected. In preparing for the settlement the Government assumed that the two years' supply sent with the First Fleet would meet the settlers' wants until they themselves had made arrangements for their own support. So confident was it in their capacity to do this that it advised Phillip not to employ all the convicts who accompanied him in raising provisions "because of the natural increase of corn and other vegetable food as well as of animals". He was instructed to reserve all surplus produce for the use of convicts who were to follow shortly afterwards. That confidence persisted; in August 1789 Grenville, after reporting the despatch of stores in the *Lady Juliana*, added, "a further proportion will accompany the convicts who are to be sent in the Autumn but I cannot help flattering myself that after that period very little farther aid will be wanted from this country for the subsistence of the convicts".[817] The results were otherwise, for neither of the settlements during Phillip's term produced sufficient animal meat or flour to support its inhabitants.

Acting upon his instructions the Governor, while at the Cape of Good Hope on his way to New South Wales, had purchased livestock to form the beginning of a common supply for the colony. According to Captain Hunter these included two bulls, six cows, 44 sheep, four goats, and 28 hogs.[818] Some of the officers also bought animals with the intention of stocking farms of their own. The passage to Port Jackson does not seem to have been excessively destructive to these beasts; a return dated 1 May 1788 gives the following account of livestock in New South Wales at the time:

OWNER	BULLS	COWS	SHEEP	GOATS	HOGS	PIGS
Government	2	2	13	1	20	–
Governor	–	2	5	–	10	–
Lieutenant Governor	–	–	–	1	1	7
Marine officers & men	–	1	–	12	10	17
Staff	–	–	11	5	7	1
	2	5	29	19	48	25

Shortly afterwards the bulls and the cows wandered into the bush and were not found until after Phillip's departure. One calf was speared by the natives, two goats were killed "by some of our own people", five sheep were destroyed apparently by native dogs, and the remaining sheep failed to thrive. Then the accident to the *Guardian* caused the killing off of what was left. Some pigs, nevertheless, remained and since a fear of the natives prevented their being turned into the bush they, after some of them had been distributed to the convicts, were carried to Norfolk Island. There it appears they "flourished greatly",[819] so much so that in February 1791 Ross, who was then in charge of the island, drew up instructions for the granting of "one grown sow to every three convicts, or one small sow pig to each convict as far as it would admit",[820] but for breeding purposes only as the sows were again to become the property of the Government if their possessors left the island; moreover, any destruction of them was to be punished as robbing or killing of the public stock. Provision was also made for the distribution of all future sows, save two in each litter, until every male and female convict on the island should be supplied with stock. Meantime, the inhabitants of both settlements lived on salt provisions.

Before leaving England Phillip had been instructed to secure cattle "from the islands" as soon as a vessel could be spared for that purpose, but the *Sirius* was wrecked before she could be employed in that way and the *Supply* was unfitted for that work. His urgent appeals for livestock did not fail to produce sympathetic attention at Westminster; in February 1791 Grenville informed him that the *Daedalus*, a supply ship accompanying an expedition then proceeding to Vancouver, would be instructed to carry livestock from the islands, but that vessel was still at Monterey (North America) when the Governor left the colony. Phillip himself had recommended the use of a two-deck warship having one of her decks cleared of guns. Finally the *Gorgon*, in 1791, shipped livestock from the Cape to Sydney as follows:[821]

	BOUGHT AT THE CAPE		LANDED AT SYDNEY	
	MALE	FEMALE	MALE	FEMALE
Cattle	3	25	0*	17
Sheep	4	62	3	56
Swine	1	10	1	4

* A bull calf survived the voyage

Then the following year the *Atlantic* purchased a supply of stock in Calcutta with the following results:[822]

	BOUGHT	DIED ON VOYAGE
Bulls	2	0
Cows	1	0*
Calves	1	1
Rams	2	0
Ewes	18	8
Goats	20	13

*The cow died shortly afterwards

But as the cattle in this case were of the buffalo breed they would have no dealings with the black cattle from the Cape. Thus at the time of Phillip's return both soldiers and convicts had still to hope for a time when fresh meat would be available.

Agricultural implements and seed of various kinds were carried from England by the first expedition. The seed was augmented by purchases made at Rio and the Cape yet little serious cultivation was attempted in the first year. In May 1788 Phillip predicted that not more than eight acres would be sown with wheat and barley that season; two months later he reported that the Lieutenant Governor had about four acres under cultivation while he himself had from eight to ten acres in wheat and barley but, at the same time, he expressed the belief that all the "corn raised in that and the following year would necessarily have to be kept for seed because of the difficulties that were being experienced".[823] Very little of the English wheat had "vegetated" and a considerable quantity of the barley from the same source had rotted in the ground because of being heated during the passage. All the wheat and barley placed on the *Supply* tender at the Cape had been destroyed by weevil. The wheat sent to Norfolk Island had likewise failed.

Phillip therefore decided to sow the ground a second time with seed intended for use in the succeeding year. Thus he had left not enough seed to sow a single acre. Ants and field mice increased the difficulty, and most of the tools provided had proved to be "as bad as ever were sent out for barter on the coast of Guinea". The nature of the country near Sydney opposed rapid advance since the removal of the large gum trees was itself a task that taxed the endurance of many convicts. Norfolk Island was described by King in 1788 as one entire wood of huge pine trees without a single acre of clear land, but the nature of its soil pointed to successful cultivation in the future. Exploration to the west of Sydney also revealed more suitable land near the head of the harbour. There, in November 1788, the Governor established a force of marines and convicts in country "as fine as any he had seen in England". This settlement he named Rose Hill after George Rose, an Undersecretary of the Treasury. Its success caused rapid development.

To supplement the produce of the public farm at Rose Hill the convicts were encouraged to establish vegetable gardens in the land which surrounded the houses allotted to their use. In 1791 the native name Parramatta was assigned to the area. In the following year another settlement, named Toongabbie, was established three miles further westward. The increasing importance of these extensions can be gauged from the following figures for the numbers of inhabitants on 8 December 1792:

Sydney	1161
Parramatta & Toongabbie	1906
Norfolk Island & at sea	1136
TOTAL	4203

Their agricultural development was also rapid; in December 1789 Rose Hill yielded "about 200 bushels of wheat and 60 of barley together with a small quantity of flax, Indian corn, and oats", all of which was preserved for seed. Two years later the maize return alone, notwithstanding a long drought and an estimated loss of 1500 bushels by theft, was 4844½ bushels, of which 2649½ bushels were distributed "as bread".[824] In 1792 the area under cultivation exceeded 1500 acres. One thousand of these formed the public farm which was stationed in the new westerly settlements; another 100 acres were described as garden ground; the remaining cultivated areas were in the possession of free settlers, whose influence in agriculture began to be felt in that year. So promising was the outlook that the Governor was constrained to say, "I flatter myself that the time now approaches in which this country will be able to supply its inhabitants with grain". But he was not to see that time; before the year closed he sailed for England.

Norfolk Island failed to fulfil the hopes entertained of its productiveness. In 1790 an officer of the *Sirius* declared the island to be as rich in soil and vegetation as any part of the world. A few months later Phillip reported that sown wheat and barley had produced 25 fold and more could be expected. Potatoes yielded a great increase and could provide two crops a year. Indian corn, sugar cane, vines, and oranges were also thriving in March 1790; between 28 and 32 acres were under cultivation on the public account and about 18 acres had been cleared for gardening purposes by free settlers and convicts.[825] These encouraging reports caused Grenville, in the following year, to suppose that the island would soon be able to produce sufficient wheat, Indian corn, potatoes, and vegetables to supply both the original settlements.

But this expectation was not realised, for Ross, in February 1791, reported that grubs and caterpillars had been "so multitudinous" that they alone had destroyed 21 acres of wheat and 33 acres of maize. Blight and "the fly" had accounted for a few more but 1800 bushels of potatoes had been secured from ten acres planted. The same officer, in January 1791, with the idea of encouraging industry and ridding the Government of some responsibility (at the time of distributing the swine among the colonists, as already described), issued orders assigning portions of land not exceeding one acre a head to those who showed a disposition to work. This they were to be allowed to work for themselves two days every week, contingent however upon a future reduction of their flour allowance.[826] Phillip gave his assent to the scheme although he expressed a doubt concerning the practicability of the proposal since he suspected that the convicts were not being given sufficient time to establish themselves. His suspicion was well founded as King, before the close of the year, had to abolish this "acre plan" because of the general discontent it had produced.

Writing in September 1792, King reported the following cultivation for public purposes on the island:

PLACE	WHEAT	MAIZE	
Arthur's Vale	106	17	acres
Queensborough	26	90	acres
Phillipburgh	–	14	acres

The ground grub and the reduced food ration had prevented more extensive operations but in the following year he hoped to be able to predict "with more certainty the time when further supplies would no longer be necessary".[827]

Debility, due to underfeeding, was definitely a deterrent to rapid advance in agriculture. Phillip's natural sympathy, combined with his dislike for disorder, opposed the exaction of strenuous effort from hungry workers. In March 1792 he informed Nepean that the hours of labour for those employed in clearing and cultivating the ground were only 5 to 9 in the morning and 4 to 5.30 in the afternoon. He admitted that little could be accomplished in those periods but his excuse was the complaints of hunger uttered by the convicts when called forth to labour, and his letter leaves the impression that he thought those complaints were justified. Later in the same year he reported how "pressure of hunger" had caused the death of several convicts who had eaten corn in its crude state while carrying it to the granary.

Weakness, the natural resistance evoked by compulsory labour, and the unprepared state of the settlement explain many of the delays in agriculture, but in Phillip's oft-stated opinion a very important cause of the failure was a lack of inspiring guidance and efficient supervision. This compelled the appointment of convict overseers, who naturally feared to exert a really effective authority and who were not competent to instruct those entrusted to their care. In May 1788 Phillip complained that he was "without a botanist or even an intelligent gardener". This caused the Government to despatch the following superintendents in the *Guardian*:[828]

James Smith & George Austin — gardeners lately employed in the King's Botanical Garden at Kew.

Phillip Schaffer — a former lieutenant in a Hessian corps serving in America, who was accustomed to farming. Thomas Clarke — a farmer.

Philip Divine and Andrew Hume — lately superintendents on the Hulks, who understood farming.

James Reid — an American planter.

John Barlow & J.T. Dodge — army officers.

Only five of these, whom Riou transferred to the *Lady Juliana*, reached New South Wales and of them Phillip stated that only one was a farmer. Two others reported that they had been accustomed to farming in their youth, but their knowledge did not qualify them to act as instructors of convicts. It is rather significant of the quality of these superintendents also that Riou considered them generally much inferior to the convicts who accompanied them.

The early successful cultivation at Rose Hill was due to the efforts of Henry Dodd, the Governor's servant, who directed the labour of 100 convicts in that area. His death in 1791 was another calamity suffered by the colony for, by his removal, it "lost the only person in the settlement equal to that charge". Meantime Phillip renewed his request; in June 1790 he stressed the futility of sending superintendents who were not "masters in the business in which the convicts they superintended were employed". Next month he informed Grenville that he did not desire many farmer superintendents; two would be sufficient if, in addition to being good husbandmen, they had enough spirit to discharge the trust which must be reposed in them.

But he was doomed to disappointment; in March 1792 he reflected how very different their state would then be if the colony had received "a few intelligent men". Eight months later he reported of the mainland superintendents that one had become a settler and was doing well, a second had been discharged as useless in every respect, and a third who could well be spared was soon to be discharged. And months before on Norfolk Island Mr Doidge's (or Dodge's) request to be allowed to resign had been granted by King because of "his thorough ignorance and incapacity for the place he was in". This defect extended also to other branches of labour such as bricklaying, carpentry, milling, and flax working. But in agriculture it set a definite limit to the area that could be cultivated as it was impossible "to detach a body of convicts to a distance" unless there were "a sufficient person to superintend and direct their labour", one "who should be not only a farmer but a man who would feel himself interested in the convicts' labouring successfully for the benefit of the Crown".

It was this lack of self-interested supervision which caused Phillip so repeatedly to emphasise the need of free settlers. In July 1788 he stated that time and a few families used to the cultivation of the soil would remove all their difficulties. In the same year he informed Lord Sydney that only settlers, assisted by convicts, could make the country self-supporting. Two years later he pointed out that the difficulty of cultivating outlying areas could be overcome by the importation of free settlers; in the last year of his term he was still lamenting the want of free colonists.

The delayed arrival of men of this class was not due to official opposition. That convicts should become settlers after the expiration of their sentences had been the wish of the Government from the beginning. Its belief that free emigrants from England would form useful colonists was demonstrated before the departure of the First Fleet.[829] In the instructions issued to Phillip in August 1787 he was directed to afford such settlers every encouragement by granting to each of them land at his own discretion but not exceeding in quantity the number of acres assigned to a non-commissioned officer, who was to receive 100 acres over and above the area granted to a discharged convict.[830] The settling of private soldiers was likewise to be encouraged by setting apart for them portions of land 50 acres in excess of the normal emancipated convict's allotment. Such grants were to be made free of all taxes, fees, and the like for a space of ten years, after which they were to become liable to a quit rent of one shilling for every ten acres.

The instructions given to Phillip before his departure had made provision for the rewarding of convicts emancipated for good behaviour by assigning to them the following land grants:

30 acres for a single man
50 acres for a married man
10 acres for each child at the time of the making of the grant.

This standard Phillip apparently kept in mind, as a return of land grants made near the close of 1791 shows that 30, 50, and 60 acre allotments were the rule except on Norfolk Island, where convict settlers on occasion secured only 10 acres because of the greater fertility of its soil.[831] Only two of the 87 grants recorded exceed 60 acres, viz. one for 70 and another for 140 acres,[832] but as at least 42 of the grantees were either retired marines or seamen we must conclude that Phillip refused to emphasise that distinction between emancipate and free settlers aimed at in the instructions of August 1789. This impression is deepened by his failure to distinguish, in that return, between the occupations or status of the recipients; the common title "settlers" is appended to them all.

That settlers would find it difficult if not impossible to establish themselves without assistance was realised from the beginning. Only a few months after the arrival of the first colonists Phillip impressed upon Lord Sydney the need of supplying them with convict labour "for a certain time" but in actual practice he does not seem to have encouraged the free inhabitants who accompanied him to apply for such labour.

Four years after landing, the Rev. Richard Johnson complained that the Governor had always refused to allow him the services of a man who could shoot or any help to clear the 400 acres set aside as church land, which consequently remained in its virgin state. In the following year, also, the Governor apparently grudged the assignment of 51 convicts to the Major Commandant and officers of the New South Wales Corps, and on Norfolk Island King forbade anyone to employ a convict during working hours without the consent of the Lieutenant Governor. But their unwillingness on these occasions was probably a result of a want of labourers for agricultural work, caused by sickness and the large numbers that were engaged in building, carrying, and other non-productive occupations. Then there was little incentive to assign labour while those who were assigned remained dependent upon the Government for support; the most reasonable courses were to employ it in clearing and cultivating the public farm and to encourage a form of free settlement that would assist in reducing the Government's responsibility. Both were adopted; the public cultivation has been explained; to encourage free settlement, convicts were regularly employed in clearing ground both in New South Wales and on Norfolk Island, which was handed over to marines and expirees for their own use.[833]

This was not the only assistance given to these early settlers; the marines and seamen received in addition, clothing and victuals for 18 months, agricultural tools, grain for the first year's sowing, two sows, one cock and six hens as well as necessary convict aid for the building of their huts. Emancipists seemingly enjoyed like favours; in 1791 Phillip reported that those expirees who were settling near Parramatta would receive support and clothing for 18 months, implements, seed, and two sows. There is no mention of poultry but as James Ruse, the first convict settler,[834] received six hens we may suppose that the omission to mention that item was an oversight. None of these regular grants, however, carried with them the right to receive anything like permanent convict labour. The only suggestion of that kind is in the described encouragement to be offered to Phillip Schaffer, who was given 140 acres together with the privilege of employing four convicts for 18 months, during which time they were to be supported from the public store.[835]

But it was not from settlers of the marine or convict type that Phillip expected much relief; writing in March 1792 he informed Dundas that a few intelligent farmer settlers would do more for the colony than 500 men from those classes, "very few of whom are calculated for the life they must necessarily lead in this country". Already many of them had "grown tired" or were anxious to surrender their land or had sold their little livestock to secure from the ships articles which would bring them no permanent benefit. In 1792 King discovered that many of the 50 convict settlers on Norfolk Island had asked the master of the *Pitt* to take them away and, suspecting that several of them had meant to desert their wives after leaving them their land, he summoned these suspected deserters to him and plainly told them that "if any of them endeavoured to leave the island before, or soon after, the twelve months might be expired for which they were to be victualled from the public stores they would be stopped until that twelve months' provisions should be made good to the public".[836] The possibility of the land being left to the wives particularly annoyed him as that would cause industrious settlers to suffer since "fifty of the best and most desirable lots would, in time, become the property of abandoned women burthened with children".

In the same year Phillip complained that the sole object of some in becoming settlers was to be their own masters; others hoped to raise enough money to pay their passages to England after assigning their lands to others "who took them with the same view". It was not in settlers of that kind that the Governor placed much hope. His request was for a few "intelligent good settlers" who would have an interest in their own labour and those who might be employed under them. Precept had little effect on the convicts but example could do much; therefore he desired "some good characters to whom these people might look up". If they also possessed some private capital their difficulties would be reduced. Realising, however, that all of them would experience some hardships he recommended, in February 1790, giving to each of them a farm of 500 to 1000 acres together with not less than 20 convicts supported by the Government for two years, one half of whom might be returned at the end of that period.[837] A few months later he modified that suggestion, proposing in its stead that "a certain number of convicts" supported for a like term might be assigned to the first 15 only.[838]

Dundas was prepared to trust the Governor; at the beginning of 1792 he informed him that His Majesty's servants did not think it either advisable or necessary to limit him to any given number of convicts in assigning labour to individuals, who would probably differ widely "in situation of life, character, and description". They would therefore leave the determination of that number, as well as the quantity of provisions to be allotted to each settler, to his judgment and discrimination.

The conditions suggested by Phillip seem to have been made known in England as certain offers to settle in the colony were laid before the Secretary of State during the last 12 months of Phillip's administration. Near the end of 1791 John Sutton, after a rejection of earlier extravagant proposals, volunteered to go to New South Wales with his associates consisting, he supposed, of about 15 families, on the following conditions: a free passage, a free land grant of at least 500 acres, free tools, free provisions, and convict labour supported by the Government for two years; but nothing seems to have come of the proposal. Delays in preparing the necessary shipping possibly accounted for its failure.

In January 1792 George Matcham offered to send on his own account a skilful farmer and his family, as well as other families, with the intention of making provision for his younger son who would follow some years later "with three or four thousand pounds". He asked for an immediate grant of between 10,000 and 20,000 acres,[839] two to three hundred being in the neighbourhood of Rose Hill; but again there is no evidence that anything eventuated. In the same month Dundas informed Phillip that he would give every encouragement to 15 families of Quakers who had made proposals to proceed to the colony. According to Collins, however, these families, after engaging to take their passage in the *Bellona*, were diverted from their purpose by some misrepresentations made to them respecting the country, but possibly they were the families Sutton had in mind.[840] In May 1792 an offer made by William Richards Jnr to settle in the colony on condition that the Government granted him land and allowed him to open a store had a like result.

Nevertheless certain settlers did leave England during Phillip's regime; a farmer named Jameson with his wife and child sailed in the *Royal Admiral*, which arrived in October 1792. The *Bellona* also carried 11 settlers but she reached the colony after Phillip's departure. They, according to Dundas, were "all that had offered"; thus the assistance and relief expected of free inhabitants were not experienced. Meantime, however, the supply of settlers from local sources had increased. A return dated December 1792 gives the following figures:

SETTLERS FROM	PARRAMATTA	NORFOLK ISLAND
Free people (i.e. marines & seamen)	11	54
Convicts	53	60
Total		178

The behaviour of the convicts during these years of stress fails to brand them as violent criminals. One serious attempt to mutiny was suspected on Norfolk Island; in February 1789 the *Supply* tender conveyed 27 convicts to that settlement and returned with the report that the resident convicts had plotted to seize the commandant and marines, take possession of the first ship that arrived, and sail for Otaheite. The plan was divulged by a woman and admitted by the convicts concerned, who comprised all of their class on the island except three. The leader was sent to Sydney but escaped hanging as no attempt had been made to put the plan into execution. The remainder were ordered back to their various occupations and the additional 27 convicts accepted. In February 1790 Phillip reported that seven convicts, including a woman, had been hanged since the establishment of the settlement.[841] But five of them, including the woman, undoubtedly suffered the supreme penalty because of robberies they had committed, and it is possible that the other two were guilty of no more serious crimes.

In the same letter Phillip also recorded the execution of six marines who had been convicted of stealing, while a seventh, who had been "the first projector of the scheme", had saved his neck by turning King's evidence. Another found guilty of a rape on an infant had had his capital sentence changed to transportation to Norfolk Island for life. Thus, by comparison with the marines, the convicts appear in a rather favourable light. It is true that only two months later the Governor declared that seven-eighths of them deserved nothing better than starvation, but that criticism was inspired by their indolence and not by crime. In his official account of the colony shortly before his departure he wrote, "In speaking of these people it is but just to observe that I can recollect very few crimes during the last three years but what have been committed to procure the necessaries of life".[842] His earlier correspondence confirms this; it refers to stealing of vegetables, gambling for provisions, selling of clothes and the like; serious crimes are conspicuously absent.[843]

Early in 1790 also he complained that for several months the robbing of gardens and poultry yards had been an almost nightly occurrence; he had therefore established a night watch which had so fully answered its intended purpose that for three months there had not been a single robbery. At the close of 1791 King also declared that those on Norfolk Island were experiencing daily and nightly robberies in gardens and other property. There, however, the trouble could in large measure be traced to deserters who had taken to the woods and had been compelled to raid to sustain life. But it is only fair to the convicts to state that this evil practice of stealing was not limited to the convicts alone; on the mainland at least, Phillip suspected that the marines were also guilty of it.

The comparatively good behaviour of the criminal class was not due to any unusual severity in the discipline adopted to preserve order. If executions be taken as a measure of the punishment inflicted its severity declined in the course of time, as the number of hangings decreased after the first year; that year witnessed four, the second only two, although a third followed soon afterwards. Nor is there reason to believe that Phillip's doubts concerning the true efficiency of execution were dispelled during the period.[844] His belief that the threat of handing over incorrigible offenders to the cannibals of New Zealand would be a greater deterrent was not put into practice, but an opportunity for effecting the method in a modified form presented itself shortly after landing. In May 1788 he reported that six men had been condemned to die for robbing the store but only one had been executed. Of the remainder he wrote, "They are to be exiled from the settlement and when the season permits I intend that they shall be landed near the South Cape where, by their forming connexions with the natives some benefit may accrue". No further mention of the plan is recorded; possibly a lack of shipping caused the Governor to forgo this form of punishment.

The want of free overseers, the refusal of the marines to act as superintendents, and the compulsory employment of convicts in that capacity have already been explained. What authority the last named possessed is not described but it apparently was sufficient to prevent their charges from "straggling" away when they were supposed to be working. The employment of men of the same class as constables, however, sheds interesting light on the difficulties of the administration and the character of some of the convicts. As mentioned above, the robbing of gardens had led to the creation of a night watch in Sydney. This consisted of 12 convicts,[845] divided into four parties, fully authorised to visit places suspected of association with crime and to arrest, for examination, persons suspected of complicity. Among other duties it was to take cognisance of convicts who sold, gambled, or bartered clothes or provisions, to detain any soldier or seaman found loitering or in a convict hut after the "taptoo" had sounded, and to take them to the nearest guard hut for examination. Neither fee nor gratuity was to be given to them but future reward for diligence was promised to them.

The fact that in the following three months not a single robbery was committed attests to the efficiency of the system but it soon provoked a dispute between the civil and the military authorities. One night a marine was detained after being discovered in the convicts' quarters. The following day Major Ross declared that the detaining of a marine who had not committed an unlawful act was an insult to the whole corps. Later he added that its members would not be controlled by convicts while they (the marines) had bayonets in their hands. The watch's orders were therefore amended in such a way as to prevent the detention of any marine unless he were found rioting or committing some illegal act.

On Norfolk Island the efforts of the administrator were hampered by a limitation of authority which forbade any more serious penalties than confinement and corporal punishment. Early in 1791 King complained that unless some criminal court or martial law were established it would be impossible to prevent constant robberies. The likely shortage of food, after the destruction of the *Sirius*, caused Ross to adopt the second alternative for some months, but a criminal court was not created.[846] Only a few weeks before his departure Phillip reported to Dundas that the inconvenience which attended the lack of a criminal court on Norfolk Island was increasing with the number of settlers and that daring robberies were being committed with impunity because of the difficulties attendant upon sending the accused and witnesses to Sydney.[847] To check this evil a night watch was also established in this settlement, but its powers were wider as it had authority to shoot persons wandering about after 8 p.m. Even this failed to put an end to the trouble; at last, in 1792, King provided the owners of gardens with firearms. As a result James Clarke, who had taken to the woods, was shot and killed by Leonard Dyer, whose garden he was robbing.

In other respects also Phillip found himself hampered. Nearly four years after his arrival one of his stated reasons for desiring free settlers was a "want of people capable of acting as magistrates". The services of a paid Provost Marshal were never at his disposal. The person chosen to fill that position deserted before the sailing of the First Fleet. In his stead Mr Henry Brewer, a midshipman of the *Sirius*, was appointed and "for near five years" he acted as Provost Marshal without fee or emolument of any kind.

One common attribute of later convict punishment, viz. the wearing of distinctively marked clothing, seems to have been unknown in the colony. This is suggested by the distribution of convict clothing to other classes in the settlements. Thus several of the inferior officers for a time wore boots and other articles sent out for the criminal section of the community. In December also King forbade by proclamation the buying of clothes from a convict by any person, "civil, military, or settler". But more conclusive evidence is supplied by Phillip himself who, after describing the impossibility of preventing convict clothing from passing into the hands of others, proposed that it should be marked by weaving into the materials of which it was made, stripes of different colours.[848] Again, in June 1792, he recommended the same course to prevent what was intended for the convicts from being sold to soldiers or settlers; "some distinguishing mark", he continued, "should be put on everything intended for the use of convicts".

Two other forms of criminal punishment, the wearing of irons and flogging, are scarcely mentioned in the records. There is nothing to suggest that the convicts were constantly watched; the knowledge that desertion would be followed by starvation or return was a better check on such action than chains would have been. Moreover, as the convicts were allowed to use tools, they could easily have found a means to rid themselves of their irons. On Norfolk Island in 1792, however, four men found guilty of robbing gardens were sentenced to receive 300 lashes each and to be kept at hard work in chains until the expiration of their periods of servitude. They suffered 100 lashes but were forgiven the remainder of their punishment two days later as King found that they were newcomers. That same officer also reported that during the period of martial law on the island, corporal punishment was inflicted by the only general court martial held. How often other courts met must be largely a matter of conjecture but the fact that Phillip states that Captain Hunter assisted the Judge Advocate one day each week while the *Sirius* was in harbour encourages the belief that they met frequently.

The Governor's other statement that neither kindness nor severity could make some convicts industrious points also to rather summary punishment of a corporal character, but the lack of references to cruelty and the general tone of the correspondence are arguments in favour of humane treatment rather than brutality. Ross certainly experimented for a short time with one unpleasant form of punishment on a few imprisoned convicts; he gave orders that they were to receive no more food than the surgeon thought absolutely necessary to sustain life.[849] He had to confess however that its results had been disappointing as far as checking villainy was concerned.

The encouragement of good behaviour by pardon was scarcely tried; as stated in an earlier chapter the felons on the *Guardian* were pardoned on Lieutenant Riou's recommendation; otherwise only three seem to have been emancipated before the conclusion of their sentences: one a convict who saved the *Sirius* from burning after she had run aground, another because of his industry in teaching others to make bricks, and a woman who secured the desired favour by marrying an overseer. Had free settlers existed they might have employed emancipists and supported them, but there was little incentive to set men free when they remained a charge on the Government after the receipt of their freedom.

Serious religious and moral instruction seem also to have received less attention than they might have. Phillip went as far as to instruct King to cause the prayers of the Church of England to be read every Sunday on Norfolk Island, and to enforce a due observance of religion. And King, amid his various troubles, did order all to attend public worship every Sunday at 10 a.m. under penalty of forfeiting, for failure to comply with that order, two pounds of meat if the offender were an overseer, and one and a half pounds if only a convict. But about the same time he complained that the island had no clergyman and there is no evidence that he ever received the services of one.[850] The correspondence of the Sydney chaplain leads us to suppose that he felt that Phillip might have given him more assistance. Four years after his arrival he was still forced to conduct his services "wholly exposed to the weather". As a result many of the officers frequently apologised for their non-attendance, but what he complained most of was the thinness of his congregations due to the absence of more than one-half to two-thirds of the convicts, "especially the women". His health had been impaired by the lack of suitable places of worship and he feared that he would soon be forced "to give up and leave these miserable people to spend their Sabbaths in a manner wholly like heathens".[851]

Of the convict women little is recorded. In spite of the paucity of their numbers at the time of the arrival of the First Fleet Phillip soon expressed his opposition to the suggested plan of importing native women from the islands. In his first letter he told Sydney that they would simply "pine away in misery" if they were introduced. Four months later he repeated this opinion although he now admitted that the majority of the convict women were "very abandoned wretches". In spite of that he expressed the view that more would have to be sent if additional male convicts were transported to the settlement. The disproportion between the sexes, however, was considerably reduced by the arrival of the *Lady Juliana* with her 220 women in 1790.[852]

From the scattered references to the employment of the women generally it seems that their services were sometimes directed towards agriculture. In July 1790 Phillip reported that a few were working in the fields and more would be when the opportunity offered. In the following year also, Ross described how women maintained by male convicts would not be expected to do more than hoe the ground and pick off grubs and caterpillars,[853] but the majority apparently were engaged in domestic duties. Phillip, in the letter just referred to, predicted that the "greatest part of them would always find employment in making their own and the men's clothes and in attending to their children". The Secretary of State seems to have been satisfied with these prospective duties as he authorised the Governor to employ the women in a manner most conducive to the advantage of the settlement, and commended his already successful exertions "in the promotion of the marriage connexion between the unmarried people". That many did marry is certain; the Governor, in June 1792, stated that they generally married and, bearing in mind Phillip's aversion to anything like indiscriminate intercourse between the sexes, this is supported by the number of births, which normally exceeded deaths in spite of the trying conditions.[854]

One task allotted to the women convicts, viz. that of minding huts, might have opened the way to some immorality. The Governor in 1792 informed Nepean that he could find full employment for all the women as hut-keepers or at labour in the fields and Ross, in the Proclamation already referred to, stated that his reason for the limitation of work to be assigned to women supported by men was "the further encouragement of such male convicts as are desirous to maintain the females". What this exactly meant and how such women were treated are not explained, but that the intention of the administration was to promote right living is beyond question; but it must be admitted that the scattered state of the huts, the lack of supervision, and the character of many of the convicts were influences tending to frustrate the Government's purpose.

The omission of references to illegitimate births in Phillip's correspondence is rather significant as its presence would manifestly have increased his responsibility by throwing upon the Crown the duty of feeding the children concerned. That much of the married life in the settlements was deficient in true affection is demonstrated by a General Order of 4 April 1791, which forbade persons having wives or children incapable of maintaining themselves to leave the colony without previous provision having been made for their maintenance.[855] King also, when censuring 50 expirees who attempted to leave Norfolk Island, declared that he had been informed that many of them intended to desert their wives and families. Marriages of convenience were evidently not unknown in the settlements.

The marines and soldiers formed an insurance against serious rebellion on the part of the convicts. Otherwise their usefulness was very limited. The inability of the Aborigines to endanger the colony's existence was recognised almost from the beginning; on Norfolk Island there were none. The captain's guard, established at Rose Hill, was soon reduced to one lieutenant and 12 privates who were retained merely to protect the public store. In the production of the necessaries of life the military department, as a whole, played no real part although Major Ross did employ a few marines on Norfolk Island to clear ground for cultivation. If they exercised any moral influence over their fellow criminal colonists it passed unobserved. In the organisation of a police system for Sydney they proved a nuisance by resisting the Governor's orders. They were suspected of stealing vegetables and were accused of seeking the women convicts' quarters. Within a few months of arrival one of their number was sentenced to receive 100 lashes for striking a comrade; another later died as a result of a quarrel with his fellows. As settlers "the great part of them" proved extremely troublesome. Two who received land had to be arrested, one for beating the watch, the other for cruelly flogging a convict overseer "when employed about his work".[856]

Again and again their officers obstructed Phillip's attempts to develop the colony; Major Ross charged them with a shameful inattention to the building of the marines' barracks; they would have nothing to do with the supervision of the convicts' labour unless it was being employed for their own advantage, and they denied that their duty required them to sit as members of a criminal court or of a general court martial, an opinion that was later directly contradicted by the Home Authorities. In February 1790 Phillip reported that of the 16 officers doing duty in the colony, five had been put under arrest (four of them remained in that state for three years) and two others had been suspended, for unofficerlike behaviour, by Major Ross, whose treatment of the Judge Advocate and of Captain Hunter, in his capacity as a Justice of the Peace, had been such as to cause both of these men to tender their resignations.

It is not surprising then that Phillip should have declared that some change was needed to avoid general confusion. Many of his troubles vanished with the departure of the marines after the arrival of the New South Wales Corps but, judged by standards of magnanimity and humanity, the officers of both the marines and the Corps fell short of Phillip and King. They grumbled about the equality of the food ration, which the Governor himself shared with them and with the convicts. They complained that the convict settlers received greater land concessions than they themselves did, ignoring the fact they were only temporary inhabitants. Phillip suspected that Major Ross's scheme to remove the convicts from the public store on Norfolk Island would produce hardship, and Ross had to suspend it in the same year because of the general confusion it caused. Thus unless we are prepared to admit that the naval officers were weak or unduly lenient it is difficult to condone all the actions of their military brethren. The magnanimity of the naval officers is one of the most striking features of the whole experiment.[857]

In one respect New South Wales failed to fulfil all that was hoped of it. Before the colony was established, its distance from the British Isles and from the usual trade routes had been advanced as arguments in its favour because of the difficulty this would place in the way of unlawful return, but criminal ingenuity soon found a means of escape. Realising that captains of reduced crews would welcome assistance for their homeward voyage, convicts tendered their services secretly to masters of departing ships. The possibility of such action had been foreseen as early as 1787 and had caused the insertion of a clause in Phillip's instructions forbidding any intercourse between convicts and visiting shipmen. Phillip himself included a like prohibition in the instructions he gave to King before his departure for Norfolk Island. These orders were not entirely effective; immediately after landing, in January 1788, some of the convicts tramped to Botany Bay and offered their services to the commander of the French ships *Astrolabe* and *Boussole*.[858] Their offers were rejected but Surgeon White believed that one French criminal, named Peter Paris, escaped from the settlement in that way.

The problem was made more difficult by the lack of records concerning the convicts' periods of transportation, which were not sent until 1791.[859] Several soon declared that their terms had expired and claimed the right to board departing ships. As early as April 1790 Phillip asked for instructions concerning these self-styled expirees who, by July of the same year, numbered 30. He emphasised the necessity of forcing them to work if they remained in the country; otherwise they would become a burden on the Government. He pointed out at the same time that ship-masters would be pleased to accept the services of able healthy convicts while they would have little reason to welcome the unfit on board their vessels. Thus the colony's burden would only increase as time passed. In the following month a convict named Joseph Sutton was found concealed on the *Neptune.*

These reports produced something akin to consternation at Westminster. Grenville admitted that the return of expirees could not be prevented legally but as it was unlikely that persons of that type would follow honest pursuits after their return it was extremely desirable that every inducement should be held out to cause them to remain in New South Wales.[860] He therefore gave Phillip authority to grant them not only land but also victuals out of the public store while they were establishing themselves. The result was far from satisfactory; in November 1791 Phillip lamented the departure of a much-needed carpenter expiree in the *Royal Admiral,* adding that unless the owners forbade such action "the settlement would never keep a carpenter, cooper, or any valuable man" because ship-masters "tempted them away".[861] Next year he reported the embarkation of 22 men and nine women, whose sentences had expired, on board the *Pitt.*

Before this, however, the Lords of the Treasury had been moved by Phillip's complaints to act. They adopted the practice of inserting a clause in every transport contract, subjecting the contractor to a heavy penalty if he were found guilty of carrying away from the colony any convict or seaman. The *Royal Admiral* sailed with the knowledge that a final settlement of accounts would not be made until the Governor had certified that no convict had been taken on board. William Richards, at a later date, agreed to forfeit 2000 pounds for any breach of his contract. The number that escaped in this way was small but not negligible, for between July and December 1791 Phillip reported the names of 34 convicts whose terms had not expired and who had probably been carried out of the colony.[862]

A few other adventurous spirits hazarded escape by taking to the bush. On the mainland, as early as July 1788, Phillip stated that 11 male convicts and one female convict were missing, but a realisation of the difficulty of maintaining life away from the settlement discouraged such attempts until the arrival of the *Queen.* Then some of her Irish convicts revived the practice because of a belief that China lay only 150 miles away. Desertions of this kind ended in death or return to punishment after extreme privation. On Norfolk Island also a few took refuge in the woods. There they were guilty of making night-time raids on the gardens of the workers, and caused the Government considerable trouble, but the situation of that island made permanent escape practically impossible.

One party gained notoriety by setting forth from Sydney in an open boat, on 28 March 1791. It consisted of eight male convicts including William Bryant, with his wife and two children aged three years and 18 months. According to Collins, before Bryant stole the boat he secured a quadrant, compass, and chart from the master of the *Waaksamheyd*, which carried provisions from Batavia to Sydney.[863] Their movements are obscure; two of the men died on board the Dutch East Indiaman *Hornwey*, one fell overboard, and Bryant and one child died in Batavia after the Dutch Governor of Timor had handed them to Captain Edwards of HMS *Pandora*. The remnant was placed on board HMS *Gorgon*, where the other child died; the remainder were tried in the Old Bailey and although they were found guilty of an offence without benefit of clergy were allowed to complete their sentences in England.[864]

The Bryant adventure was not the only attempt to escape in this way; another is recorded, and more convicts might have risked their lives on the sea had boats been available, but boat-building was regulated in such a way as to prevent escape that way.[865] Phillip's fear of the possibility of such attempts is demonstrated by his statement in 1792 that a boat "received in frame" would have to be idle until proper men could be found to man it, as convicts could not be trusted. Very few, however, escaped in this way, and if to these be added all those who fled to the bush or returned by sea the total is relatively very small. As a penal settlement New South Wales was not perfect but it was, at least, effective.

History has revealed more than one example of the immutable linking of the name of an individual with an undertaking. Phillip's name stands in that relation to the New South Wales venture. His continued courage in spite of temporary depression, and his optimism in spite of repeated disappointments, overcame difficulties which evoked nothing but complaints from others who accompanied him. His choice of Lieutenant King to administer Norfolk Island was no small factor in the success of that settlement. His humanity in directing convicts stands in vivid contrast to the attitude assumed by certain later rulers in penal settlements. His continued enthusiasm justly merited and received the approbation of the Home Authorities, who urged him to remain in spite of repeated requests to be allowed to return to England because of ill health and domestic difficulties. When at last he sailed in the *Atlantic* at the close of 1792 he went in the hope of returning to the colony if the cause which obliged him to leave it should be removed by the voyage or the assistance he might find in London. There however he resigned his governorship on the ground that he suffered from a complaint that could not be treated in the settlement.[866]

In 1793 Phillip reached England. In the same year the arrival in New South Wales of the *Bellona*'s eleven free settlers confirmed, as far as the colony was concerned, the Government's determination to establish free settlement within it and to give a changed character to the new possession. A generation had passed since the Old Empire stood at the pinnacle of its power, after the signing of the Peace of Paris. It had fallen and another had sprung into existence to take its place but the attitude of Englishmen towards convict punishment had not altered. Transportation had become a tradition; to even the more enlightened men of the period, such as Burke, Fox, and Sir Charles Bunbury, it was still the only effective method of solving the problems caused by the existing criminal code and its resultant overcrowding of gaols. Even the passing of an Act in 1779 which ordered the building of two penitential houses to provide a means of reforming criminals in England had no effect; they were not built. The fact of the matter was that the majority of Englishmen did not want them. They thought what the members of the 1785 Committee thought: that transportation was the most satisfactory remedy for moral ills. Had they expressed their ideas they would have revealed them as being still in close agreement with those of Hakluyt when he wrote, more then 200 years before, "the pety theves might be employed for certain years in the western parts in sawing and felling timber and in planting sugar canes".

Appendices

THE FIRST three appendices were discovered among the Bentham Papers in University College, London, by Mr A.T. Milne, M.A. who kindly brought them before my notice. By then, however, the third chapter of this work was written. They therefore have not been incorporated into the text of this thesis but their value compels their inclusion here for purposes of comparison. They show the results of a private inquiry into the hulk system conducted by Bentham and his friends. The third has been abridged but it is otherwise practically a transcript of Bentham's notes. The conditions it reveals are, if anything, a little more pleasing than those set forth in Chapter 3, the difference possibly being due to the omission of some unpleasant detail.

Appendix 1
Diet on the Hulks, 1785
Bentham MSS. Portfolio 107

Copy of a paper given to Mr Townshend by Sir Rob. Boyd. A table of diet expended daily by the convicts on board the *Ceres* hulk; the amounts are for each mess of six men.

26 November 1785

	BREAKFAST	DINNER	SUPPER
Sun.	A pint of barley made into three quarts of soup	Seven pounds of salt pork or 8 lbs of beef with 6 lbs of biscuit or a loaf of bread weighing 7 lbs and 5 quarts of beer	Half a pint of peas and half a pint of barley made into three quarts of soup
Mon.	Ditto	Half a bullock's head with a loaf of bread weighing 7 lbs	Ditto

199

	BREAKFAST	DINNER	SUPPER
Tue.	Ditto	Two pounds of cheese with a loaf of bread weighing 7 lbs and 5 quarts of beer	A quart of oatmeal made into Burgoo
Wed.	Ditto	Half a bullock's head with a loaf of bread weighing 7 lbs	Half a pint of peas and half a pint of barley made into 3 quarts of soup
Thu.	Ditto	Ditto	Ditto
Fri.	Ditto	Ditto	Ditto
Sat.	Ditto	Two pounds of cheese with a loaf of bread weighing 7 lbs and 5 quarts of beer	A quart of oatmeal made into Burgoo
EACH MAN PER WEEK	7 pints of soup, 1 pint a day	Beer, 1 pint. A pound of butcher's meat. 18 oz of bread or more	A pint

Appendix 2
Diet on the Hulks, 1790

Bentham MSS. Portfolio 107

Gosport, 29th June 1790

Sir (Rev. Mr. Townshend)

Agreeable to your desire I have procured you a statement of the allowance of provisions to the convicts.

They are all divided into messes consisting of six in number and the provisions below is for one mess and is the allowance for those working on shore. If they are not at work they have but 6 pounds of bread.

I am, Sir, your most humble servant

Robert Dads.

Four days in the week each mess has every day:

Beef	6 pounds
Bread	8 pounds
Beer	5 quarts
Cheese	none

The three other days each mess has for dinner peas and barley boiled into a soup and also:

Bread	8 pounds
Beer	5 quarts
Cheese	2½ pounds

N.B. They have also every day as much greens and potatoes, cultivated by themselves, as they can eat, and thick meal-gruel (called, I believe, Burgoo) for breakfast and supper.

Appendix 3
Conditions on the Hulks, 1778

Bentham MSS, Portfolio 117, ff.I.2

(Abridged description of the hulks by Jeremy Bentham, January 1778)

Above 300 convicts on board the two ships, room for 50 more, many boys — some of them under 12 years.

About 150 employed on shore in making a wharf, a terrace for cannon and a proof. No one allowed to enter without an order. Part of the terrace is preparing to receive cabbages for the use of the convicts. The rest employed in raising ballast or in hospital.

In winter always dine late and do not quit the ship afterwards; always go on board for meals.

A heavy chain round each man's ankle fixed to another fastened round the middle. Some have only a rope, the sick have a chain only on one leg, some none at all. They were formerly chained two and two and to their beds at night. Now neither of these is done.

The chains at first very light but made heavier in consequence of escapes. Those round the ankle at one time lined with list, not now as it prevented officers from seeing when the irons were sawed.

Between 40 and 50 to guard them.

Punishments. Whipping and running the gauntlet, rarely inflicted, not once a month.

All well clothed, uniform a dark brown jacket and trousers, those in the ditch furnished with boots by the Ordnance Board.

The convicts go all over the ship (*Censor*) but a space is to be enclosed for the Officers and crew.

Every other port to be shut in winter, the rest to have strong iron grates.

The beds raised about 2 ft from the floor and 2 or 3 ft apart in one row along the ship's side asunder. They are of straw covered with canvas and furnished with blankets and pretty clean rugs.

No fire or candle allowed at night but the place is abundantly warm; fires kept burning all day; the ship often washed with vinegar, hardly any disagreeable smell between decks, bathing allowed at first but now prohibited as unwholesome.

Mr. Campbell thinking of some employment for bad weather when it is impossible to leave the ship; nothing can be done at night for fear of fire; he mentioned picking oakum.

Three meals a day. Hot rice for breakfast. Ox cheek 1 lb per man and 1 lb bread for dinner. Cheese and the remains of the bread for supper. Two banyan (burgoo) days a week when they have rice for dinner instead of meat. The water all filtered. No strong liquor, nor provisions, nor money allowed to be given by friends except to the sick and then under inspection.

A very considerable sickness which Campbell says is concealed as much as possible — chiefly putrid fever and low spirits and some swelled legs, no ague, mortality greatest among country convicts.

The surgeon of an artillery battalion attends them every day and Dr. Irvine, the surgeon general, once a week.

The forecastle of the *Censor* fitted up tolerably neat and clean for a hospital, beds very close, almost touching. Barrington superintends the place.

A Methodist preacher, belonging to Lady Huntingdon, petitioned to attend the convicts. Service every Sunday and attended to with great decorum. The parson has distributed about 15 pounds worth of bibles.[867] He preaches $1\frac{1}{2}$ hours at a time.

Appointment of overseer nominally by Quarter Sessions of Middlesex, really by Treasury.

A coroner has lately sat on the dead bodies.

The men remarkably silent at work, don't talk, no swearing. Campbell declares they do more work by one half than common workmen, for six months have not cost the public 500 pounds more than the value of their labour; allows that he has a good bargain.

He is going to erect a brewery in the *Censor*.

About 50 have been discharged, some by application to Court of King's Bench, the greater part by *letters of remission* from the King, the latter do not receive the bounty; before recommending a pardon Campbell sees the friends and satisfies himself that some feasible plan for the man's subsistence is arranged.

Some are going into the 50th Regt. but Lord Sandwich won't receive any into the navy. Improper objects often sent by Quarter Sessions; an old man sent from Cornwall at an expense of 20 pounds for stealing a game cock — another with one arm, several unable to work. One man there who was sentenced for one year only. Such judgment must be void, the statute allowing no less than 3 years.

Mr Campbell declined going down with us into the hospital and soon called us out.

Windows not above a foot square.

Appendix 4
Irish Transportation

The practice of transporting social criminals[868] had begun before the advent of the Hanoverian line of kings. The Irish Act, 2 Ann, c.12, provided for the transportation of those convicted of felonies above the value of 20s. The influence of English custom is seen in the Irish Act 6 Geo. I, c.12; its close resemblance to the British Act 4 Geo. I, c.11, which played so important a part in organising the English system, is shown in its provisions which prescribed transportation as the punishment for those who had received a Royal Pardon after conviction of a non-clergyable offence, or had been found guilty of felonies punishable by burning in the hand. The same measure also gave authority to magistrates to contract for the removal of such offenders. Different statutes later extended the influence of the system, e.g. the Irish Act 5 Geo. II, c.10 declared the stealing of lead or iron bars to be transportable offences. The bond requirement of English practice was adopted at least as early as 17 Geo. II, c.4. That measure required the contractor, with two solvent persons, to give bond or recognizance to a sheriff, in 10 pounds a head, to convey on board and transport the criminals concerned.

The Irish counterpart of the British Act which established the hulks was 17 & 18 Geo. III, c.9 which authorised hard labour on the Liffey or in houses of correction, but no hulk of the English type seems to have been established.

The American refusal to accept convicts produced a congestion within Irish prisons also. This caused the two unfortunate attempts (mentioned in Chapter 10) to land convicts on Newfoundland and Antigua in 1789 and 1790 respectively. Each produced complaints which were addressed to the British Government. The second attempt resulted in a reprimand, forwarded to Ireland by Evan Nepean, in which that Undersecretary stated that the British Government had hoped that the Irish authorities would have refrained from putting the transportation laws into effect, after the return of the "Newfoundland convicts", until some plan had been arranged for the disposal of such offenders.[869] In January 1790 the Rt Hon. Robert Hobart wrote from Dublin seeking information concerning a cheaper method of conveying convicts to Botany Bay "as the great expense now attending would create much difficulty here".[870] Two plans were proposed: the sending of Irish convicts to England to be treated as English convicts, and the removal of Irish convicts from Irish ports by English contractors. Both were adopted; the Irish women convicts who sailed in the *Kitty* went to Portsmouth; the *Queen* collected her Irish felons at Cork. The rule adopted in the latter instance entrusted to the British Government the contracting for the transportation while the Irish were required to pay a share of the cost according to their proportion of the whole.[871]

The procedure within Ireland was explained by Hobart in March 1790. He records that orders were sent to the various sheriffs to transmit their convicts to Dublin on 29 September 1789. A few days before that date (18 September) the Lord Mayor of that city executed a charter with the owner of the ship *Duke of Leinster* whereby the convicts were to be clothed, fed, and landed in North America in return for a payment of 5 pounds a head.

Any attempt to estimate the number of convicts carried from Ireland is rendered exceedingly difficult by the destruction of the Irish records due to the blowing up of the Four Courts of Dublin. Some idea can be formed from the events of 1789-92. Seventy-nine convicts were returned from Newfoundland late in 1789, but possibly more had been sent to that settlement. Eighty-nine were removed in the

Duke of Leinster before the close of the same year. Within a few months the Irish Government was complaining of gaol overcrowding. The *Queen* carried at least 155 to Sydney Cove in 1791 and less than 12 months later another 234 were shipped on board the *Boddingtons* and *Sugar Cane.*

Appendix 5
Scottish Transportation

Strictly speaking, transportation as a sentence was unknown in Scotland before 1766. Banishment however was the regular mode of disposing of certain offenders from a much earlier date. Thus in 1424 "thiggars", who refused to work, were ordered to be burned in the hand and banished. Measures of 1427, 1449, and 1648 also prescribed banishment as the punishment for those who failed to pay customs duties or who were "sorners" or sheep-stealers. But the term "transportation" was in common use at the time; those who received the sentence of banishment were ordered to be kept in custody until arrangements could be made for their "transportation"; that term, however, referred only to the actual conveyance of the guilty.

In 1700 the members of the Scottish Parliament showed their dislike for transportation by considering a draft of an Act to prohibit it and by suggesting that a clause of like effect should be added to a Bill introduced to prevent "wrongous" imprisonment. Eighteen years later the British Parliament definitely exempted Scotland from the provisions of the Act 4 Geo. I, c.11, which organised transportation in England.

According to Professor Oswald Dykes of the University of Edinburgh, the Scottish hostility towards transportation was due to a fear of arbitrary punishment by the Executive and a realisation of the helplessness of any court to act in the case of an offender who had been sent oversea; in other words, to a fear similar to that which produced the English Habeas Corpus Act of 1679. This may be accepted as the basic cause of Scottish resistance, but it is possible that political grievances also influenced those of the North in the early years of the 18th Century. In 1699 the attempted Scottish Darien settlement failed, partly, according to the Scots, because of a lack of English support; and the friends of those who had shared in the '15 rebellion perhaps feared the effect of a measure which might make easier the removal of returning rebels. The British Act 25 Geo. III, c.46, however, provided for the transportation of Scottish offenders, and Scottish and English felons sailed together to New South Wales in the *Pitt* and *Royal Admiral.* But their number, compared with those of England and Ireland, was almost negligible.

Appendix 6
Details of Transportation to North America by Government Contractor, 1763-72

Convicts carried to North America by the government contractor, 1763-72, taken from the Treasury In-letters, T.1 series.

		SUM PAID TO CONTRACTOR	NUMBER TRANSPORTED
		(pounds)	
1763	24 August	605	121
	3 December	570	114
1764	1 March	830	166
	12 June	685	137
	27 September	1050	210
1765	18 February	580	116
	9 July	775	155
	27 September	765	153
1766	5 February	645	129
	8 July	840	168
	7 November	915	183
1767	3 March	735	147
	2 June	875	175
	3 December	970	194
1768	18 February	725	145
	16 May	895	179
	21 July	510	102
	31 October	715	143
1769	7 February	765	153
	12 May	565	113
	21 September	675	135
1770	6 February	600	120
	? April	910	182
	24 July	910	182
1771	21 February	630	126
	23 May	630	126
	31 July	845	169
1772	3 March	1140	228
	TOTALS	£	NO.
		21355	4271
	Average per annum	2373	475

Appendix 7
Details of Transportation to North America Numbers of Males and Females 1769-71

The relative numbers of males and females transported to America as shown by figures taken from the Treasury In-letters, T.1. series.

	SHIP	MALE CONVICTS	FEMALE CONVICTS
1769 20 January	*Thornton*	117	36
9 August	*Douglas*	117	18
1770 11 December	*Justitia*	88	38
1771 16 April	*Thornton*	95	29
TOTALS		417 (78%)	121 (22%)

Appendix 8
Cost of Hulks

Cost of the hulks according to a statement found in C.O. 201/5.

YEAR	AMOUNT		
	£	s	d
1777	1,879	10	6
1778	9,075	3	11
1779	13,586	17	0
1780	14,348	2	9
1781	15,487	17	0
1782	14,719	4	0
1783	14,452	17	3
1784	12,212	11	6
1785	13,578	14	4
1786	31,299	10	0
Granted for 1787	21,560	5	7
1788 C	30,083	10	$2\frac{1}{2}$
B	4,533	6	6
1789 C	48,417	13	5
B	8,180	14	4
1790 C	33,228	15	6
B	6,888	7	6
	293,533	1	$3\frac{1}{2}$
1791 C + B	12,721	16	2
TOTAL	£306,254	17	$5\frac{1}{2}$

Appendix 9
Officers of Marine Companies who Sailed to Sydney Cove, 1787-88

Major-Commandant	Robert Ross
Captain	James Campbell, John Shea
Captain-Lieutenant	James Meredith, Watkin Tench
First Lieutenant	James Maxwell, John Creswell, John Poulden, John Johnstone, James M. Shairp, George Johnstone,

	Robert Kellow, Thomas Davey, Thomas Timins
Second Lieutenant	Ralph Clarke, William Faddy, William Collins
Adjutant 2nd Lieut	John Long
QM 1st Lieutenant	Jas. Furzer
Judge Advocate	David Collins

Appendix 10
First Fleet, Return of Convicts Before Sailing

A return of convicts in the First Fleet dated 6 May 1787, i.e. a week before sailing. The intended numbers are placed in brackets; C.O. 201/2.

SHIP		MEN	WOMEN	CHILDREN M	F
Alexander[872]	(M 210)	195	–	–	–
Charlotte	(M 100, F 24)	86	20	1	1
Scarborough	(M 210)	205	–	–	–
Friendship	(M 80, F 24)	76	21	3	1
Prince of Wales	(F 50)	2	47	–	2
Lady Penrhyn	(F 102)	1	101	2	3
TOTALS		565	189	6	7

Appendix 11
Moneys Paid to William Richards Jnr

An account of moneys issued to William Richards Jnr by the Hon. Commissioners of H.M. Navy for conveying convicts embarked with Captain Phillip; C.O. 201/5.

SHIP	£	s	d
Alexander	7,204	18	3
Scarborough	4,228	2	5
Charlotte	3,449	18	2
Lady Penrhyn	3,473	0	4
Fishburn	5,946	8	0
Prince of Wales	4,693	15	11
Golden Grove	5,232	6	7
Borrowdale	4,109	9	2
Friendship	3,315	8	0
Victualling & other charges	12,865	9	3
TOTAL	54,518	16	1

Appendix 12
Cost of Transporting and Maintaining Convicts

Cost of transporting and maintaining convicts, taken from Appendix O, 28th Report of a Select Committee on Finance, Reports of the House of Commons, 1810, iv, p. 504.

	EXPENSE OF							
	FIRST SETTLEMENT & TRANSPORTATION			VICTUALLING			CLOTHING		
1786	£28,339	1	10	†			†		
1787	23,779	7	1	†			†		
1788	7,393	4	4	261	5	0	—		
1789	39,588	3	4	21,124	14	2	12,853	1	0
1790	8,202	13	11	1,840	9	3	18,401	10	4
1791	47,356	0	0	25,682	1	5	25,602	10	5
1792	34,233	14	11	17,261	9	0	31,139	3	4

† This expense is included under Transportation

To the above must be added Bills drawn, expense of Civil and Military establishments, and the expense of the Marines. The totals then are:

1786	£ 28,346	3	6
1787	29,242	11	10
1788	18,008	9	2
1789	88,057	18	2
1790	44,774	4	6
1791	129,019	19	11
1792	104,588	2	3

Appendix 13
Criminal Status of Convicts Sent to New South Wales, 1787-1792

At least three schools of thought exist concerning the criminal status of the convicts that proceeded to New South Wales during the period 1787-1792. There are those for whom the word "convict" (which was an abbreviation of the phrase "convicted person") conjures up pictures of notorious villains, murderers, destroyers of life and property. Others regard these early offenders as comparatively innocent persons who were the victims of a harsh and unreasonable criminal code which outrageously punished the most trivial offences. The third group believes that they were inherently law-abiding citizens and country folk whom economic distress forced into petty crimes.

The beliefs of the first class may be quickly dismissed; murderers, violent assailants, and violent burglars normally ended their careers on the gallows.

A decision regarding the opinion of the third school cannot be given here as the subject does not fall within the purview of transportation. The only relevant facts worthy of mention which this research has revealed are a lack of reference to hunger or necessity in the records of the trials, and an absence of cases of theft of food. These omissions, of course, are no proof that need did not explain some of the crimes that were committed. Phillip, when he reported thieving of the Government's stores in 1788, declared his belief that it would not have happened had the convicts received more food.

In an attempt to shed some light upon the second view a number of the convicts' offences have been traced and tabulated from the records of the Old Bailey. These were committed by persons arrested in London and Middlesex, and extended over a number of years. The criminals concerned sailed in different ships; their names were selected without any knowledge of their lives or previous actions. The results of the 236 cases investigated are as follows:

	TOTAL	(WOMEN)	VALUE OF GOODS £1 or less	5s or less
Stealing without force from:				
a shop, e.g. shoplifting	69	(32)	36	14
a house, e.g. that of servants, lodgers	58	(36)	33	11
a person, e.g. picking a pocket	26	(9)	15	12*
* Each a single handkerchief				
a warehouse	5		4	0
a ship	4		2	2
a cart	2		1	1
Stealing without comment	8	(2)	7	4
Stealing a boat	4	(all for the same offence)		
Stealing clothes from line	5	(1)	5	5
Horse or sheep stealing	1		0	0
Entering & stealing from				
a house	32	(5)	10	0
a shop	1		1	1
Highway offences	8		2	1
Stealing from a person with force	7	(6)	0	0
Forgery	2		1	0
Receiving stolen goods	2	(1)	1	0
TOTAL	234	(92)	118	51
Returning from transportation	1			
Resisting a customs officer with force	1			
No. of cases investigated	236			

The six women guilty of stealing with force were a very undesirable sextet. Their offences are described in this way to distinguish them from the ordinary picking of a pocket. Two of them dragged a drunken man into a low house and robbed him of 22 pounds; a third enticed another drunken man into a yard and took his watch. Two others stole during drunken brawls. The last forcibly stole a violin and clothes from another woman.

The picture that the table reveals is certainly not a pleasant one, but it does not contain cut-throats. Rather it is a presentation of comparatively minor thefts; one-half of those transported had stolen goods to the value of only one pound or less; a little over ten percent of the total succeeded in taking more than five pounds each.

Country case records are usually indefinite. They frequently contain the words "petty larceny" or "grand larceny" without any comment. Country offences, however, seem to have been similar to those of the metropolis but with some additions: they included a fairly high proportion of thefts of horses, cattle, and sheep. Thus of 22 convicts in Reading gaol on 4 August 1786, eleven had been sentenced to death for the following crimes:

Horse stealing	5	House breaking	2
Highway robbery	3	Sheep stealing	1

The remainder had been sentenced to transportation for stealing. The goods stolen included rabbits, wheat, a shirt, stockings, money, linen, lead, an ass, and clothing.

Seven years' transportation was the normal sentence for such offences as stealing a crown piece (5s), a watch, a blanket, and other goods of like value.

One of the most complete lists is that of Gloucester gaol for 1 November 1786. It is as follows:

Stealing cloth	4	Stealing a sheep	3
Stealing a watch	2	Stealing yarn	1
Stealing cider	2	Stealing a horse	3
Stealing wool	1	Stealing a calf	2
Stealing a hatchet	1	Highway robbery	3
Stealing iron	2	Receiving stolen goods	1
Stealing apparel	4	Burglary	3
Stealing money	1		

Reference Notes

REFERENCE NOTE ABBREVIATIONS:

		HRA	*Historical Records of Australia*
Ad.,Adm.	Admiralty	HRNSW	*Historical Records of N.S.W.*
C.O.	Colonial Office	S.P.	State Papers
Cal.	Calendar	T.	Treasury
H.O.	Home Office	W.O.	War Office

PREFACE

1 Irish and Scottish transportations were in reality distinct systems for some years after the Seven Years' War. This thesis does not attempt a complete exposition of either. They are discussed briefly to explain their amalgamation with the English system.

2 In this work the term "convict" does not include religious and political offenders. Basil Sollers makes it clear that the colonists carefully distinguished between these two classes of offenders and the common thieves, pickpockets, etc. who formed the true convict class. To the last-mentioned group he has assigned the term "social convicts", a term occasionally used in this thesis.

1. INTRODUCTION

3 *A Discourse on Western Planting*, 1584. Hakluyt's Collection of Voyages. Goldsmid Edition XIII, p.195.

4 *A History of New Holland*, Wm Eden, 1787; Introduction. Wm Eden (1st Lord Auckland, 1744-1814) Undersecretary, diplomatist, and an authority on legal and economic questions.

5 *Archives of Maryland (Assembly)*, XXXV, p.213.

6 State of New York, Messages from the Governor, I, p.248.

7 Archives of Maryland, Gov. Sharpe's Letters, III, p.413.

8 The demand led to the kidnapping and sale of innocent English adults and children; Beer, G.L.: "Old Colonial System", I, p.33.

9 MacCormac, E.I.: *White Servitude in Maryland*, p.92. "The English kings ever solicitous about the want of labourers in America kindly consented to send over all their unmanageable subjects".

10 Smith, A.E.: *Transportation in the 17th Century* (unpubl.) *passim.*

11 *Middlesex Records*, II, p.224.

12 *Egerton Papers*, Camden Society, p.116. On 6 April 1586, Walsyngham declared that one of the galleys was ready; *ibid.*

13 Smith, A.E.: *op. cit., passim.*

14 Blackstone: Commentaries; adapted by Kerr, 1862. vol. I, p. 120.

15 18 Chas. II, c.3.

16 22 Chas. II, c.5.

17 22 & 23 Chas. II, c.7.

18 See p.12.

19 Ballagh, J.C.: *White Servitude in Virginia*, p.37.

20 Records of the Virginia Company, I. p.212.

21 Butler, J.D. in *American Historical Review*, II, p.16.

22 Cal. S.p.Domestic, 1638-39, p.425.

23 Cal. Treasury Papers, 1676-79, p.826.

24 Cal. Treasury Papers, 1714-41; index Forward. Guildhall Archives, MSS 57, 9b.

25 Cal. Treasury Papers, 1742-5, p.5. See also, *ibid.*, 1739, p. 18.

26 Forward at first received only 3 pounds a head; see Cal. Treasury Papers, 1714-19, p.389.

27 Reid's Certificate; T.1/340. The Guildhall records show that the contract system was in existence in Charles II's reign. See the contract of Wm Nevett and Thos Walsh in the 22nd year of his reign; Guildhall Archives, MSS 57, 9b.

28 Cal. Treasury Papers, 1729-30, p.655.

29 Cal. Treasury Papers, 1742-45; index Reid, Andrew. Private contractors often carried much smaller numbers; see table p.8.

30 There is no doubt about this at a later period; see p.23.

31 Guildhall Archives, MSS 57, 8a.

32 Corbett to Reid, 5 April 1744; Ad. 2/1054.

33 Corbett to Winnington, 23 March 1743-4; Ad. 2/1054.

34 For a more detailed treatment of this see pp.21-24.

35 Guildhall Archives, MSS 57, 8a.

36 Maryland Archives (Council), XXV, pp.425 *et seq.*

37 Guildhall Archives, MSS 57, 8a.

38 Butler, J.D.: *American Hist. Review*, II, pp.12-33. Basil Sollers applies the title "social convicts" to those guilty of theft, perjury, forgery etc. to distinguish them from those convicted of armed rebellion or breaches of the laws controlling religion. He states that the colonists distinguished between the two classes of offenders.

39 *Ibid.*, p.23.

40 Guildhall Archives, MSS 57, 8a.

41 State of New York, Messages from the Governor, vol. II, pp. 245-9.

42 Tailfer, Pat.: *Narrative of the Colony of Georgia*, p.24n.

43 Sollers, Basil: *Maryland Historical Magazine*, vol. II, p.23.

44 Cal. S.p.America and West Indies, 1661-8, p.257.

45 Cal. S.p.Colonial, 1677-80, p.572.

46 MacCormac, E.I.: *op. cit.*, pp.106-7.

47 McNutt, W.S., author of the unpublished thesis, "British Rule in Nova Scotia 1713-84", assured me he never discovered that convicts were carried directly from England to Nova Scotia.

48 See p.29; the figure is taken from the Calendar of Treasury Papers.

49 *Maryland Gazette*, 30 July 1767, quoted by Williams, G.W. in *Negro Race in America*, vol. I, p.244.

50 In 1776 the House of Commons, desiring the number of convicts transported during seven years ordered returns from the counties; *Commons Journal*, vol. 36, p.15.

51 Cal. S.p.America and West Indies, 1661-8, p.313.

52 Cal. S.p.America and West Indies, 1717-18, p.681.

53 Archives of Maryland, XXXVIII, p.320.

54 Massachusetts Acts and Resolves I.452 and II.245. Maryland passed a similar measure in 1728; Bacon, T.: *Laws of Maryland*, 1728, ch. XXIII.

55 Cal. S.p.America and West Indies, 1669-74, p.59.

56 Sollers, Basil: *op. cit.*, p.29.

57 Keith, C.P.: *Chronicles of Pennsylvania*, II, p.651.

58 *Ibid.*, p.859.

59 *Ibid.*, p.651.

60 Maryland Archives, Sharpe Papers I, p.328.

61 Maryland Archives (Council) XXXI, p.118.

62 Minutes of the Council and General Court of Colonial Virginia, p.288.

63 MacCormac, E.I.: *White Servitude in Maryland*, p.102.

64 Cal. S.p.America and West Indies, 1717-18, p.681.

65 *Virginia History Magazine*, XXX, p.250.

66 Cal. Treasury Papers, 1732, p.96.

67 Sollers, Basil: *op. cit.*, p.34. Bacon's *Laws of Maryland*, 1751, ch. 11.

68 Documents re the Colonial History of New York, VII, p.87.

69 Shipping Returns, Maryland; C.O. 5/750. No entries exist for the period July 1759 to July 1761.

2. TRANSPORATION TO THE AMERICAN COLONIES, 1763-1776

70 Old Bailey Session Papers for the years quoted.

71 Herein called the Old Bailey Session Papers.

72 Traitors and rebels were also transported but were carefully distinguished from social convicts by the colonists. See Sollers, Basil: *op. cit.*, p.46 and Tomlins's Law Dictionary, "Felony".

73 Blackstone: *op. cit.*, I, p.116n.

74 Howard, J.: Prisons, 2nd edition, p.436. These figures, it will be noticed, are greater than those of the preceding paragraph. Possibly the printed

"Proceedings" did not include all cases that passed through that court.

75 Leading magistrates condemned the existing penal code. Sir John Fielding, after explaining that mercy often changed a sentence of death to transportation, declared that it was "a change for which there are but few instances where humanity would not cheerfully hold up both her hands"; Cal. H.O. Papers, 1773-75, p.11.

76 See Table of Pardons, next paragraph.

77 John Bentham petitioned on the condition that he submitted to an amputation; 17 June 1767; S.P.44/89. The High Sheriff and Grand Jury "at Lancaster" petitioned for John Jones's life; *ibid.*, 44/92. On behalf of the "neighbourhood" Lord Talbot petitioned for the life of Lewis Witham; *ibid.*, 44/92. The judges themselves, after sentencing offenders to death, respited large numbers (one-half, according to Blackstone; quoted by Colquhoun: *op. cit.*, p.6) and successfully recommended milder punishment.

78 Rochford to Morgan; S.P.44/92.

79 Cal. H.O. Papers for the years quoted; the arrangement of the Calendars makes mathematical accuracy difficult.

80 Thus William Rowley who stole fifteen guineas was convicted of stealing 39 shillings; Old Bailey Session Papers, 1787, No. 476.

81 *Ibid.*, Nos. 368, 560, and 782.

82 E. Davies on 15 April 1786 complained to Lord Sydney, when reporting sheep-stealing, "we seldom or ever have an execution but for murder"; H.O. 42/8.

83 This was Colquhoun's opinion of the law; *op. cit.*, p.6.

84 Treason, highway robbery, and misdemeanours were never clergyable. Stephens: *History of Criminal Law*, "Benefit of Clergy".

85 After 1487 a person who could read could commit murder once with no other punishment than branding. The reading test was abolished in Anne's reign; *ibid.*

86 Blackstone Commentaries; *op.cit.*, IV, p.430. Whipping was sometimes an alternative to branding.

87 Colquhoun believed that London sheltered at least 3000 receivers who were one of the most potent causes of crime; *op. cit.*, p.10.

88 See Appendix 5.

89 12 Geo. I, c.29.

90 7 Geo. II, c.21.

91 16 Geo. II, c.31. Assisting escape was common at the time. The prison system made it easy for friends to convey saws, even crowbars, at times, to the imprisoned.

92 18 Geo. II, c.27.

93 25 Geo. II, (2), c.10.

94 10 Geo. III, c.48.

95 12 Geo. III, c.48.

96 13 Geo. III, c.59.

97 To plead pardon in the succeeding court was the normal practice of the time.

98 Blackstone: *op. cit.*, IV, p.434.

99 Colquhoun: *op. cit.*, p.439. Hawkins, Wm.: *Pleas of the Crown*, 7th edn, IV, p.282 gives a similar list.

100 Colquhoun: *op. cit.*, p.445. The Old Bailey was, of course, only one among several courts in the metropolis.

101 The figure for sixteen assizes taken at random from the Assize Returns of the Western Circuit during three years are: Sentenced to transportation for felony with benefit of clergy, 84; without, 21; Assizes 24/25.

102 See p.10.

103 Many of these were then sentenced to seven years' transportation, others received 14 years or life sentences.

104 The age of the convicts is inferred from the data supplied by the Hulk records; see p.50.

105 See p.10.

106 Numbers of prisoners in English gaols, in the Spring of 1776 were: Debtors 2437; Felons 994; Petty offenders 653; Total 4084 (Howard: *op. cit.*, p.22).

107 They were required to enlist or serve abroad in the Navy, in Jamaica, in Antigua, in regiments of foot, etc. Cal. H.O. Papers, 1760-65, pp.109-15.

108 In other words, London, Middlesex, and the counties of the Home Circuit.

109 Articles of Agreement, 7 April 1763; T. 54/39.

110 The convicts of London and Middlesex were commonly sent from Newgate; Howard: *op. cit.*, pp.196 and 202.

111 The latter agreement also required transportation after every assize. A convict who escaped was evidently not transported.

112 The writing of the document makes spelling uncertain. The number of Justices varied considerably, being sometimes as low as four, in others as high as ten. The Gaol Book of the City of York reveals similar procedure; Assizes, 42/8.

113 Halifax to the Lords of Trade, 5 November 1763; C.O. 5/65.

114 Unfortunately the Board does not tell how it conducted this inquiry. Possibly it questioned the Colonial Agents.

115 I.e. 40 pounds a head.

116 The Treasury convict certificates prove that the contractors entered into bonds with Clerks of Gaol Delivery, Clerks of Assizes, Clerks of the County, and of the Peace etc.; T. 1/422.

117 Before the sessions, indicted prisoners were regularly carried from the other metropolitan gaols to Newgate.

118 Howard: *op. cit.*, pp.186 and 189.

119 Cambridge paid £6 6s, Leicester £10, Horsham £2 2s; Howard: *op. cit. passim*. But one contractor paid an Exeter gaoler two guineas for each convict; *ibid.* p.345.

120 Thus William Eden informed the Recorder of London on 20 January 1776, that eight discharged women "could be marched back to Newgate as on former occasions"; S.p.44/93.

121 This practice was old; 4 Geo. I, c.11, according to its preamble, was inspired by the failure of persons to transport themselves.

122 Howard: *op. cit.*, p.19. "Surely prisoners ought to be conveyed in carts" was his comment.

123 On 20 July 1763 Lord Halifax directed the Secretary at War to send a guard to Coventry to prevent a feared attempt at rescue during removal; S.p.44/139.

124 See p.8.

125 Howard: *op. cit.*, p.391.

126 List of convicts, 20 January 1769; T.1/470.

127 Cal. Home Office Papers, 1766-69, p.137.

128 Howard: *op. cit.*, p.25n.

129 Sydenham to Shelburne, 24 August 1768; S.p.44/232. His name suggests some relationship with Jonathan Forward, and Prof. Adams in his "Guide to the Public Records" names him Forward. See however Shelburne to Treasury, S.p.44/328, where Shelburne calls him Sydenham.

130 Shipping Returns 1766-70; C.O. 5/1450.

131 *Commons Journals*, 36/928.

132 Contract in Oxford County Hall Archives, dated 22 March 1728-9.

133 Shelburne to Admiralty, 24 August 1768; S.p.44/232.

134 In 1770 the Sheriffs of London and Middlesex were ordered to detain certain convicts "from a transport ship totally lost, til the Contractor, Mr James Baird of Glasgow, should have a vessel to transport them"; Cal. Home Office Papers, 1770-72, p.169.

135 The ruling is signed by D. Ryden and W. Murray, 8 November 1746; Adm. 7/298.

136 Cal. Home Office Papers, 1766-69, p.171. Several others occur in the same volume.

137 Cal. Home Office Papers, 1760-72. In addition a number of conditional pardons, viz. for military service, were secured.

138 Howard: *op. cit.*, p.13.

139 Cal. Home Office Papers, 1773-5, p.11.

140 Courts occasionally uttered this view; John Ludlow on 21 March 1768 was transported "solely with a view to his reformation". Cal. Home Office Papers, 1766-69, p.405.

141 To obtain facts about the gaols of England the House of Commons questioned Howard or required returns from the various counties.

142 See Quarantine dispute, pp.24-25.

143 *Commons Journals*, 37/311.

144 *Ibid.* Campbell was the partner of Stewart, the government contractor.

145 Guildhall Archives, MSS. 57.8a.

146 The *Little Nancy* was of 52 tons; Shipping Returns; C.O. 5/750, 1449 and 1450.

147 Lists of convicts; T. 1./429, 465 and 483.

148 Howard: *op. cit.*, p.7. But Howard also encourages the belief that the Government contributed half a crown a week towards their upkeep; see *ibid.*, p.299.

149 Sollers, Basil: *Maryland Historical Magazine*, II, p.41.

150 Sharpe to Hamersley, 27 July 1767; Sharpe's Letters, III, p. 413.

151 Shipping returns C.O. 5/750 give the following instances: 17 January 1759, *Tryal*, 12 men, 91 convicts; 12 December 1757, *Thetis*, 16 men, 118 convicts.

152 Howard: *op. cit.*, p.25n.

153 See p.17.

154 Howard: *op. cit.*, p.302.

155 *Ibid.*, p.263.

156 *Ibid.*, p.11.

157 Medical opinions that I have obtained support this view. Campbell said he usually lost 5 to 6 out of 150.

158 Sharpe to Hamersley, 27 July 1767; Sharpe's Letters, III, p. 412.

159 Bacon's Laws of Maryland, 1766, ch. XXXIII.

160 Hening: *Virginia Statutes at large*, November 1766, VIII, p. 260.

161 To direct the measure against convicts alone would have made disallowance easier.

162 Sharpe to Hamersley, 4 September 1767; Sharpe's Letters, III, p.421. The letters are quoted in Williams, G.W.: *Negro Race in America*, I, p.244 *et seq.*

163 Sharpe to Hamersley, 27 July 1767; Sharpe's Letters, III, p. 412.

164 Hamersley to Sharpe, 24 August 1767; Sharpe's Letters, III, p.419.

165 Hillsborough to Sharpe, *ibid.*, p.524 and Cal. Acts of the Privy Council Colonial, 1766-83, pp.115-6.

166 The Commissioners' reasons can be found in *Massachusetts Historical Collections*, Fourth Series, X, p.691.

167 Sharpe to Hamersley, 27 July 1767; Sharpe's Letters, III, p. 412.

168 Moore to Gentlemen, 5 September 1784; Burdon, J.A., Honduras Archives, I.

169 Sharpe to Hamersley, 4 September 1767; Sharpe's Letters, III, p.421.

170 Eddis, William: *Letters from America*, pp.66-7.

171 Guildhall Archives, 19 September 1719, MSS. 57.8a.

172 *Ibid.*, 18 May 1721. The women apparently lacked occupations. "Dark" was the prevailing colour.

173 Calvert to Sharpe, 23 December 1755; Sharpe's Letters, I, p. 330 and Campbell's evidence, *Commons Journals*, 37, p.310. The services, not the persons, of the convicts were sold.

174 Oxford County Hall Archives; Sessions Records, 28 March 1763.

175 *Commons Journals*, 37, p.310.

176 Lists of convicts 1763-72 scattered among the T.1 bundles; see Appendix 6.

177 Campbell to Nepean, 29 January 1787; C.O. 201/2.

178 *Commons Journals*, 36, p.932 and 37, p.314.

179 The respective populations of Great Britain and Ireland were approximately 10.5 and 4.5 millions. Lecky: *England in the 18th Century* (1890), VIII, p.234. Scotland's number of convicts was probably very much smaller.

180 *Commons Journals*, 40, p.1161 *et seq.*

181 Lecky: *op. cit.*, VI, p.253.

182 *Commons Journals*, 37, p.310.

183 Bacon's Laws of Maryland, 1728, ch. XXIII.

184 Hewett to Halifax, 17 July 1763; S.p.44/139.

185 Cal. Home Office Papers, 1773-5, p.11.

186 Eddis, William: *Letters from America*, p.67.

187 Sollers, Basil: op.cit, p.46.

188 MacCormac, E.I.: *op. cit.*, p.106.

189 Fiske, J.: *Old Virginia and her Neighbours*, II, p.198.

190 Williams, G.W.: *Negro Race in America*, I, p.247.

191 *Maryland Gazette*, 30 July 1767, under the name A.B.

192 Quoted by Phillips, A.: *A Voyage to Botany Bay*, p.6.

193 Cal. Home Office Papers, 1766-69, p.115.

194 Cal. Home Office Papers, 1773-75, p.93.

195 Fielding to Suffolk, 1 February 1773; Cal. Home Office Papers 1773-75, p.11

196 *Gentleman's Magazine*, 1766, p.386.

197 Campbell declared that Colonial Laws forbade sale for longer periods whatever the sentence of the convict.

198 See pp.24-25.

199 See the *Virginia Historical Magazine*, vol. 30, pp.250, 260.

200 Campbell to Nepean, 29 January 1787; C.O. 201/2.

201 *Virginia Gazette*, 25 April 1776.

3. THE HULKS

202 Eden to Recorder of London, 29 November 1775; S.p.44/91.

203 Eden to Campbell, 12 January 1776 and Campbell to Robinson, 11 and 19 December 1776; T. 1/521.

204 *Morning Chronicle*, 20 December 1775.

205 Eden to Campbell, 12 January 1776; S.P.44/93.

206 Suffolk to Campbell, 21 January 1776; S.P.44/93.

207 Campbell may have been using more than one ship.The *Gazetteer* of 28 February 1776 stated that the *Justitia* was receiving felons.

208 Suffolk to Campbell, 5 June 1776; S.P.44/93.

209 *Ibid.* The men were to enter the sea or land forces or transport themselves. No condition attached to the women's pardons.

210 *Gazetteer*, 7 March 1776. The vessel's name is not given.

211 *Gazetteer*, 12 January 1776.

212 *Gazetteer*, 7 March 1776.

213 The *Daily Advertiser* of 12 January 1776 reported that eight persons convicted of grand larceny were burnt in the hand and imprisoned for six months.

214 Howard found this the case all over England.

215 Colquhoun: *op. cit.*, p.445. "In the choice of difficulties the system of Hulks was suggested and adopted".

216 Parliamentary Register (Commons), 1775-76, p.473.

217 *Ibid.*

218 *London Magazine*, 1776, p.369.

219 16 Geo. III, c.43. See also *Commons Journals*, XXXV, p.810.

220 The areas of work were to be defined by Trinity House.

221 Eden to Chamberlayne, 5 July 1776; S.P.44/93.

222 There is nothing to show that Campbell ever received anything but his salary. That was paid regularly.

223 According to the Maryland Port Entry Books she was of 305 tons.

224 *Commons Journals*, 36, p.926.

225 *Annual Register*, 1776, p.164 (Chronicle).

226 Suffolk to Home Circuit Justices, 21 August 1776; S.P.44/93.

227 Weymouth to High Sheriffs, 6 July 1776; S.P.44/143.

228 Campbell's proposal was to provide a ship for 1004 pounds a year, six lighters for 600 pounds a year, and convict maintenance at nine pence a head per day; Campbell to Treasury, 11 March 1777; T. 1/529.

229 The *Gentleman's Magazine* for 1777, p.226, calls the temporary hulk the *Tayloe*.

230 Agreement between the Treasury and Campbell, 2 February 1778; T. 54/42. The Treasury minutes erroneously state the annual payment to be £3483 17s 6d.

231 *Parliamentary History*, XIX, p.970.

232 Report of Convicts; T. 1/539(2).

233 *Annual Register*, 1776, p.163 (Chronicle).

234 Eden to Campbell, 12 December 1776; S.p.44/93.

235 *Commons Journals*, 36, p.928.

236 Reports of Convicts; T. 1/539(2).

237 Treasury Minute, 21 January 1777 (T. 29/46) and Campbell to Sydney, 15 July 1784 (T. 1/608).

238 *Commons Journals*, 36, p.931.

239 *Commons Journals*, 36, p.931. Erskine here described himself as Campbell's principal deputy.

240 *Ibid.*, p.927.

241 Howard: *op. cit.*, pp.323 and 201.

242 *Commons Journals*, 36, p.926.

243 *Ibid.*, p.929. The contract did not mention a surgeon.

244 The facts of this section are taken from the evidence in *Commons Journals*, 36, pp.926 *et seq.*

245 Ditto.

246 *Commons Journals*, 36, p.927.

247 Report of Convicts, Jan.-Feb. 1778; T. 1/539(2).

248 Eden to Milne, 27 July 1776 (S.p.44/141) stated that Campbell had been instructed to deliver 3000 tons at the wharf near the Hospital.

249 *Commons Journals*, 36, p.932.

250 *Commons Journals*, 36, p.931.

251 *Gentleman's Magazine*, 1777, p.226.

252 *Commons Journals*, 36, pp.926-32.

253 This was evidently an error. The Government paid 3560 pounds, not 4560, for the 120 convicts; see p.37.

254 *Parliamentary History*, XIX, p.920.

255 See also Appendix 3 for Bentham's evidence.

256 A writer in the *Annual Register* of 15 July 1776 interpreted the Act in such a way as to forbid visitation without the consent of the overseer. All the evidence supports his interpretation.

257 *Gentleman's Magazine*, 1777, p.22. Dignam was sentenced to five years' hard labour for defrauding; see *Annual Register*, 1777, pp.172 and 177.

258 18 Geo. III, c.62 and *Commons Journals*, 36, p.997.

259 Agreement between Treasury and Campbell, 1 August 1778; T. 54/42.

260 *Commons Journals*, 37, p.308.

261 The *Censor* being a warship was probably less roomy than her tonnage implied.

262 I.e., April 1778 to February 1779; Reports of Convicts; T. 1/539(2).

263 Return of Convicts; T. 1/539(2).

264 *Ibid.*

265 *Gentleman's Magazine* 1778, p.494.

NOTES

266 Mayor to Campbell, 8 July 1778; S.P.37/12.

267 *Commons Journals*, 37, p.306.

268 *Ibid.*

269 Dr William Smith believed brackish water caused the fluxes. Campbell showed that it came from the source which supplied the Navy.

270 *Commons Journals*, 37, p.310.

271 Mackworth had stated that the effluvia from the hospital descended to the men because it was on the top deck.

272 Dr William Smith had recommended more vegetables, and ox cheek three times a week only.

273 *Commons Journals*, 37, pp.308 *et seq.*

274 One was to provide for 600 males, the other for 300 females. They were not erected, nor were the hulks inspected.

275 Earlier contracts each provided for a single ship.This was the first general contract.

276 Agreement between Treasury and Campbell, 5 November 1779; T. 54/43.

277 Agreement between Treasury and Campbell, 16 August 1780 and 13 August 1781; T. 54/43.

278 Rose to Nepean, 3 January 1783; H.O. 35/4.

279 Nepean to Burke, 29 April 1783; S.P.44/330.

280 North to Campbell, 12 August 1783; H.O. 13/1.

281 North to Campbell, 24 August 1783 (H.O. 13/1) but for 200 felons.

282 Sydney to Campbell, 23 January 1784; H.O. 13/1.

283 Assize certificates; H.O. 47/3. The Act providing for this was 19 Geo. III, c.74.

284 Reports of Convicts; T. 1/626 and 641.

285 Campbell to Sydney, 2 June 1784; H.O. 42/4.

286 *Parliamentary History*, XXIV, p.755. Fox had complained that he was loathe to condemn those sentenced only to transportation to hard labour also.

287 Campbell's Warrant, 20 November 1784; H.O. 13/2.

288 Campbell to Rose, 30 November 1784; T. 1/600.

289 *Ibid.*, and Report of Convicts, January-April 1785; T. 1/619.

290 Report of Convicts, October-January 1786; T. 1/626.

291 Report of Convicts, April-July; T. 1/622. See also p.55.

292 Campbell to Treasury, 11 March 1777; T. 1/529.

293 Treasury Minute, 3 September 1779; T. 29/48.

294 See Appendices 2 and 3.

295 Campbell to Robinson, 12 August 1779; T. 1/548.

296 Sydney to Treasury, 23 July 1784 (T. 1/608) and Report of Convicts, July-October 1786 (T. 1/637).

297 Lord Beauchamp introduced the rumour. *Parliamentary History*, XXV, p.431, April 1785.

298 Campbell to Nepean, 5 March 1785 (T. 1/619) and Sydney to Treasury, 20 March 1785 (T. 1/619).

299 Report of Select Committee, 28 July 1785. *Commons Journals*, 40, p.1161.

300 See the Das Voltas experiment, p.106.

301 Confession of Charles Keeling, undated; H.O. 42.4.

302 Sydney to Treasury, 20 April 1785; T. 1/619.

303 Sydney to Treasury, 18 November 1785; T. 1/599.

304 Cowdry to Nepean, 11 March 1786; H.O. 42/8.

305 Agreement between Treasury and Bradley, 10 March 1786; T. 55/44.

306 Loxdale to Sydney, 12 July 1785; H.O. 42/7.

307 Grand Jury of Leicester to Sydney, 29 July 1785; H.O. 42/7.

308 "Whitehall" to Admiralty, 22 August 1785; H.O. 28/5.

309 Campbell to Nepean, 20 September 1785; H.O. 42/7.

310 Sydney to Treasury, 11 November 1785; T. 1/616. But in both T. 27/38 and Ad. 1/4289 it is recorded as received on the 10th.

311 Return of Convicts sent 8 December 1785 (H.O. 42/7) and Sydney to Treasury, 19 January 1786 (H.O. 36/5).

312 Townshend to Stephens, 3 February 1786 (Ad. 1/4152) and Sydney to Treasury, 14 March 1786 (H.O. 36/5).

313 Sydney to Treasury, 8 March 1786; H.O. 36/5.

314 Agreement between Treasury and Bradley, 10 March 1786; T. 55/44. Ditto for Campbell, 18 March 1786; T. 55/44. Each had proposed 130 pounds a month but had reconsidered his offer. Until the signing of the contract the Admiralty Victualling Board maintained the convicts.

315 Sydney to Treasury, 7 February 1785; T. 1/613. Each received 1 shift, 1 pair of men's stockings, 1 pair of shoes, 1 gown, 1 apron, at a cost of one guinea. Eight of the nine acknowledged receipt by a mark only.

316 Hill to Campbell, 18 December 1785 (H.O. 42/7) and 22 January 1786 (H.O. 42/8).

317 Report of Convicts, February–May 1786; T. 27/38.

318 Report of Convicts, April–July 1786; T. 1/634.

319 Coroner's Bill, 11 July 1786; T. 1/637.

320 Report of Convicts, November–February 1786; T. 1/634.

321 Accounts and Papers, 1792, XXXV, 751, pp.9-12. The first convicts were landed in Sydney Cove in 1788 but the system was not assured until experience had demonstrated the possibility of remaining there.

322 *Gentleman's Magazine*, 1784, pp.712-13. The lawyers had some doubts concerning the legality of the action but returned a verdict of "Not Guilty".

323 See p.50.

324 *Parliamentary History*, XXIV, p.755.

325 See T. 1/641 and 644.

4. WEST AFRICAN MILITARY EXPERIMENTS

326 See Martin, E.C.: *The British West African Settlements*; and C.H.B.E. vol. I.

327 Miles to Committee, 8 December 1779; T. 70/32.

328 Martin, E.C.: *op.cit.*, p.74.

329 Abstract of Charge of an Establishment, 28 October 1778; C.O. 267/6.

330 The figures for 1781 were:

Cape Coast Castle	58	Wydah	5
Annamaboe	12	Commenda	8
Tantumquerry	6	Dixcove	8
Winnebah	7	Appolonia	9
Accra (with Prampram)	14		
		Total	127

Crooks, J.J.: *Records of the Gold Coast Settlement*, p.51.

331 Governor and Council to Committee, 25 September 1778; T. 70/32.

332 *Ibid.* to *ibid.*, 24 December 1780; T. 70/32.

333 *Ibid.* to *ibid.*, 17 July 1780; T. 70/32.

334 Minutes of Council at Cape Coast, 20 October 1781; T. 70/152.

335 Martin, E.C.: *op. cit.*, p.5. Miles in writing to Germain on 8 July 1782 described 4 Leeward and 7 Windward forts besides Elmina; C.O. 267/7.

336 Eyre to Rochford, 10 May 1769; W.O. 1/874.

337 Rochford to Secretary at War, 19 May 1769; W.O. 1/874. The area referred to was Senegal.

338 *Ibid.*, as enclosure.

339 *Ibid.*, as enclosure.

340 McNamara to Germain, 5 August 1776; C.O. 267/16.

341 Clark to Germain, 4 July 1777; C.O. 267/16.

342 "Observations on transporting convicts from the hulks at Woolwich to Africa", 26 January 1779; S.P.37/13.

343 See p.50.

344 *Commons Journals*, 37, p.311.

345 *Ibid.*, p.314.

346 *Ibid.*, p.314.

347 Martin, E.C.: *op. cit.*, p.99.

348 Germain to Wall, 20 March 1780; C.O. 5/263.

349 Jenkinson to McKenzie, 27 December 1780; W.O. 4/112.

350 Jenkinson to Hon. Rich. Rigby, 11 April 1781; W.O. 4/113.

351 Treasury Minute, 7 April 1781; T. 29/50.

352 Clarke to Germain, 12 June 1782; C.O. 267/20.

353 *Ibid.*

354 Weuves to Committee, 29 April 1782; T. 70/33.

355 Miles to Committee, 30 August 1783; T. 70/33.

356 McKenzie's Petition, undated; C.O. 267/7.

357 McKenzie to Germain, 5 July 1782; C.O. 267/7. McKenzie's trial established the ratio 16:5 between the numbers of convicts and volunteers in one fort; Crooks, J.J.: *Gold Coast Records*, p. 71.

358 Company Minutes, 10 May 1781; T. 29/50. The question was raised in the House by Sir George Saville, 10 April 1770; *Parliamentary History*, XVI, p.942.

359 Camplin to My Lord (Germain?), 24 May 1781; C.O. 267/20.

360 See p.67.

361 Miles to Knox, 27 March 1781; C.O. 267/20.

362 Germain to Africa Committee, 27 April 1781; C.O. 5/263.

363 Germain to Admiralty, 15 June 1781; Ad. 1/4145.

364 Committee Minute, 13 June 1781; T. 70/145.

365 *Leander's* log; Ad. 51/527.

366 Weuves to Committee, 20 March 1782; T. 70/33. And Crooks: *op. cit.*, pp.51-5.

367 Among these was Lieutenant Cranston; Crooks; *op. cit.*, p.61.

368 *Ibid.*, pp.56-9.

369 Miles to Germain, 8 July 1782; C.O. 267/7. Weuves reported 40 on the ship, probably an exaggeration; Weuves to Committee, 29 April 1782; T. 70/33.

370 Weuves to Committee, 29 April 1782; T. 70/33.

371 Miles to Germain, 8 July 1782; C.O. 267/7. The arms were sold for brandy; Miles to Committee, 22 June 1782; T. 70/33.

372 See pp.72-73. Commodore Thompson declared he could account for only 8 out of 350, one and a quarter years after their arrival; Lemaine Enquiry, 2 May 1785; H.O. 7/1. Both figures seem to be exaggerations.

373 Council Enquiry, 23 July 1782; T. 70/153.

374 McKenzie's petition, undated; C.O. 267/7. Lysaght to Clarke, 28 July 1782; C.O. 267/7.

375 Butchart's Enquiry, 11 June 1782; T. 70/153.

376 Clarke to Germain, 12 June 1782; C.O. 267/20.

377 Council Enquiry, 23 July 1782; T. 70/153.

378 Council Minute, 2 May and 23 July 1782; T. 70/153.

379 Miles to Committee, 28 September 1782; T. 70/33.

380 Crooks: *op. cit.*, p.71. His petition for release, dated 23 August 1785, is in H.O. 42/7.

381 Council Minutes, 10 June 1782; T. 70/153.

382 Council Enquiry, 23 July 1782; T. 70/153.

383 Governor & Council to Committee, 30 August 1783; T. 70/33.

384 Directions to Goree, 3 June 1783; T. 267/20.

385 Pardon Warrant, 17 February 1781; S.P.44/96.

386 Miles to Committee, 7 December 1782; T. 70/33.

387 Miles to Germain, 8 July 1782; C.O. 267/7. The Council Enquiry showed that two of the forts under McKenzie's care never received any stores; Council Enquiry, 23 July 1782; T. 70/153.

388 Miles to Committee, 28 September 1782; T. 70/33.

389 See p.77.

390 Miles to Committee, 30 August 1782; T. 70/33.

391 Committee Minutes, 20 June 1781; T. 70/145.

392 Miles to Committee, 14 February 1783; T. 70/33.

393 Treaty of Peace; Crooks: op.cit, p.74.

394 *Ibid.*, p.69.

395 *Ibid.*, p.83.

396 Committee Minute, 2 October 1782; T. 70/145. The number is not stated.

397 *Ibid.*, 6 November 1782; T. 70/145.

398 Miles to Committee, 7 December 1782; T. 70/33.

399 Miles to Committee, 1 February 1783; T. 70/33.

400 Governor & Council to Committee, 30 August 1783; T. 70/33.

401 Committee to Governor & Council, 8 December 1782; T. 70/69.

402 *Ibid.* to *ibid.*, 25 November 1782; T. 70/69.

403 Governor & Council to Committee, 31 March 1784; T. 70/33.

404 Committee to Governor & Council, 27 December 1784; T. 70/69.

405 Governor & Council to Committee, 9 July 1785; T. 70/33. Convicts seemed normally to lack useful trades.

406 Committee to Governor & Council, 2 November 1785; T. 70/69.

5. AMERICAN EXPERIMENTS, 1783-1785

407 Rose to Nepean, 3 January 1783; H.O. 35/4.

408 Campbell had lost financially on his last transportation; see Campbell to Robinson, 28 July 1776; T. 1/521.

409 Sollers, B.: *op. cit.*, p.45.

410 North to Treasury, 5 November 1783; T. 1/590. See also Moore to Treasury, 13 July 1786 (H.O. 42/9), where he states that he carried 143.

411 See p54.

412 North to Treasury, 15 December 1783; S.P.44/330.

413 North to Campbell, 12 August 1783; H.O. 13/1.

414 Campbell to North (enclosure), 11 October 1783; T. 1/594.

415 *Gentleman's Magazine*, 53, p.800.

416 Stephens to Nepean, 24 September 1783; H.O. 28/3.

417 North to Treasury, 5 November 1783; T. 1/594.

418 North to Treasury, 15 December 1783; S.P.44/330.

419 Sollers, B.: *op. cit.*, p.45.

420 Treasury to Campbell, 3 January 1783; T. 27/34.

421 Nepean to Gullet, 18 October 1783; H.O. 13/1.

422 *Parliamentary History*, XXIV, p.755.

423 Estimate of a contract, undated; T. 1/581.

424 George Moore's proposed contract, undated; H.O. 42/5.

425 See p.54.

426 North to Campbell, 24 August 1783; H.O. 13/1.

427 Nepean to Campbell, 21 November 1783; H.O. 13/1.

428 Sydney to Campbell, 23 January 1784; H.O. 13/1.

429 Sydney to Treasury, 12 April 1784; H.O. 36/4. Moore himself, at a later date, declared he carried 179; Moore to Treasury, 13 July 1786; H.O. 42/9.

430 See pp.60-61. In 1787 Moore assigned the responsibility for the convicts he had not transported to Thomas Quayle. The criminals included seven women; see p.132.

431 Confession of Chas. Keeling, 24 April 1784; H.O. 42/4.

432 Cadman to Stephens, 14 April 1784; H.O. 28/4.

433 Moore to Nepean, 24 April 1784; H.O. 42/4.

434 Sydney to Admiralty, 29 May 1784; H.O. 28/4.

435 North to Treasury, 5 November 1783; S.P.44/330.

436 Nepean to Moore, 17 April 1784; H.O. 13/2.

437 Moore to Gentlemen, 16 May 1784; Enclosure under 5 September 1784; Burdon, Sir H.A.: *Archives of British Honduras*, vol. I.

438 Lemaine Enquiry, 27 April 1785; H.O. 7/1.

439 Hill's Narrative, 4 July 1788; C.O. 123/11.

440 Burdon: *op. cit.*, p.12.

441 *Ibid.*, p.18.

442 *Ibid.*, p.137.

443 *Ibid.*, pp.143-5.

444 Hoare reported about 90 convicts; Hoare to White, 12 September 1784; C.O. 123/3. Hill in his narrative gives 86; 4 July 1788; C.O. 123/11.

445 Conde de Florida Blanca to Don Antonio Valdez, 30 May 1789, C.O. 123/7, quoted by Burdon: *op. cit.*, p.173.

446 Despard to Nepean, 3 December 1785; C.O. 137/86.

447 White to Nepean, 26 November 1785; C.O. 123/3.

448 Hoare to White, 12 September 1784; C.O. 123/3.

449 *Ibid.*

450 White to Nepean, 25 January 1785; C.O. 123/3.

451 Half-pay officer to Moore, 2 December 1784; C.O. 123/3.

452 Resolutions of the 9th Aug. 1784; Burdon: *op. cit.*, p.146.

453 Hoare to White, 12 September 1784; C.O. 123/3.

454 Sydney to Clarke, 5 October 1784; C.O. 137/84.

455 Hill's Narrative, 4 July 1788; C.O. 123/11.

456 Case of H. Jones, 22 September 1784; Burdon: *op. cit.*, p. 147.

457 Half-pay officer to Moore, 2 December 1784; C.O. 123/3.

458 Capt. Arnott's complaint, 2 October 1784; Burdon: *op. cit.*, p.148.

459 Arnott v. Hill, 5 October 1784; *ibid.*, p.148.

460 Hill's Narrative, 4 July 1788; C.O. 123/11.

461 *Ibid.*

462 Lemaine Enquiry, 27 April 1785; H.O. 7/1.

463 Moore to Treasury, 13 July 1786; H.O. 42/9.

464 Moore to Treasury, 13 July 1786; H.O. 42/9.

465 Nepean to Despard, 15 September 1785; C.O. 137/85.

466 Moore to Treasury, 13 July 1786; H.O. 42/9.

467 Moore to Nepean, 14 August 1786; H.O. 42/9. Colquhoun: op. cit., p.461 reports that Moore was paid £1512 7s 6d but he gives no details.

468 In the Lemaine Enquiry Nepean declared that convicts were not sent to Nova Scotia because it had protested strongly; 27 April 1785; H.O. 7/1.

469 As late as 1789 the Irish attempted to land felons in Newfoundland; see p.167.

6. AFRICAN SCHEMES, 1785-1786

470 Lemaine Enquiry, 2 May 1785; H.O. 7/1.

471 Description of Lemaine — enclosure in Sydney to Treasury, 9 February 1785; T. 1/614.

472 Frazer to Nepean, 26 August 1784; H.O. 32/1.

473 Richard Bradley who later bought the island said it was 7 by 2 miles. John Roberts described it as 6 by ⅓ miles, two-thirds being under water in the rainy season.

474 Viz. conveyance and clothes, 4000; six months' rations, 1500; tools and implements, 1000; merchandise, grain etc. 3500.

475 Proposal of John Barnes — enclosure in Sydney to Treasury, 9 February 1785; T. 1/614.

476 Heatley's proposal, 4 February 1785; *ibid.*

477 Calvert to Nepean, 4 February 1785; T. 1/614.

478 Sydney to Treasury, 9 February 1785; T. 1/614.

479 Sydney to Treasury, 12 February 1785; T. 1/614.

480 Navy Board to Rose, 28 February 1785; T. 1/616.

481 Bailey's evidence, 25 April 1785; Lemaine Enquiry; H.O. 7/1.

482 Recorder's list of convicts, 2 March 1785; H.O. 47/3.

483 Campbell to Nepean, 5 March 1785; T. 1/619.

484 See p.57.

485 *Parliamentary History*, XXV, p.391. Cf. Burke's figures with those of the Committee on p.105.

486 *Ibid.*, p.431.

487 Seventy-eight were taken from Newgate; see p.103.

488 *Commons Journals*, 40, p.870.

489 Lemaine Enquiry; Bailey's evidence, 26 April 1785; H.O. 7/1. The subsequent evidence is to be found in the same volume.

490 His evidence is an almost exact reproduction of the "Description"; see p.95.

491 The women apparently were not removed.

492 Recorder's List, 3 May 1785; H.O. 47/3.

493 Loose leaf note without signature or date; H.O. 42/1.

494 See p.105.

495 Seven traders to Sydney, 12 May 1785; T. 1/614.

496 R. Bradley to Sydney, 29 November 1785; T. 1/627. The account was for 1499 barrs, or £374 15s, a barr being worth 5s.

497 Bradley's Instrument of purchase attested that he had bought the Island of Lemaine from Sanno Tambo Sabally, Slattee and Master of the town of Lemaine and its dependencies with the assent of his Bullanda or headmen for the sum of 100 barrs and an annual rent of 30 barrs, "say 10 iron barrs, 10 barrs of spirits, and 10 barrs of powder" on the condition that His Majesty should admit the natives of Lemaine "to cut grass cane and to gather tamarinds and lalou after requesting the permission of the white inhabitants to do it"; Instrument enclosed in Bradley to Sydney, 9 November 1785; T. 1/614.

498 See p.29.

499 "Whitehall" to Admiralty, 22 August 1785; H.O. 28/5.

500 Stephens to Nepean, 25 August 1785; H.O. 28/5.

501 Sydney to 51 areas etc., 11 March 1786; S.P.44/415.

502 Sydney to Clerks of Assize, 3 April 1786; S.P.44/415.

503 Sydney to Sheriffs etc., 24 June 1786; S.P.44/415.

504 Nepean to Steele, 10 June 1786; T. 1/632.

505 Navy Board to Stephens, 13 June 1786 (Adm. Navy Board 2213) and Steele to Navy Board, 10 June 1786 (T. 27/38). Macaulay's tender was 15 guineas a head, Calvert's 20 pounds and demurrage etc.; see their letters to Nepean on 10 May and 1 June respectively; T. 1/632.

506 Sydney to Treasury, 18 August 1786; T. 1/639.

507 *Ibid.*

508 A comparison of the suggested forms of government is impossible as no record of the system proposed for Das Voltas remains. Possibly none was ever arranged.

7. UNOFFICIAL PROPOSALS

509 Report of 1785 Committee, *Commons Journals*, 40, p.1161; and H.O. 42/7.

510 Sir Watkin Lewes's scheme, undated; H.O. 42/7. The proposal is included with others bearing the date 1785 but it might have been presented earlier. It refers to the report of the 1779 Committee.

511 The sale was not to be restricted to the Navy absolutely.

512 Donaldson to Sir John Sinclair, 1 May 1786; H.O. 42/8.

513 Plan for treatment of convicts without name or date; H.O. 42/7.

514 The opposition of the owners troubled him little since "private interest ought always to give way to public good". See also footnote 2 of the Introduction.

515 Preface to *A History of New Holland* (1787) by G. Barrington.

516 And yet he condemned the practice of punishing by death those who returned unlawfully from transportation, on the ground that "such severity was inconsistent with that leading principle which forbids penal laws to attack the natural sentiments of the heart"; *ibid.*

517 "au nombre provisionel de 300 hommes".

518 De Lynden to Sydney(?), 17 October 1785; H.O. 28/5.

519 The Archives of the Hague contain no reference to this incident.

520 Howe to Sydney, 13 October 1785; H.O. 28/5.

521 Margetson to Nepean, 15 July 1785; H.O. 42/7.

522 Dalrymple's Statement re. the Caffree Coast, undated; T. 1/624. Dalrymple was probably Alexander Dalrymple, a noted writer and official in the East India Company. He left Madras on 13 February 1785.

523 Blankett to Nepean(?), November 1786; H.O. 42/10.

524 A Serious Admonition to the Public, 1786, including a letter by Alex. Dalrymple. The Admonition is not signed by Dalrymple but it is probable that he wrote it.

525 *Parliamentary History*, XXIV, p.758.

526 Copy of paper left by Colonel Call, undated; H.O. 42/7. A Mr Call, who had visited Africa, was questioned by the 1785 Committee; see p.101.

527 In the latter part of his plan he suggested Norfolk Island as a possible site for a settlement; *ibid.*

528 This indicates that this plan followed the Report of the 1785 Committee of Enquiry.

8. PREPARATIONS FOR NEW SOUTH WALES[529]

529 The term "Botany Bay" is purposely omitted where possible to correct

the almost general though erroneous belief that convicts were transported to Botany Bay.

530 Nepean to Steele, 10 June 1786; H.O. 36/5.

531 Sydney to Lord Mayor of London; 2 February 1787; H.O. 43/2.

532 See pp.106-107.

533 Higgins to Sydney, 4 August 1786; H.O. 42/9. The facts for this paragraph have been selected from the two volumes H.O. 42/8 and 9.

534 Potter to Sydney, 29 May 1786; H.O. 42/8.

535 Lloyd to Sydney, 13 August 1786; H.O. 42/9.

536 Nowell to Sydney, 15 August 1786; H.O. 42/9.

537 Lord Mayor to "My Lord", 8 July 1785; H.O. 42/7.

538 *Commons Journals*, 37, p.311. Banks, as botanist, accompanied Captain Cook on his voyage to New Holland in 1770 when Botany Bay was discovered and named.

539 Matra's Proposal, 23 August 1783; C.O. 201/1. Matra believed the hulk system cost England £20,000 a year and therefore a colony would be economical. He had been a midshipman in Cook's *Endeavour*, then a British Consul at Teneriffe, later an American Loyalist. See *Australian Encyclopaedia*, Matra.

540 A reference to the Manila Galleon.

541 Supplement to Matra's Proposals, 6 April 1784; C.O. 201/1.

542 Arden to Sydney, 13 January 1785; C.O. 201/1.

543 His suggestion was that the East India Company's ships should land the convicts at New South Wales and then proceed to Formosa or China. It is probable that Young had read Matra's plan and that Sir Joseph Banks was a common source of inspiration to both writers.

544 See p.100.

545 Lemaine Enquiry, 9 May 1785; H.O. 7/1.

546 Lemaine Enquiry, 10 May 1785 and 25 May 1785; H.O. 7/1.

547 *Ibid.*, 25 May 1785.

548 Howe to Sydney, 26 December 1784. Howe was First Lord of the Admiralty. It is not certain that his view was divulged to the Committee. The information was forwarded to Sydney.

549 Lemaine Enquiry, 12 May 1785; H.O. 7/1.

550 *Ibid.*

551 See p.117.

552 Sydney to Treasury, 18 August 1786; C.O. 201/2.

553 Cook, on his last voyage, did not visit the mainland of Australia. He discovered Botany Bay during his first voyage. On the second and third he avoided the continent. His description can be seen in his "Journal of a Voyage round the World".

554 Enclosure in Sydney to Treasury, 18 August 1786; C.O. 201/2.

555 *Parliamentary History*, XXVI, pp.211-2.

556 *Ibid.*, p.215.

557 Narrative of the late expedition to Botany Bay, by an officer just returned, p.iii. This work must be treated with the greatest caution.

558 Hunter, J.: *Journal of Pt. Jackson etc.*, pp.17-18.

559 Barrington, G.: *History of New Holland*, Introduction, p.iv.

560 Phillip, A.,: *Voyage of Gov. Phillip to Botany Bay* (1790), p. 6.

561 Phillip to Nepean, 11 May 1787; C.O. 201/2.

562 Sparrow to Nepean, 30 October 1786 (H.O. 42/9) and Singleton to Nepean(?), 5 November 1786 (H.O. 42/10).

563 *Gentleman's Magazine*, 56, p.903.

564 *Ibid.*, pp.915-7.

565 *Ibid.*, pp.1018-9. Eden declared that if there were terrors to be faced they were not more than the convicts ought to expect.

566 See p.107.

567 Steele to Board, 26 August 1786; T. 27/38.

568 Minute, 29 August 1786; Adm. Navy Board 2621.

569 Enclosure in Sydney to Treasury, 18 August 1786; T. 1/639.

570 Minute, 27 November 1786; Adm. Navy Board 2622. The contract itself has yet to be found. Richards, however, signed the lists of convicts as contractor; Richards to Nepean, 1 April 1787; C.O. 201/2.

571 Campbell's evidence, Lemaine Enquiry, 12 May 1785; H.O. 7/1.

572 Rose to Chairman of E.I. Coy., 15 September 1786; T. 27/38.

573 Minute, 25 September 1786; Adm. Navy Board 2622. It will be observed that two ships bore the same name.

574 *Ibid.*, 10 October 1786.

575 *Ibid.*, 14 October 1786.

576 See Appendix11. The *Prince of Wales* was added later; see p.134.

577 Brough to Navy Board, 9 September 1786; Adm. Navy Board 1286.

578 Minute, 18 October 1786 (Adm. Navy Board) and Rose to Stephens, 21 October 1786 (Ad. 1/4287).

579 Sydney to Treasury (enclosure), 18 August 1786; T. 1/639.

580 Admiralty to Board, 6 September 1786; Ad. 2/262.

581 Minute, 13 October 1786; Adm. Navy Board 2622. Both ships were armed; the *Sirius* (*Berwick*) carried 14 six-pounder carriage guns, 6 eighteen-pounder carronades, and 8 swivels.

582 Admiralty to Board, 12 October 1786; Ad. 2/262.

583 Minute, 1 November 1786; Adm. Navy Board 2622.

584 Minute, 29 November 1786; Adm. Navy Board 2622. Captain Teer was the officer appointed by the Board to supervise the preparations.

585 Teer to Board, 7 December 1786; Adm. Navy Board 243. The fifth transport (*Lady Penrhyn*) was intended for women and therefore received less attention in strengthening.

586 Nepean to Rose, 18 December 1786; T. 1/639.

587 Stephens to Board, 25 January 1787 (Ad. 2/1178) and Minute, 26 January 1787 (Adm. Navy Board 2347).

588 Minute, 26 February 1787; Adm. Navy Board 2347.

589 Steele to Board, 26 August 1786; T. 27/38.

590 Teer to Thomas, 8 December 1786; Adm. Navy Board 243.

591 Minute, 7 December 1786; *ibid.*

592 Sydney to Treasury, 18 August 1786; T. 1/639.

593 Howe to Sydney, 3 September 1786; C.O. 201/2.

594 Introduction to Phillip, A.: *Voyage of Gov. Phillip to Botany Bay*, and *Australian Encyclopaedia*, Phillip, A.

595 Admiralty to Phillip, 16 December 1786; Ad. 2/117.

596 Admiralty to Board, 12 October and 27 October 1786; Ad. 2/262.

597 Sydney to Treasury, 18 August 1786; T. 1/639 or C.O. 201/2.

598 Stephens to Tupper and Hughes, 8 October 1786; Ad. 2/1177. The marines volunteered for three years on condition of being returned or discharged within the colony.

599 Return of Marines, 6 May 1787; C.O. 201/2. The appointment of the Judge Advocate, David Collins, raised the total to 212. See also Appendix 9.

600 Steele to Board, 26 August 1786; T. 27/38.

601 Minute, 27 November 1786; Adm. Navy Board 2622.

602 Steele to Board, 9 September 1786; T. 27/38.

603 Undated and unaddressed note by Sir Charles Middleton; C.O. 201/2. Middleton, later Lord Barham, was presiding over the Navy Board at the time.

604 Unsigned and undated estimate; C.O. 201/2.

605 Steele to Navy Board, 9 September 1786; T. 27/38.

606 Phillip to Nepean, 28 September 1788; *Historical Records of Australia*, vol. 1, p.86.

607 Nepean to Rose, 22 December 1786; T. 1/639.

608 Richards to Nepean, 5 April 1787; C.O. 201/2.

609 Ross to Stephens, 13 April 1787; C.O. 201/2.

610 Stephens to Ross, 13 March 1787; Ad. 2/1178.

611 Board to Shortland, 20 April 1787; Adm. Navy Board 2347.

612 Nepean to Middleton, 18 April 1787; C.O. 201/2.

613 Jos. Thomas to ?, 19 April 1787; C.O. 201/2.

614 Phillip to Nepean, 8 May 1787; C.O. 201/2.

615 Nepean to Phillip, 10 May 1787; C.O. 201/2.

616 See p.98.

617 Order in Council, 6 December 1786; H.O. 31/1.

618 *Ibid.*

619 Two barons of the Exchequer (Eyre and Hotham) altered the destination of 19 women, sentenced to Africa or America on 22 December 1786; H.O. 31/1.

620 Order dated 10 June 1787; C.O. 201/2.

621 Minute, 15 December 1786; Adm. Navy Board 2622.

622 Nepean to Clerks, 13 December 1786; H.O. 13/4.

623 Nepean to Middleton, 9 December 1786; C.O. 201/2.

624 Richards to Nepean, 5 April 1787; C.O. 201/2.

625 Minute, 18 October 1786; Adm. Navy Board 2622.

626 Board to Treasury, 5 September 1786; T. 1/639.

627 Sydney to Treasury, 18 Ausust 1786; T. 1/639.

628 Minute, 8 December 1786; Adm. Navy Board 243.

629 Sydney to Treasury, 22 December 1786; H.O. 36/5. Phillip had suggested an extra ship; see Phillip to Nepean, 12 December 1786; T. 1/639.

630 Minute, 27 December 1786; Adm. Navy Board 2622.

631 Report of Convicts, October–January 1787; T. 1/641.

632 Stephens to Board, 5 December 1786; Ad. 2/1178.

633 *Historical Records of NSW*, vol. 1, pt 2, p.44.

634 Report of Convicts, October–January 1787; T. 1/641. The *Alexander*'s log records the receipt of only 184.

635 Alexander's log; *HRNSW*, ii, p.399.

636 Paul to Nepean, 16 and 26 October 1786 (H.O. 42/9) and Sydney to clerks etc., 24 November 1786 (H.O. 13/4). At Plymouth they went on board the *Dunkirk* hulk.

637 I.e. in the neighbourhood of Portsmouth.

638 *Alexander*'s log, 19 and 20 January 1787; *HRNSW*, ii, p.399. The ships had lain in the Galleons Reach while in the Thames.

639 *Sirius*'s log, 30 January 1787; Ad. 51/832a. See also the *Alexander*'s log for 29 January.

640 Teer to Middleton, 15 December 1786; Adm. Navy Board 243.

641 *Prince of Wales*'s log, 23 February 1787; *HRNSW*, ii, p.403.

642 John Johnstone to Phillip, 11 January 1787; C.O. 201/2.

643 Phillip to Nepean, 11 January 1787; C.O. 201/2.

644 Rose to Nepean, 24 October 1786 and Rose to Board, same date; T. 27/38.

645 Minute, 25 October 1786; Adm. Navy Board 2622.

646 Minute, 21 November 1786; *ibid.*

647 White to Phillip, 7 February 1787 (C.O. 201/2) and Phillip to Stephens, 7 February 1787 (Ad. 1/2308).

648 Minute, 12 February 1787; Adm. Navy Board 2347.

649 Board to Treasury, 19 February 1787; T. 1/643.

650 Minute, 6 March 1787; Adm. Navy Board 2347.

651 Phillip to Sydney, 12 March 1787; C.O. 201/2.

652 Phillip to Nepean, 18 March 1787; C.O. 201/2.

653 *Alexander*'s log, *HRNSW*, ii, 399. The other ships were disinfected also.

654 Sydney to Phillip, 20 April 1787; C.O. 201/2.

655 Phillip's Instructions, 25 April 1787; C.O. 201/2. Sir Charles Middleton recommended that the right to purchase should be given to Phillip and "not to any agent belonging to Richards", a check of the amount expended being kept by the Navy Board to balance accounts with Richards; Middleton to ?, 4 May 1787; C.O. 201/2.

656 Enclosure in Sydney to Treasury, 18 August 1786; T. 1/639.

657 Minute, 26 December 1786; Adm. Navy Board 2622.

658 Phillip to Nepean, 18 March 1787; C.O. 201/2.

659 Minute, 9 April 1787; Adm. Navy Board 2347. A little later a number of worsted caps were also supplied for the women, "whose hair it might be necessary to cut off", a common punishment for refractory women.

660 Phillip to Sydney, 5 June 1787; *HRNSW*, i, pt 2, p.107.

661 *HRNSW*, *ibid.*, pp.138, 329.

662 Minute, 11 May 1787; Adm. Navy Board 2347.

663 Bowes's Diary; *HRNSW*, ii, p.389.

664 Dalrymple, A.: A Serious Admonition to the Public, p.33.

665 Stephens to Ross and to Smith, 13 March 1787; Ad. 2/1178.

666 Phillip to Sydney, 16 May 1788; *HRNSW*, p.138.

667 *Lady Penrhyn*'s log, *HRNSW*, ii, p.406.

668 Tench, W.: *Narrative of an Expedition to Botany Bay*, p.47.

669 Undated note by Middleton; C.O. 201/2.

670 Nepean to Phillip, 18 April 1787; C.O. 201/2. His words were, "this business, which I must suppose, has given you nearly as much perplexity as it has your faithful servant".

671 Between August and October 1786, prisoners in Ipswich, Lancaster, and Gloucester gaols petitioned to be transported; H.O. 42/9.

672 Teer to Board, 7 December 1786; Adm. Navy Board 243.

9. THE VOYAGE TO NEW SOUTH WALES

673 Court of Directors, 9 February 1787; C.O. 201/2.

674 *Ibid.*, 4 April 1787; C.O. 201/2.

675 Phillip to Nepean, 11 May 1787; C.O. 201/2.

676 Sydney to Treasury, 22 December 1786; H.O. 36/5.

677 Phillip to Stephens, 12 May 1787; Ad. 1/2308.

678 Phillip to Nepean, 20 May 1787; C.O. 201/2.

679 1789 edition, viz. 850, 778, and 777 on pp.VII, 13, and LV.

680 List of persons victualled, 12 November 1787; T. 46/22.

681 State of sick, 4 June 1787; *HRNSW*, i, pt 2, p.107.

682 Phillip does not refer to Ann Wright's death; see p.140.

683 At least five children were born after the fleet left Teneriffe.

684 Phillip to Nepean, 2 September 1787; C.O. 201/2.

685 *Ibid.*

686 Phillip to Stephens, 6 August 1787; Ad. 1/2308.

687 Phillip to Nepean, 2 September 1787; C.O. 201/2.

688 Phillip to Stephens, 10 March 1787; Ad. 1/2308.

689 Phillip, who apparently doubted the suitability of Botany Bay, had secured permission to do this before leaving England. See Sydney to Admiralty, 5 May 1787; C.O. 201/2.

690 King's journal, *HRNSW*, ii, pp.533-6.

691 Hunter, J.: *Journal of Transactions at Pt Jackson* (1793), p. 29.

692 Phillip to Stephens, 16 November 1788; *HRNSW*, i., pt 2, p. 214.

693 Return of sick, 30 June 1788; C.O. 201/2.

694 Returns of sick, 4 June and 30 August 1787; C.O. 201/2.

695 Victualling Lists, 12 November 1787; T. 46/22. Vegetables, although not mentioned in the table, must be added to these amounts; see Phillip to Nepean, 2 September 1787; C.O. 201/2.

696 Middleton to Nepean, 11 December 1786; C.O. 201/2.

697 A week before sailing there were 195 on board; see Appendix 10.

698 Tench, W.: *Narrative of an Expedition to Botany Bay*, p.8.

699 Phillip to Nepean, 2 September 1787; C.O. 201/2.

700 Bowes's Diary, *HRNSW*, ii, p.389. John Irving (or Irvine), a convict, also acted as an Assistant Surgeon; see Return of Convicts, 26 April 1787; C.O. 201/2.

701 Those who died before departure are not reckoned in this result. It is only fair to point out that both White and Balmain, as well as Hunter, stated that the *Alexander's* sickness on the Mother Bank had been exaggerated.

702 A comparison with an American voyage is hardly fair as Campbell had to take *every* transportable felon.

703 This may be an exaggeration, as it is recorded of Rio only; Collins, D.: *Account of the English Colony in NSW* (1798-1802), p.XXIII.

704 Phillip, A., undated memo; C.O. 201/2.

705 White, J.: *Journal of a Voyage*, 1790, p.76.

706 *Ibid.*, p.45.

707 *Sirius's* log, 21 May 1787; Ad. 51/832a.

708 White, J.: *op. cit.*, p.44.

709 King's Journal; *HRNSW*, ii, p.527.

710 A few charges of unchastity were directed against marines, seamen, and convict women. Bowes in his diary on 19 April 1787 records that five women were put in irons for being found in the company of the Second Mate and some sailors. At Rio also, Cornelius Connell, a private marine,

received 100 lashes for "improper intercourse" with some of the female convicts.

711 Southwell Papers, *HRNSW*, ii, p.674.

712 Tench, W.: *Account of the Settlement*, p.3.

10. TRANSPORTATION 1789-1793

713 Phillip's Instructions, 25 April 1787; C.O. 201/2.

714 Treasury Minute, 5 November 1788; T. 29/60.

715 *Ibid.*

716 Treasury Minute, 24 April 1789; T. 29/60. Phillip's despatch arrived at the end of March; *HRA*, i, p.728.

717 These dates have been selected from various sources which, on occasion, differ slightly. The Third Fleet left in three divisions.

718 28th Report on Finance, 26 June 1798.

719 The figures have been collected principally from the volumes C.O. 201/4, 5, 6, and 7, from H.O. 28/8 and 35/2, and from various journals.

720 The first however was concluded in the name of George Whitlock "on behalf of the owners", 27 August 1789; C.O. 201/6. George Macaulay was contractor for the *Pitt* voyage; *HRNSW*, i, pt 2, p.526. The *Kitty* and *Bellona* were really store ships.

721 Phillip to Sydney, 13 February 1790; *HRA*, i, p.158.

722 Long to Scrope Bernard, 17 March 1792; H.O. 35/12.

723 Navy Board to Treasury, 29 May 1792; H.O. 35/12.

724 Contract between Richards and James Bowen, 19 November 1792; C.O. 201/7.

725 Enderby to (?), 13 October 1790; C.O. 201/6.

726 Proposal by Edmund Hill, 11 April 1792; T. 29/63.

727 Macaulay's offer, 13 January & 4 February 1792; T. 29/64.

728 Minute 10 September 1789; Adm. Navy Board 2631.

729 *Ibid.*

730 Dundas to Treasury, 23 June 1791 and Long to Board, 6 August 1791; T. 27/42.

731 Agreement between Board and Richards, 2 February 1789; C.O. 201/4.

732 Agreement between Board and Whitlock, 27 August 1789; C.O. 201/6.

733 Minute, 18 November 1790; Adm. Navy Board 2635.

734 Board to Rose, 11 April 1792; H.O. 25/12.

735 Agreement between Richards and Bowen; 19 November 1792; C.O. 201/7.

736 Grose to Nepean, 17 July 1791; C.O. 201/6. He contradicted his report almost immediately.

737 King to Sir H. Martin, 10 February 1792; C.O. 201/7.

738 Summary of Evans's attempt to punish contractors, undated; C.O. 201/7.

739 Contract between Richards and Bowen, 19 November 1792; C.O. 201/7.

740 Agreement between Board and Richards, 2 February 1789; C.O. 201/4.

741 Board to Treasury, 7 February 1792; H.O. 35/11.

742 At Teneriffe soap was bought to replace "what the convicts had received from the marines"; Phillip to Nepean, 2 September 1787; C.O. 201/2.

743 Sydney to Treasury, 24 April 1789; T. 29/60. These agents were not responsible for the navigation of the ships.

744 Minutes, 8 January and 7 February 1791; Adm. Navy Board 2636.

745 List of escapes on the *Pitt*, undated; C.O. 201/7.

746 Board to Woodriff, 4 January 1792; Adm. Navy Board 2640.

747 Minute, 1 June 1789; Adm. Navy Board 2630.

748 Richard Kent and Alexander Jamieson were appointed to the *Boddingtons* and *Sugar Cane*. These were additional to the contractor's surgeons.

749 Aitken to Teer, 1 May 1789; Adm. Navy Board 243.

750 *Accounts and Papers*, 1792, xxxv. 751, p.74.

751 *Accounts and Papers*, 1792, xxxv. 751, p.74.

752 Young to Stephens, 24 April 1791; H.O. 28/8. Both Phillip and King commended this summary justice.

753 Nairne's list of escapes, October–December 1791; C.O. 201/7.

754 Long to Bernard, 21 March 1792; H.O. 35/12.

755 Richards to Nepean, 20 October 1792; C.O. 201/7.

756 Alley's affidavit, 10 October 1792; C.O. 201/7.

757 See p.156.

758 Richards to Nepean, 19 April 1789; H.O. 35/10.

759 *Ibid.*

760 See p.155.

761 Evans to Sir (perhaps J. King), 17 and 20 January 1792; C.O. 201/7.

762 Summary of Evans's attempt to punish the contractors, undated; C.O. 201/7.

763 Dundas to Phillip, 10 January 1792; C.O. 201/5.

764 King to Phillip, 10 January 1792; C.O. 201/5.

765 *Accounts and Papers*, 1792, xxxv. 751, p.73 *et seq.*

766 Phillip to J. King, 4 October 1792; C.O. 201/7.

767 *Accounts and Papers*, 1792, xxxv. 751, p.78.

768 Lieutenant Riou declared that Shapcote had acted about as foolishly as any man could, but there is good reason to believe that Riou's judgment was biassed at the time, as he had lost his ship only a short time before.

769 Hill to Wather, 26 July 1790; *HRNSW*, i, pt 2, p.366.

770 Sam. Gale's evidence, *Accounts and Papers*, 1792, xxxv. 751.

771 Instructions of Messrs Camden, Calvert & King to Trail; *ibid.*

772 Johnson to Thornton, undated; C.O. 201/6; *HRNSW*, i, pt 2, p. 387.

773 During the voyage the *Surprise* lost 14% while the *Neptune* and *Scarborough* lost 35% and 28% of their convicts, respectively.

774 The Third Fleet, whose death rate was much lower than that of the Second, did not touch at Rio.

775 Banks to Richards, 18 August 1791; *HRNSW*, i, pt 2, p.522.

776 Enclosure in Phillip to Grenville, 5 November 1791; C.O. 201/6.

777 Dundas to Phillip, 15 May 1792; C.O. 201/6.

778 See p.157.

779 Minute, 8 December 1789; Adm. Navy Board, 2631.

780 Estimate of cost of transportation, December 1789; C.O. 201/4.

781 Phillip to Nepean, 28 September 1788; C.O. 201/5.

782 Grenville to Phillip, 24 December 1789; C.O. 201/4.

783 Yeo to Nepean, 23 November 1789; H.O. 28/6. In 1790 an attempt to land 89 convicts in the West Indies was made; see Nepean to Hobart, 18 March 1790; H.O. 100/29.

784 Hamilton to Nepean, Dublin Castle, 25 October 1792; C.O. 201/7.

785 Shelton's account Nos. 2 & 3; A.O. 3/291.

11. NEW SOUTH WALES, 1788-1793

786 *Historical Records of New South Wales*, vol. i, pt 2, pp.423, 560, 676. These figures take no account of the crews of ships or of natives within the settlements.

787 Phillip to Sydney, 9 July 1788; *HRNSW*, vol. i, pt 2, p.147.

788 Phillip to Sydney, 12 February 1790; *ibid.*, p.297.

789 J. King to Phillip, 15 May 1792; *ibid.*, p.621. Throughout the period the Acting "Provost-Marshal" acted also as Superintendent of Works; *ibid.*, p.139.

790 Phillip to Dundas, 4 October 1792; *ibid.*, p.654. The smaller number transported in 1792 and the temporary cessation of transportation in 1793 presented an opportunity for overtaking the housing difficulty.

791 King to Phillip, 19 September 1792; *ibid.*, p.658.

792 Phillip to Sydney, 12 February 1790; *ibid.*, p.299. The officers cultivated public or building land on the understanding that it was to be surrendered when needed for those purposes.

793 Phillip to Dundas, 4 October 1792; *ibid.*, p.654.

794 Phillip to Sydney, 9 July 1788; *ibid.*, p.146.

795 Phillip to Grenville, 17 July 1790; *ibid.*, p.361.

796 *Ibid.*

797 Phillip to Dundas, 19 March 1792; *ibid.*, p.596. Between 1 January and 31 December 1792, 436 convicts died.

798 Phillip to Nepean, 6 August 1790; *ibid.*, p.390.

799 Hill to Wathen, 26 July 1790; *ibid.*, p.368.

800 Phillip to Sydney, 28 September 1788; *ibid.*, p.188. By "necessaries" White meant sugar, barley, oatmeal, spice, portable soup etc.

801 Economy, however, caused them to deduct from the total an amount equal to that secured by Phillip from the Cape.

802 Grenville to Phillip, 24 December 1789; *ibid.*, p.285.

803 Phillip to Grenville, 15 December 1791; *ibid.*, p.569. The greater part of that had either died or escaped.

804 Phillip to Nepean, 29 March 1792; *ibid.*, p.611.

805 Lieutenant Fowell to his father, 31 July 1790; *ibid.*, p.382.

806 Letter of an Officer, 1790; *ibid.*, p.397. The lack of pork on Norfolk Island was met by the slaughter of "puffins" already explained.

807 King to Phillip, 4 October 1792; *ibid.*, p.660.

808 Ross to Stephens, 10 July 1788; *ibid.*, p.173.

809 Grose to Lewis, 22 October 1792; *ibid.*, p.672.

810 Phillip to Grenville, 25 June 1790; *ibid.*, p.353.

811 See table, p.155.

812 Ross administered Norfolk Island from March 1790 to November 1791. Before and after that period Lieutenant Philip Gidley King was in charge.

813 White to Skill, 17 April 1790; *ibid.*, p.332.

814 This resulted in the sending of the *Waaksamheyd* from Batavia to Port Jackson with provisions.

815 It had, however, a ten months' supply of beef.

816 *HRNSW*, vol. i, pt 2, pp.450, 560, 676. Under the heading "flour", rice was also included.

817 Grenville to Phillip, 24 August 1789; *ibid.*, p.261. In describing his difficulties regarding cultivation Phillip once declared that Captain Cook's meadows must have been marshes viewed from a distance.

818 *Hunter's Journal*, p.26. A few breeding sows had also been brought from England. Sundry geese, turkeys, fowls, and rabbits were also imported.

819 Phillip to Grenville, 17 July 1790; *HRNSW*, vol. i, pt 2, p. 362.

820 General Order, 9 February 1791; *ibid.*, p.447.

821 King to Buckingham, 24 October 1791; *ibid.*, p.529.

822 Phillip to Dundas, 2 October 1792; *ibid.*, p.643.

823 For administrative purposes at the beginning of the settlement Phillip and Ross divided the convicts between themselves. The land cultivated formed a common farm. Ross was so discouraged by early failures that he declared it would be cheaper to feed the convicts on turtle and venison at the London Tavern than send them to New South Wales. White described the country as one fit only for execration and curses. Phillip meant wheat when he used the term "corn". He described Indian corn as maize.

824 Phillip to Dundas, 2 October 1792; *ibid.*, p.645. A note in Phillip's

writing suggests that 600 bushels of wheat also were raised; p.611.

825 King's description, January 1791; *ibid.*, p.431. The evidence suggests that the cultivation was done by hand. No beasts of burden, except one or two horses, existed in the settlements. Some waggons, placed on the *Guardian*, had had to be thrown overboard.

826 General Order, 8 January 1791; *ibid.*, p.445, also p.321.

827 King to Phillip, 19 September 1792; *ibid.*, p.658. In two other respects also Norfolk Island disappointed its founders: a flax industry did not develop due to an inability to work the flax, which King declared could only be overcome by introducing Maoris from New Zealand, and the pine timber was found to be unsuitable for naval use.

828 Grenville to Phillip, 24 August 1789; *ibid.*, p.261.

829 Phillip's Instructions, 25 April 1787; *ibid.*, p.91.

830 Instructions, 20 August 1789; *ibid.*, pp.256-9.

831 Return of Land Grants, 1791; *ibid.*, p.540. Twenty-seven received 30 acres or less but as there were 44 convicts named in the list, 17 at least must have received 50 acres, which was the next area in size.

832 That of Phillip Schaffer, one of the Superintendents who had sailed in the *Guardian*.

833 One half to two acres of cleared land were included in the grants given in the year 1791.

834 This settler was given 1½ acres of cleared and dug ground in November 1789, with a promise of 30 acres if he were industrious. These he apparently received shortly afterwards although the grant is dated 30 March 1791. He was supported from the Public Store until 25 February 1791. He then married. Phillip in November 1791 stated that he (Ruse) wished to take both his wife and child off the store "next Christmas"; Phillip to Grenville, 5 November 1791; *ibid*, p.536. The records do not distinguish between emancipists and expirees.

835 Encouragement to settlers, November 1791; *ibid*, p.539. On Norfolk Island King assigned two convicts to each settler for three weeks to assist him in the building of his hut.

836 King to Phillip, 19 September 1792; *ibid.*, p.657.

837 Phillip to Sydney, 13 February 1790; *ibid.*, p.306. Phillip stressed the fact that free settlers, by offering employment to expirees, would encourage them to remain in the colony.

838 Phillip to Sydney, 17 June 1790; *ibid.*, p.349. The suggested period of support he reduced to 18 months in March 1792. His opposition to an inrush of free settlers was revealed by his attitude towards reported discoveries of precious metals. He stated, "I gave no encouragement to search after what, if found, in our present situation, would be the greatest evil that could befal the settlement".

839 In April he reduced this to 12,000 acres.

840 Collins, *op. cit.*, i, p.262.

841 Phillip to Sydney, 17 February 1790; *HRNSW*, vol. i, pt 2, pp. 293-301.

842 Phillip to Dundas, 2 October 1792; *ibid.*, p.645.

843 So, in February 1790, he wrote, "The convicts have lately behaved better than I ever expected". On one occasion, however, he declared that those who had some little education were the greatest villains of all.

844 See p.150.

845 The appended list gives only eight names.

846 Only one court martial was held and it imposed only corporal punishment. But about the same time Ross proclaimed that those who neglected work, or deserted, would be "adjudged to suffer death".

847 Phillip to Dundas, 4 October 1792; *ibid.*, p.655.

848 Phillip to Nepean, 18 November 1791; *ibid.*, p.556.

849 *HRNSW*, vol. i, pt 2, p.440 or *HRA*, vol. i, p.236.

850 The Rev. J. Crowther, the second chaplain appointed, returned to England from the Cape after the accident to the *Guardian.*

851 Johnson to Phillip, 23 March 1792; *HRNSW*, vol i, pt 2, p. 602.

852 See p.144 for the number of women in the First Fleet.

853 Ross's General Order, 8 January 1791; *ibid.*, p.447.

854 Thus up to February 1790 Phillip reported 87 births and 77 deaths. Ross in February 1791 declared that since his arrival in Norfolk Island there had been 15 births and 12 deaths (eight being due to drowning). A Return dated December 1792 shows that there were 255 children in the various settlements.

855 General Order, Port Jackson, 4 April 1791; *ibid.*, p.485.

856 The former was required to find security for good behaviour for 12 months, the latter was ordered "to pay eighty pounds to the King and five pounds to the person whom he had beaten". Lieutenant King's letter suggests that he would have preferred heavier sentences.

857 On one occasion, however, a marine officer set an example to Phillip. In December 1790, as a result of a spear-throwing by the natives, the Governor ordered a party of marines to seize, alive or dead, six of the Aborigines to check the practice. Lieutenant Dawes, chosen to accompany the party, refused to obey the orders of both his senior officer and of Phillip, and yielded only when the Rev. Mr Johnson "thought he might obey the order". After the service, however, he informed Phillip that "he was sorry he had been persuaded to comply with the order".

858 These exploring ships arrived while the First Fleet was in Botany Bay. They refitted in that harbour.

859 Grenville to Phillip, 19 February 1791; C.O. 201/5.

860 *Ibid.* This is an interesting comment on Grenville's belief in the moral efficacy of transportation.

861 Phillip to Nepean, 18 November 1791; *HRNSW*, vol. i, pt 2, p. 558.

862 Phillip to Nepean, 14 December 1791; C.O. 201/6.

863 Collins, *op. cit.*, pp.155-6. The wife, Mary Bryant is named Mary Brand

in the list of convicts in Phillip's *Voyage to Botany Bay.*

864 Since the preparation of this work a log of this voyage has been found among the Bentham Papers in University College, London.

865 Thus, in the instructions given to King, appears the following: "You are not to build or to permit the building of any vessel or boat . . . whose length of keel exceeds twenty feet, and if any that exceeds 20 ft be driven on the island you are to cause it to be scuttled".

866 Phillip complained of a pain in the side caused by sleeping in the open while exploring in New South Wales.

APPENDICES AND BIBLIOGRAPHY

867 Bentham records that this preacher gave prizes of "half a crown gin" to encourage a study of the bibles.

868 I.e., not religious or political offenders.

869 Nepean to Hobart, 18 March 1790; H.O. 100/29.

870 Hobart to Nepean, 8 January 1790; H.O. 100/29.

871 "Whitehall" to Hobart, 5 January 1791; H.O. 100/32.

872 Death removed several from the *Alexander*; see p.144-5.

873 The Public Record Office reference numbers are inserted here to help to explain and identify the references included in footnotes of this work.

874 Since the completion of the above, the reference number Ad. 106 has been applied to the Adm. Navy Board section.

Bibliography

1. Contemporary Manuscript Records

a. General

The following sources[873] stored in the Public Record Office (PRO) London contain information relevant to the whole period 1763-1793:

T. 1/422-621	Treasury In-letters
T. 27/28-44	Treasury Out-letters general
T. 29/35-65	Treasury Board Minutes
T. 31/245-368	Accounts general
T. 52/55-80	King's Warrants
T. 53/49-60	Warrants relating to money
T. 54/39-47	Warrants not relating to money; these contain the hulk Contracts

b. North America (in the PRO)

S.P. 36/158-9	Petitions, George II's reign
S.P. 37/2-10	Letters and Papers, George II's reign 1763-74
S.P. 44/87-92	Criminal correspondence — pardons 1761-76
S.P. 44/138-43	Entry Book, Domestic, Secretaries' Letter Books, Pitt, Egremont, Halifax, Holdernesse, Bute etc.
S.P. 44/149	Undersecretaries' miscellaneous correspondence 1766-71
S.P. 44/231-2	Entry Books, Naval Correspondence 1760-84
S.P. 44/328	Treasury Letter Book 1763-75
S.P. 45/32	State Papers, various, Colonial 1768-82
T. 28/1	Treasury Out-letters 1762-78
T. 47/11	Weekly Emigration Returns from England 1775-6
T. 64/133	Contracts 1756-94
T. 64/312	Correspondence re sailing to America 1767-77
C.O. 5/257-63	Dispatches, Letters from Admiralty etc. 1780-83
C.O. 5/709-10	Shipping Returns, Georgia 1752-67
C.O. 5/750	Shipping Returns, Maryland 1754-65
C.O. 5/1449-50	Shipping Returns, Virginia 1762-70
C.O. 5/1330-4	Board of Trade, Correspondence to Virginia 1760-81
C.O. 217/56-8	Secretary of State's Correspondence re Nova Scotia 1781-6

C.O. 218/9   Instructions to Governor Parr 1782-3
C.O. 389/31-2   Board of Trade, commercial correspondence etc. 1760-76
C.O. 389/39   *Ibid.* 1761-82
C.O. 389/51-52   *Ibid.* 1760-85

c. England (in the PRO)

S.P. 37/11-4   Letters and Papers, George III 1775-80
S.P. 37/23-26   *Ibid.* , Treasury Correspondence 1776-81
S.P. 41/26-7   Secretary at War's Letters 1773-8
S.P. 42/49   Lords of Admiralty's Letters 1774-7
S.P. 44/92-6   Criminal correspondence 1772-6
S.P. 44/143   Secretaries' Letter Book 1775-82
S.P. 44/330   Treasury Letter Book 1775-83
S.P. 44/414   Miscellaneous Circular Letters 1761-86
H.O. 13/1-4   Pardons, Criminal Reports 1782-6
H.O. 28/1-4   Admiralty Correspondence 1782-4
H.O. 32/1   Foreign Office Correspondence 1782-9
H.O. 35/1-7   Treasury Correspondence, Colonial 1781-6
H.O. 36/1-5   Treasury Entry Books, Colonial 1776-87
H.O. 38/1-2   Warrant Books 1782-7
H.O. 42/1-10   Letters & Papers, George III 1782-6
H.O. 43/1-2   Domestic Letter Book 1782-5
A.O. 3/291   Shelton's Accounts for Contracts etc. 1786-93
Assizes 24/25   Transportation Books, Western Circuit 1743-70
Assizes 30/3   Returns, Western Circuit 1740-90
Assizes 33/4   Gaol Books, S.E. Circuit 1765-70
Assizes 34/75   Record Books, George II and George III
Assizes 42/8   Gaol Books, N.E. Circuit 1762-74
F.O. 95/5   Correspondence, Holland 1781-1837
F.O. 97/246   Correspondence, Holland 1785-6

In the Guildhall of the City of London: Transportation Bonds and Contracts 1667-1737; Certificates of landing of felons 1718-36

In the Oxford County Hall: Sessions Papers 1728 & 1763

In the Archives of the City of Bristol: Quarter Session Conviction Records
1728-76

d. Africa (in the PRO)

S.P. 37/13-4   Letters and Papers, George III 1779-80
S.P. 41/28-9   Military Correspondence 1779-82
S.P. 44/198-200   Military Correspondence 1775-80
H.O. 7/1   Lemaine Enquiry 1785
H.O. 28/5   Admiralty Correspondence 1785-7
H.O. 36/5   Treasury Entry Books 1785-6
H.O. 47/1-3   Correspondence on Criminals 1784-5
T. 70/32-3   Africa Co. In-letters 1773-99
T. 70/69   Africa Co. Outward Letter Book 1764-87
T. 70/145   Africa Co. Minutes 1780-87
T. 70/152-3   Africa Co. Acts of Cape Coast Castle 1770-99

T. 70/155-9   Africa Co. Reports of Select Committees 1770-84
T. 70/485-96   Africa Co. Accounts & Journals 1779-85
T. 70/634   Africa Co. Ledgers, Forts & Settlements 1763-84
T. 70/1455-6   Africa Co. Register of Servants 1760-1815
T. 70/1539-47 Africa Co. Detached Papers 1780-82
C.O. 267/6-7   Secretary of State's Correspondence re Sierra Leone 1753-
               83
C.O. 267/11   *Ibid.* re African Forts 1755-83
C.O. 267/16   *Ibid.* re African Forts 1773-7
C.O. 267/18-20 *Ibid.* , Dispatches 1778-84
C.O. 268/3-4   *Ibid.* re Senegambia 1771-81
C.O. 391/87-9 Minutes of Board of Trade 1781-2
W.O. 1/682   Conditional Pardons 1777-81
W.O. 1/867   In-letters, various 1780-81
W.O. 1/874-7   *Ibid.* 1767-83
W.O. 1/891   Orders in Council 1777-83
W.O. 1/1008-12 In-letters 1780-81
W.O. 2/34-5   Out-letters, regimental 1767-91
W.O. 4/110-16 Out-letters, Sec. at War 1780-81
W.O. 5/63   Out-letters, general 1780-82
W.O. 17/228   African Corps 1778-1812
W.O. 24/509   10 Coys of 4th, 5th & 49th Regiments 1780-81
W.O. 25/705   Staff Returns, Africa 1782-1815
W.O. 34/111-42 Amherst Papers 1778-82
Ad. 1/4144-6   Secretary of State to Admiralty 1781

e. Honduras (in the PRO)

C.O. 5/263   Secret Dispatches 1778-83
C.O. 123/2-4   Secretary of State's Correspondence 1779-86
C.O. 123/10-11 Transactions by E. Despard 1784-90
C.O. 137/84-5   Secretary of State's Correspondence re Jamaica 1783-5
S.P. 44/330   Domestic, Treasury and Accounts 1775-83

In the Royal Empire Society's Library:
  Honduras Almanac 1738-1828
  Extracts from Proceedings of Magistrates 1775-85
  Miscellaneous Papers re Honduras 1783-6

f. New South Wales (in the PRO)

H.O. 6/1   Criminal circuit Letters 1784-9
H.O. 10/1-2   Convicts NSW 1788-1819
H.O. 11/1   Convict Registers 1787-1809
H.O. 13/5-9   Entry Books, Criminal Correspondence 1787-94
H.O. 26/1-2   Newgate Registers 1791-3
H.O. 28/5-13   Admiralty Correspondence 1787-94
H.O. 29/1-2   Admiralty Entry Books 1779-93
H.O. 31/1   Orders in Council 1782-91
H.O. 35/7-13   Treasury Correspondence, Colonial 1786-93
H.O. 36/6-8   Treasury Entry Books 1787-95

H.O. 38/3-5	Warrant Books 1787-94
H.O. 42/9-27	Domestic Letters & Papers George III, 1786-93
H.O. 43/2-4	Domestic Letter Book 1785-94
H.O. 47/6-17	Judges' Reports 1787-93
H.O. 48/1	Law Officers' Reports 1782-91
H.O. 102/51-2	Petitions, Criminals 1783-93
T. 40/14-7	Treasury Commissions 1786-93
T. 46/22	Victualling List, Garrison NSW 1787
T. 60/27-8	Order Books 1786-94
A.O. 3/154	Accounts various, Van Diemen's Land 1754-1837
A.O. 16/44	Warrant of Establishment 1787-1824
B.T. 1/1-10	Board of Trade In-letters 1791-3
B.T. 3/1-4	Board of Trade Out-letters 1786-93
B.T. 6/58	Miscellaneous NSW 1792-1806
Ad. 1/2308	Admiralty In-letters, Phillip's 1785-9
Ad. 1/3824	Admiralty In-letters, Ross's 1787-92
Ad. 1/3914	Admiralty In-letters, East India House 1782-95
Ad. 1/4152-59	Admiralty In-letters, Secs. of State 1786-93
Ad. 1/4289-90	Admiralty In-letters, Treasury 1783-95
Ad. 1/4352	Admiralty In-letters, Secret 1756-1800
Ad. 1/5177-8	Admiralty In-letters, Orders in Council 1784-92
Ad. 2/117-25	Ad. Out-letters, Orders etc. 1786-93
Ad. 2/262-71	Ad. Out-letters, Lords' Letters 1786-93
Ad. 2/586-603	Ad. Out-letters, Secretary's Letters 1786-93
Ad. 2/756-71	Ad. Out-letters, Orders, Sec.'s Common Letters 1786-93
Ad. 2/1177-82	Ad. Out-letters, Orders re Marines 1786-93
Ad. 2/1342-6	Ad. Out-letters, Orders, Secret Orders 1789-93
Ad. 3/102-11	Admiralty Board's Minutes 1786-93
Ad. 3/125-7	Papers re Transports 1787-92
Ad. 7/172	Estimates 1771-1818
Ad. 7/181	Estimates 1782-92
Ad. 7/342-3	Memorials and Reports 1775-99

Adm. Navy Board:[874]

243	In-letters from Deptford 1784-9
1286-99	In-letters miscellaneous 1786-93
2213-7	Out-letters to Admiralty 1786-93
2347	Out-letters to Transport Agents 1784-90
2621-48	Board Minutes 1786-93
2407-8	Deptford Yard Letter Book 1786-93
Ad. 110/34-8	Ad. Victualling Board Out-letters 1786-93
Ad. 111/105-12	Ad. Victualling Board Minutes 1786-8
Ad. 36/10978	*Sirius*'s Log 1786-92
Ad. 51/832a	Captains' Logs of the same
C.O. 201/1-9	Secretary's Correspondence re NSW 1784-93

Chatham Papers:

G.D. 8, CLXXI	Richards to Pitt 1786-92
G.D. 8, CCXLVI	Admiralty and Navy Board to Pitt
G.D. 8, CCCXLII	Campbell to Pitt 1789

P.C. 2/130-2   Privy Council Registers 1785-7

g. Scotland (in PRO)

S.P. 54/11-3   Scottish Letters & Papers 1716-18
S.P. 55/6-7   Letter Book, Scottish 1717
S.P. 55/11   Letter Book, Scottish 1714-25
S.P. 55/13   Letter Book, Scottish 1742-6
H.O. 102/50-2   Circuit Letters 1784-93

h. Ireland (in the PRO)

H.O. 100/23-34 Correspondence, civil & military 1788-92
T. 14/17   Out-letters, Ireland 1787-95

2. Contemporary Printed Records

a. For the Introduction

For this section of the work the following printed records were invaluable:

Calendars of State Papers; Domestic, Home Office, Treasury, America, and the West Indies

Acts of the Privy Council, including the Colonial Series and the Unbound Papers

See also the following records of the various colonies.

b. The Period 1763-93

The following voluminous works, though useful, contain little information concerning transportation:

KINGSBURY, S.M.: *Journals of the Virginia Coy.* (1906)
Virginia — *Journals of the House of Burgesses and of the Council*
Maryland — *Proceedings of the Assembly, Council, and Provincial Court*; also the *Correspondence of Gov. Sharpe*
North Carolina — *Colonial Records of North Carolina*
New Jersey — *Documents in re. the colonial history of New Jersey*
New York — Documents in re. the colonial history of New York
Massachusetts — *Historical collections*
PALMER, W.P.: *Calendar of Virginia papers*
ATKINS, T.B.: *Archives of Nova Scotia*
Historical Manuscript Commission, xiii. Reports, pts 3-4, pp. 542-3, Grenville to Hobart, 25 November 1789
EDDIS, W.: *Letters from America 1769-77* (1792)
DOUGLAS, William: *British Settlements in North America 1749-50*

Statutes — the following are interesting because they reveal the influence of disallowance on colonial convict legislation:

HENING, W.W.: *Statutes at large of Virginia* (1923 etc.)
BACON, Thomas: *Laws of Maryland* (1765 etc.)
BIOREN, J.: *Laws of Pennsylvania*
WRIGHT & POTTER: *Acts and resolves of Massachusetts Bay, 1769-86*
Periodicals — *The Virginia Gazette, The Maryland Gazette*

c. England

Egerton Papers (Cam. Soc.) Walsyngham to Egerton 6 April 1786, pp. 116-7
COBBETT, William: *Parliamentary History*
Parliamentary History of England by "Several Hands"
Parliamentary Register
The London Gazette
FORTESCUE, Sir J.: *Correspondence of George III* , Nos. 4413-4, 4419-20 (1928)
Journals of the House of Commons — these contain the Reports of Select Committees on Gaols, Transportation, and the Hulks; see particularly vols. 36/926, 37/311, 40/1161
Journals of the House of Lords

Periodicals — *London Magazine, Annual Register, Gentlemen's Magazine*

Newspapers — facts concerning the cessation of the American transportation and the beginnings of the hulk system can be found in the periodicals mentioned and in the following London newspapers (Burney Collection, British Museum): *Daily Advertiser, Morning Post, Morning Chronicle , Lloyd's Evening Post, The Gazetteer* etc.

d. Africa

CROOKS, J.J.: *Records of the Gold Coast Settlement* (1923)
Report of Select Committee of 1785 in re. Lemaine and Das Voltas; *Coms. Journal*, 40/1161 and H.O. 42/7

e. Honduras

BURDON, Sir J.A.: *Archives of British Honduras*, vol. 1 (1931)

f. New South Wales

The following Parliamentary Papers contain much useful information (British Museum):

Extracts of Letters and Accounts in re. the Settlements of New South Wales, 8 April 1791
Accounts and Papers in re. convicts on the hulks and transported to New South Wales, 10-26 March 1792
28th Report of a Select Committee on Finance in re. Police, convicts etc., 26 June 1798

Printed Records:

BLADEN, F.M.: *Historical Records of New South Wales*. The second volume contains the Macarthur Papers, Lieutenant King's Journal, the Southwell Papers, Logs of the various transport vessels, Surgeon A. Bowes's Journal, and numerous newspaper articles
WATSON, F.: *Historical Records of Australia*

Pamphlets and Books:

COOK, J.: *A Journal of a Voyage round the World* (1771)
DALRYMPLE, A.: *A Serious Admonition to the Public on the intended thief colony at Botany Bay* (1786)

EDEN, *William: Discourse on Banishment* (in BARRINGTON, below)
ANON.: *Historical narrative of the discovery of Botany Bay* (1786)
A returned officer's narrative of the late expedition to Botany Bay (1789); unreliable
PHILLIP, A.: *Voyage of Governor Phillip to Botany Bay* (1790)
BARRINGTON, G. *The history of New Holland* (1787); the real author assumed
    the name of a famous convict, Geo. Barrington
BARRINGTON, G.: *The history of New South Wales* (1802)
HUNTER, J.: *Historical journal of transactions at Port Jackson* (1793)
WHITE, J.: *Journal of a voyage to New South Wales* (1790)
TENCH, W.: *Account of the settlement at Port Jackson* (1793)
TENCH, W.: *Narrative of an expedition to Botany Bay* (1789)
BENTHAM, J.: *Principles of penal law*, pt ii, book v; Works of Bentham, Bowr-
    ing Edition (1838) vol. i, pp. 490-7; this was written a year or two after
    the events

3. Later Sources

a. America

The first three books are directly concerned with transportation; the remainder refer to it

SMITH, A.E.: *Transportation in the 17th Century* (unpubl. at the time of the
    preparation of this work)
BALLAGH, J.C.: *White servitude in Virginia* (1895)
MacCORMAC, E.I.: *White servitude in Maryland* (1904)
FISKE, J.: *Old Virginia and her neighbours* (1897)
NEILL, E.D.: *History of Virginia* (1886)
BRUCE, P.A.: *Economic history of Virginia in the 17th Century* (1896)
SCHARF, J.T.: *History of Maryland* (1878)
BEER, G.L.: *Old colonial policy* (1912)
CHANNING, Ed.: *History of America* (1923)
DOYLE, J.A.: *The English in America* (1882-1907)
WILLIAMS, G.W.: *The Negro race in America* (1883)
HERTZ, G.B.: *Old colonial system* (1905)
LATIMER : *Annals of Bristol in the 18th Century* (1893)
ANDREWS: *Guide to materials for American history in the Public Record Office of
    Great Britain* (1912)
MacNUTT, W.S.: *British rule in Nova Scotia, 1713-1784* (unpubl.)

Periodicals — the following historical journals contain a number of very useful articles: *American Historical Review, Maryland Historical Review, The Virginia Magazine of History and Biography*

b. England, Africa, and Honduras

Only the first of the following works is directly concerned with transportation:

LANG, J.D.: *Transportation and colonisation* (1837)
Cambridge history of the British Empire, vol. i (1929)
ROSE, J.H.: *William Pitt and national revival* (1911)

MARTIN, E.C.: *British West Africa settlements* (1927)
CLARIDGE, W.: *History of the Gold Coast* (1910)
BURDON, Sir J.: *Introduction to historical archives of British Honduras*, vol. i (1931)

c. New South Wales

Cambridge history of the British Empire (Australian Volume)
Australian Encyclopaedia
RICHARDS, Thomas: *Official history of New South Wales* (1883)
BARTON, G.B.: *History of New South Wales from the records* (1889)
SCOTT, Ernest: *Short history of Australia* (1927)
RUSDEN, G.W.: *History of Australia* (1883)
MILLS, R.C.: *Colonisation of Australia 1829-1842* (1915)
LUCAS, Sir Charles: *Historical geography of the British Dominions*, Australian Volume by J.D. ROGERS (1925)

The following two anonymous works must be treated with the greatest caution:

ANON: *A concise history of New South Wales* (1804)
ANON: *A new history of Botany Bay* (1821)
Royal Australian Historical Society's *Journals and Proceedings*; see particularly Prof. G.A. WOOD's article on convicts in vol. 8, pp. 177-208

4. The Legal Foundation of Transportation

Statutes at Large of Great Britain, and of Ireland
Acts of the Scottish Parliament
BLACKSTONE, Sir Wm: *Commentaries on the laws of England,* edited by R.M. KERR (1862)
HAWKINS, William: *A treatise of the pleas of the Crown* (1795)
KELYNG, Sir J.: *Reports of Crown cases* (3rd edn, 1873)
STEPHEN, J.F.: *History of the Criminal Law* (1883)
STEPHEN, J.F.: *Laws of England* (1928)
TOMLINS, Sir T.E.: *Law dictionary* (1835)
See also HOWARD and COLQUHOUN below

5. English Social Conditions

Many works might be recommended; the following are useful:
LECKY, W.E.H.: *History of England in the 18th Century* (1892)
HOWARD, J.: *Prisons* (1780)
COLQUHOUN, P.: *Police of the Metropolis* (1800)
GEORGE, Dorothy: *English social life in the 18th Century* (1925)
GRAY, B.K.: *History of English philanthropy* (1905)
GRIFFITHS, A.: *Chronicles of Newgate* (1884)
Proceedings of the Sessions at the Old Bailey, 1763-93
TRAILL & MANN *Social England* (1903)
HAMMOND, J.L. & L.B.: *The village labourer* (1920)

Commentary on Oldham Thesis

by Dan Byrnes

B RITAIN'S HANDLING and disposal of its convicts is still a field of study laced with errors, oversights, and biassed writing. This belatedly published work, which is distinguished above all by hard facts patiently gathered and objectively presented, will do much to correct the problem. Now that it is available, readers in North America, England, and Australia will find new reasons, derived from their differing cultural contexts, to appreciate this thesis's virtues. It was the first full study, by any historian, of the transportation of British convicts to both America and Australia. Oldham's earliest date for transportation by ship is 1633. He cites evidence that the idea of transporting British convicts overseas was proposed as early as 1597, and evidence that legislative material was produced as early as 1614. (Transportation to North America became more frequent from the 1720s; Australia ceased to receive convicts in the late 1860s).

Only the specialist in convict matters can appreciate the lack of informative and incisive secondary material available to Oldham when he began his research in 1931. To a modern reader some of the material he cited may seem old fashioned, and his narrative a little wooden when compared, for example, to Roger Ekirch's livelier prose (Ekirch, 1987). Despite the challenges he faced, however, Oldham surpassed the practice of his art so outstandingly that his information has still not been greatly improved upon. Nor has his incisiveness been greatly bettered.

In his search he created useful linkages between documented material, archival resources, and living scholars, including the American historian A.E. Smith, whose important work on the subject has since been published (Smith, 1934, 1947, 1965). Oldham had — or developed — an "attitude" well able to handle emotionally difficult material and the grave legal, moral, psychological, intellectual, and spiritual contradictions of the topic. This topic was in reality Crime and Punishment: an English drama made possible by a series of Acts of

251

Parliament, the action taking place first in America, then briefly in Africa, and eventually in Pacific waters at a time when the British Empire was forced to change course after the loss of what became the United States of America.

Unlike O'Brien (1937, 1950), Oldham was not particularly interested in one instance of colonisation — the Australian case — nor was he greatly interested in the American colonies *per se*. The subject he concentrated on was the *administration* of the system of transportation — the mercy and brutality, the nuts and bolts, paperwork, costs, and questions of management of large numbers of convicts sentenced to transportation, under various conditions and evolving legislation, on ships sailing over various oceans between 1718 and 1793. He held no brief for the wisdom or otherwise of decisions that were made as they were. Instead he held the paperwork up for inspection so that the effectiveness of the transportation system, its costs, and the accuracy of statements made in public and private could be objectively assessed by those who followed him. (Yet Crittenden's 1982 Bibliography of the First Fleet does not cite Oldham!).

Without acid, Oldham noted how little had been written about convict transportation to either America or Australia before he began, a note still echoed by an American, Ekirch, in 1987. One possible explanation for this neglect is that in America the word "transportation" seems to have lost its specialised meaning: conveying criminals to a penal colony. At all events, Oldham was obliged to go straight to departmental papers for his facts. There he recognised that transportation, in its milieu of cant, convention, community despair, and refusal to budget for prisons, had become institutionalised. He then described its economic roles and the effects of circumstances on the institution. In so doing, however, he resisted the temptation to which many writers still succumb, to make pungent judgements about social conditions generally for the rich and poor in England during the reign of George III (Hughes, 1987; Lloyd, 1971; Marshall, 1973).

In brief, Oldham's thesis drew attention to:

(a) The history of transportation of convicts to North America from 1718, from England, Ireland, and Scotland;

(b) The interruption to transportation due to the outbreak of the American War of Revolution in 1775;

(c) The enactment of the Hulks Act in 1776, and the consequent placement of convict hulks on the River Thames under the superintendence of merchant and former government convict contractor Duncan Campbell;

(d) Various health issues and matters of prisoner discipline on the hulks, along with community reaction to the scheme, which remained controversial;

(e) Debacles in the resumption of transportation, and the new legislation of 1784;

(f) Recommencement of shipping convicts overseas, but this time to Australia;

(g) Governance of New South Wales, the new Australian colony, during its early years.

Throughout, he took care to provide an overview of the successive Acts of Parliament that permitted these changes to the system.

Modern students of convict transportation face two literary problems with the contemporary documents. One is the whining, self-righteous moral cant that was expressed by the upper classes concerning what they saw as the moral worthlessness of the rebellious lower classes, during a period of brutal social change exacerbated by a series of wars that alternately absorbed and abandoned unemployed Britons. The other, backing up this cant, is the authoritarian attitude of English society then. The latter is the harder to handle because it cannot be pricked with wit, and this may explain Oldham's slightly wooden style. A third form of cant — the "flash" language used by the convicts — is more entertaining. In America, where incoming convicts were separated and spread among the community, their peculiarities of speech probably soon died away; but in Australia they were largely herded together as a disadvantaged social group, so their cant has had more influence on Australian speech patterns, though lamentably at the expense of respect for a "decent education". Cockney rhyming slang is a conspicuous legacy here.

Of the questions that students of the system should ask — the how, what, when, where, and why — Oldham mostly looked for *what* had happened in the administrative context he had chosen. As his thesis has been largely unread, however, many questions that later historians might logically have been expected to ask have not been asked. Oldham, of course, did not discover all the facts, nor did Eris O'Brien (whose thesis of the 1930s is reputed to have been published more by luck than design). Both stressed the fact that one legal basis of transportation from 1718 was "the property in the service of the body of the convict". Apart from Manning Clark (Clark, 1957, 1962) few historians have dwelt at any length on this odd legal/economic entity; if they had, some arguments — for example, about the brutality and "excessive tyranny" of the system of transportation — might have been handled more rationally. Robert Hughes in *The Fatal Shore* (1987) has recently reopened this old wound. By contrast, it was Oldham's habit to stand well back and gaze objectively at allegations of brutality, a habit which gave his pungency ample scope.

The chief difference between Oldham's thesis and the work of O'Brien and many later writers is that Oldham, as his original title suggested, dwelt on the administration of the various regimes set up to handle transportable convicts. The explicit or implicit assumption in all these regimes was that economic value could and should be extracted from convict labour, either by private individuals (the legislation of 1717-18 to 1775) or by the State (the legislation of 1776-1784 and what followed). Surprisingly, however, there have still been few useful Australian studies of the role played by convicts in protracted works in the public and private sectors of the colony.

In a sense, because the King's mercy or justice could follow a convict virtually anywhere, the exploitation of convict labour under the 1784 and subsequent legislation was inherently imperialistic. Where the transported convict went, so did the King's will. George III was personally enthusiastic about transportation, as were most of his influential subjects, especially in London. The social weight pressing on the convict was overwhelming, and the era was characterised by Giles Playfair (1971) as reflecting a "punitive obsession" of widespread effect.

Marshall (1963), Lloyd (1971) and many other writers have described this period of British history. J.H. Plumb (1976) in *The First Four Georges* incidentally notes that "few empires have been founded without the aid of labour camps and convict settlements". Had he paid more attention to the settlement of Australia during the reign of George III he could have proved his point even more vigorously. Most commentators agree that Georgian England was hard and brutal.

One Londoner, Duncan Campbell (1726-1803), made a fortune from selling the "service of the body of the convict". In 1758, then in the merchant marine between London and Jamaica, he became a partner with John Stewart, the government contractor for transportation of convicts to North America. Stewart died in 1772, and Campbell inherited all their joint business, which involved carrying convicts to the colonies and backloading tobacco to England. Campbell also had sugar interests in Jamaica as a result of his marriage, about 1753, to the daughter of Dugald Campbell, a Jamaican planter. Some of Duncan Campbell's most valued correspondents in North America were colonial aristocrats — the Hon. John Tayloe of the noted Virginian plantation "Mount Airy" (Conway, 1892; Dunn, 1977) and the Fitzhughs. Two of Campbell's American agents were Tom Hodge or Hodges (Schmidt, 1986) and Matthew Ridley (Klingelhofer, 1963). Ridley, of whom Oldham was unaware, later became a minor United States diplomat. Campbell's varied and unduly neglected career throws much direct and indirect light on convict matters in America, England, and Australia; Oldham handled Campbell's roles more skilfully than any other historian.

As the influx of British convicts was only a minor feature in America's pre-Revolutionary history, its comparative neglect by historians there may be easily understood, but the writings of Blumenthal (1962), Ekirch (1984, 1985, 1987), Morgan (1985, 1987), and Schmidt (1986) are recent contributions of great interest.

Campbell's trade was interrupted by the American Revolutionary War, but in early 1776 he had discussions with William Eden. As a result of these discussions and liaisons with others, Eden saw the Hulks Act passed later that year (Thomas, 1925). Campbell contracted to guard convicts placed aboard two "hulks" anchored on the River Thames. The first hulks he supplied were the *Justitia* and the *Tayloe*, two seaworthy merchant ships he had used for years to carry convicts to the colonies. Hughes (1987) like many other writers mistakenly accepts the much popularised idea that derelict vessels were used to house "hard labour" prisoners. Ekirch (1987) describes them as warships, but few former warships were ever used for this purpose. From the outset the hulks scheme was controversial, both in and out of Parliament. Hibbert (1963) and Capper (1963) refer to the hulks, while an entertaining account is that by Branch-Johnson (1957). Curiously, the 1776 Hulks Act was objected to as being un-English. Some, including Thomas Townshend, later to become Lord Sydney, saw it as a perversion of criminal law, which advanced the power of the Crown too abruptly (Thomas, 1925). The measure withstood this pressure, however, and Duncan Campbell remained as superintendent of the Thames convict hulks until 1801; around 1803 he was replaced by magistrate Aaron Graham.

While Oldham was researching his subject, Duncan Campbell's letterbooks — now in the Mitchell Library, Sydney (Duncan Campbell, unpubl.; see References) — were in the possession of George Mackaness, a biographer of William Bligh of HMS *Bounty* fame (Mackaness, 1931). D.S. Mitchell, founder of the Mitchell Library, had sought and failed to find the letterbooks before 1900. Mackaness obtained the letterbooks from W.D. Campbell, a descendant of Duncan Campbell, presumably in the course of his research on Bligh. Mackaness appears to have held them until his death; he used them in popularising Bligh but drew little from Campbell's papers apart from alluding to his role as administrator of the hulks. W.D. Campbell has left copious notes on his family history (W.D. Campbell, undated, unpubl.; see References). In a later monograph Mackaness (1949, re-printed 1976) made some slight errors in reference to Duncan Camp-bell's family; this suggests that he had not fully sorted through the letterbooks, which, significantly, provide much day-to-day informa-tion that broadly confirms the results of Oldham's examination of more public, official, documents.

Evan Nepean, Undersecretary of the Home Office from 1782, found Campbell's long experience in handling prisoners indispensable while ways were sought for England to resume transportation. Camp-bell was never personally involved after 1776 in conveying convicts to Australia or anywhere else; his role from 1786 was confined to delivering them as required from his hulks to ships bound for New South Wales. Meanwhile he retained his Jamaican sugar plantation, "Saltspring", in Hanover Parish on the west coast of the island. From 1788 he had one of his sons, John, on ships in the East India trade, and in Kent he acquired land between Blackheath and Maidstone, in-cluding the present site of Brandshatch motor raceway. Campbell also retained links with Captain William Bligh.

From 1790 Campbell found his position as superintendent of hulks assailed by both William Richards, the shipping contractor for the First Fleet to Australia, and the penal reformer Jeremy Bentham, whose desire to create a new form of prison, the Panopticon, has been documented in works such as those by Cooper (1967), Dinwiddie (1984), Hume (1973), Milne (1981), and Wood (1933). Considering the close association of William Richards with the First Fleet there has been remarkably little study of this ship-broker and his ideas for the new colony until the recent paper by Knight (1988). Bentham and Richards both attacked Campbell (and therefore the Government) for their different reasons; this London moral battle is still not well docu-mented.

Generally it can be suggested that British scholars have not yet as-sessed the extent to which the perceived social problem caused by large numbers of transportable convicts was ameliorated by sending them to the new penal colony in New South Wales. In other avenues, too, Am-erican, British, and Australian historians retracing Oldham's steps could still find much to expand on. Britain's attempts to send convicts to Africa, particularly to The Gambia, are still not widely enough known, and Oldham's thesis does valuable work in outlining that sorry affair in detail. The episode is mentioned in more recent works by Atkinson (1984), Gailey (1964), and Gray (1966).

Meanwhile, to the dismay of almost everyone, particularly the convicts, the hulks remained full. Oldham noted that the history of the hulks had not been organised, and too few have paid them much attention since. The hulks have been viewed with abhorrence by both contemporary and later writers; Oldham shows them in a different, more pragmatic, light but helps to explain the dread in which they were held by convicts. The *London Magazine* of July 1777 depicts the *Tayloe* (wrongly named "Taylors" by the artist) and the *Justitia* in an article on the implementation of the Hulks Act. Parliamentary inquiries regularly harassed Government penal measures. As superintendent of the convicts on the hulks, Campbell had a unique, and still largely unrecognised, role as a "private enterprise criminologist".

Oldham now provides a wealth of factual evidence about how the British Government came to choose Botany Bay as the site for a new penal colony to take the place of the American colonies. In Australia there has been much argument in recent years, forming what Alan Atkinson engagingly calls "the great Botany Bay debate", about why and how a penal colony came to be established in Sydney in 1788. The *why* is still a riddle. My own view concerns the question of sovereignty: England chose New South Wales because it could be perceived as *terra nullius* — an uninhabited place presenting no legal barriers to settlement by Europeans (Frost, 1981; Bennett & Castles, 1979). The debate forms the subject of an anthology by Ged Martin (1978), an English historian then visiting Australia. Of the eleven historians whose work was anthologised, only three — Professors Manning Clark, A.G.L. Shaw, and Geoffrey Blainey — cited Oldham's thesis in that collection. Other historians contributing to the debate have been R.J. King (1952), Frost (1980, 1981, 1987), Gillen (1982, 1989), and Atkinson (1984, 1988).

History writing in Australia is not easy. Concealment of the shame of having convict ancestors led some colonists to spread misinformation which laws of defamation, particularly in New South Wales, have made difficult to dispel. Because of the country's "thief colony" image, and for many years a lack of proper information, Australians have suffered from intellectual and emotional difficulties in developing a view of their national origins. This has been compounded by academic acrimony over penal and other matters, apologies for or polemics against British imperialism, claims about Aboriginal sovereignty, and even debate about who "discovered" Australia (see Clark, 1962; Martinez-Shaw, 1988).

Many early Australian writers emphasised emotional and dramatic issues such as convict horrors, religious bigotry, feats of maritime survival, the harshness of an unfamiliar land, and a social system cruelly biassed against ex-convicts and Aborigines. This has made it harder for historians, and their readers, to view the evidence with detachment. In such a context Oldham's thesis remains as one of the most powerfully

257

rational studies of convict transportation and early Australian history generally. He was perhaps the first to recognise the relevance of the forms of business transacted by merchants and ship-owners in the convict services to both America and Australia.

At the time of Oldham's writing, the 150th anniversary of white settlement in Australia was still five or six years in the future. Since then, "from the thesis to the coffee-table book", fashions in the writing and reading of Australian history have fluctuated with an increasing sense of urgency, in a rapidly developing cultural kaleidoscope. Notably, Australians are no longer ashamed to discover a convict ancestor; they are more likely to express pride at what were formerly convict skeletons in family cupboards. With this welcome growth in personal and cultural maturity, family history has become an extremely popular field of study. In pursuing it, many Australian laymen have inevitably become interested in the history and social conditions of 18th Century Britain and the convict period in Australia — matters that were until recently avoided as belonging to the "bad old days". It is said that the first film treatment in Australia of convict history risked being banned by the authorities! Television has done much to stimulate an awakening of public interest. Late in 1978 the miniseries "Against the Wind" (Pegasus Productions, scripted by Bronwyn Binns) made its debut on commercial television, to be followed by others on colonial history. This series treated the lives of several convicts from their trip on Dennott's "Hell ship" *Britannia* to the time of Governor Lachlan Macquarie. Shortly after its broadcast the Melbourne *Age* newspaper published a critique of the series by historians at universities and schools; the journal *Historical Studies* in April 1979 published a collection of review articles on this same series.

But recent advances in history both as a discipline and — particularly as a result of celebration of Australia's Bicentenary in 1988 — a community interest, do not mean that everything is satisfactory. Concerning convictism in Australia it has been said that the art of history suffers from what Robert Hughes (1987) has called "amnesia", but which might be better described as selective memory. If university historians suffer in this way they must influence school teachers and thus the next generation of Australians. Publication of Oldham's thesis then is part of a corrective process of remembering what for so long has been forgotten. In particular, his analysis of administrative questions could benefit people descended from convicts, who otherwise would be unaware of the superstructure that governed their ancestors' destinies. Had the superstructure been probed more deeply since Oldham wrote, history might read a little differently; publication of this thesis can greatly assist such probing.

This thesis was a truly pioneering work, but tragically it remained almost unknown to all but a few experts in early Australian history. Many writers were unaware of it; A.G.L. Shaw in *Convicts and the Colonies* (1966) listed the thesis in his bibliography but gave the author's name as Trevor Oldham (who was a former Attorney-General of the State of Victoria!). The historian who paid most attention to it was L.F. Fitzhardinge of the Australian National University, who in the 1950s arranged for copies of the original version to be circulated to some Australian libraries (Fitzhardinge, pers. comm.).

When Oldham began work for his doctorate at London University, the study of Australian history was almost non-existent. In 1907 David Jordan, an American scholar associated with the early days of Stanford University, was invited to give lectures at Sydney University. He knew an American scholar, Payson Jackson Treat, who had proposed to construct a course on Australian history but who had been advised: "In the country itself [Australia], controversies were held to render such an experiment unwise" (Fredman, 1972; Mitchell, 1982). Prerequisites for the course Treat outlined were: (1) Studies in the history of relations between western nations and those of the Far East, and European colonialism in the East; then (2) Australasia, China, Japan, and the Philippines; then (3) accounts of the colonisation of Australia and New Zealand.

At Melbourne University about 1914, Ernest Scott treated Australian history with special regard; his approach has been described as "relatively free" of English academic preferences. At Sydney from 1891 to 1928 George A. Wood gave courses on Australian history, broadly under the rubric of Imperial History (Wood, 1933); he was followed from 1928 by S.H. Roberts, who developed a "systematic study". Scott's students meanwhile had fanned out, and it is said that his influence shone with the appointment of W.K. (later Sir Keith) Hancock as professor in Adelaide in 1926. Hancock recalls that the lecturers of that time

> "carried a disproportionate share of academic drudgery. I had one assistant, Wilfrid Oldham, who for many years past had been given very little time to read, think, or write. According to [the Vice-Chancellor's] theory a continuance of this arrangement might have been for the common good; because, so long as I kept Oldham's nose to the grindstone, I could keep mine in the upper air; but if I put mine to the grindstone alongside his, neither of us might create anything worth while. I could see the force of this argument but could not make it my own, for I have always felt uncomfortable when any associate or assistant of mine is denied the chance to try out his form and work to the top of it. So I took over some of Oldham's work to give him more time for reading and after a year or two I got him leave to do research in the Public Record Office in London. The common good did

259

not suffer. Oldham wrote a thesis and took a doctorate; I wrote a book."
(Hancock, 1954, pp. 108-9).

In this thesis Oldham's interest in Australia ceased as the colony, as
intended, started to become economically and agriculturally self-
sufficient; he was interested in the early New South Wales settlement
only while it remained a helpless offshoot of the British penal system
and had to be fully administered from Britain. From his cutoff date of
1793, Australia changed rapidly. (Shaw, 1966, then took up the administrative story). Viewed economically from Europe, it began as an
open gaol, then became an increasingly popular port for ships (including American ships), and soon became a more or less self-sufficient
colony, agriculturally and otherwise (Crowley, 1974; Abbott & Nairn,
1969).

In the 57 years since Oldham wrote his thesis, economic and cultural developments have been still more rapid; much has been discovered with methodological techniques, and examined from ideo-
logical viewpoints, that were not available to Oldham. For example,
there is now an extensive literature about the Aborigines in the early
colonial era, and research on women or by women writers has encouraged many different views of Australian colonial history. The title
Damned Whores and God's Police chosen by Anne Summers (1975)
speaks eloquently of the psycho-social attitude of the early colony:
women, despite their scarcity, never seemed beautiful enough in the
eyes of some beholders, and their role in colonial history was generally
ignored. Sturma's (1978) is a classic examination of community attitudes to women in early Australia, while Heney (1978) has investigated the role of women as founders of a nation, as has Robinson
(1985, 1988). Gillen's (1989) is an especially fine piece of research on
all First Fleet personnel; it even shows that some people thought to
have been early colonists never existed.

Amid the various shades and colours of Australian writing about
transportation, all given perspective now by the sweeping synoptic
vision of Manning Clark's six-volume *History of Australia*, Oldham's
pioneering work provides a mass of unassailable facts in the administrative detail of what transportation of convicts was all about; this was
the removal of felons from Britain and, regardless of their destination,
the harnessing of economic value from convict labour. By 1989, those
who were "sent down the river" to Botany Bay have been variously
construed as having been sent to a penal settlement, to an outpost of
Empire, or to a geographic variation in the rehabilitation of hearts and
reclamation of souls — a new kind of incentive to good behaviour.
Or, as by Robert Hughes (1987), to a *gulag*, an organised, brutal, highly
coercive network of terror camps designed and staffed by professionals

to deter the incautious by systematic degradation of the defiant; where one inmate could kill another so that both would be put out of their misery. Readers will now be better able to assess the relative validity of these judgements.

The former scarcity of published data in the field of transportation has led some authors into error. Hughes (*op. cit*, p. 70) made a startling mistake in naming the contractor for the First Fleet to Australia as Duncan Campbell instead of William Richards Jnr, and then describing him as a "crooked contractor"; in fact neither was crooked by the standards of the day, and Oldham finds much to praise about Richards. A similar error is embellished in Michael Talbot's 1987 novel *To the Ends of the Earth*. There, no mention is made of Richards, and Campbell is portrayed as having organised all the shipping of the First Fleet. Errors by a novelist are more pardonable than those by an historian, but a reading of Oldham's thesis could have provided either kind of writer with many new options to be explored. Questions still need to be asked about the ship-owners and their ships in the convict service to Australia. London's whaling and associated commercial operators were intimately involved in Australia's early maritime history (Byrnes, 1987, 1988; Dallas, 1969; Dunbabin, 1960; Jones, 1981, 1986; Stackpole, 1972; Steven, 1983; Sanderson, 1956). Churchward (1949, 1979) has documented American ships that visited the colony. American readers are luckier than Australian, for more information is available about ships and their owners in the service to America from the 1720s (see Coldham, 1988). On that subject Morgan (1985, 1987) outlines the part played by the Bristol firm of convict contractors Stephenson, Randolph & Cheston. Oldham's emphasis on maritime history is commendable.

As governments still find, prison management is often controversial. Details of the administration of the system of transportation are never dull: the system has always created controversy. Many Australians, as a cultural reflex, have tended to shy away from a proper appreciation of the administrative scene, but it is inextricably associated with many facets of human nature and social responses to criminal behaviour.

Given the titles published since 1933 on convict transportation to both America and Australia, and works that have analysed the English politics involved in those transportations, I am confident that Oldham's thesis will remain a reliable and steadying treatment, a truly humane treatment. As such it will be relished by historians, by family historians seeking background to an ancestor's life, and by those who are curious about the cultural obsessions that for so long sustained the custom of transportation. It is a classic vision of Crime and Punishment during the reign of George III, one in which the author's own outlook radiates a subtle human warmth together with wisdom, intelligence, and humour.

References to Commentary

ABBOTT, G.J. & NAIRN, N.B. (Eds.), 1969. Economic growth of Australia, 1788-1821. Melbourne, Melbourne University Press.

ATKINSON, Alan, 1984. The convict republic. *The Push from the Bush, a Bulletin of Social History,* No. 18.

ATKINSON, Alan, 1988. Sunshine from Frost [a review of Alan Frost's "Phillip — his Voyaging"]; *The Push from the Bush, a Bulletin of Social History,* No. 26, April 1988.

BENNETT, J.M. & CASTLES, Alex. C. (Eds.), 1979. A source book of Australian legal history, source material from the Eighteenth to the Twentieth Centuries. Sydney, Law Book Co.

BLUMENTHAL, Walter Hart, 1962. Brides from Bridewell — female felons sent to colonial America. Rutland, Vermont; Tuttle.

BRANCH-JOHNSON, W., 1957. The English prison hulks. London and Chichester, Phillimore.

BYRNES, Dan, 1987. Emptying the hulks: Duncan Campbell and the first three fleets to Australia. *The Push from the Bush, a Bulletin of Social History,* No.24, April 1987, pp. 2-23.

BYRNES, Dan, 1988. Outlooks for the English south whale fishery, 1782-1800, and the "great Botany Bay debate"; *The Great Circle,* vol. 10, No. 2, pp. 77-102.

CAMPBELL, Duncan (unpubl.). Letterbooks held in the Mitchell Library, Sydney, A3225-A3231. The holding consists of:
A3235: vol. 1 of Business Letter Books Mar 1772-Oct 1776;
A3236: vol. 2 of Business Letter Books 13 Dec 1776-21 Sep 1779;
A3227: vol. 3 of Business Letter Books 30 Sep 1779-9 Mar 1782;
A3228: vol. 4 of Business Letter Books 15 Mar 1782-6 Apr 1785;
A3229: vol. 5 of Business Letter Books 1 Dec 1784-17 Jun 1788;
A3230: vol. 6 of Business Letter Books 20 Jun 1788-31 Dec 1794;
A3231: 3 volumes of Private Letter Books.

CAMPBELL, W.D (unpubl.). W.D. Campbell was a descendant of Duncan Campbell; his copious notes on his family history are held in the Mitchell Library, Sydney, ML A3232.

CAPPER, Douglas Parode, 1963. Moat defensive: a history of the waters of the Nore Command, 55BC to 1961. London, Arthur Baker Ltd.

CHURCHWARD, L.G., 1949. Notes on American whaling activities in Australian waters 1800-1850. *Historical Studies,* vol. 4, No. 13.

CHURCHWARD, L.G., 1979. Australia and America 1788-1972: an alternative history. Chippendale, New South Wales; Alternative Publishing Co-op. Ltd.

CLARK, C.M.H. (Ed.), 1957. Sources of Australian History. London, Oxford University Press.

COMMENTARY BY DAN BYRNES

CLARK, C.M.H., 1962. A history of Australia, vol. 1. Melbourne, Melbourne University Press.

COLDHAM, Peter Wilson, 1988. The complete book of emigrants in bondage 1614-1775. Baltimore, Genealogical Publishing Co. [This title lists convict ships, ships' captains 1716-1776, and thousands of individual convicts sent from England to North America. Most of the ships of Duncan Campbell for example are listed. The ships of Stephenson, Randolph & Cheston have apparently not been listed. See Morgan, 1985]

CONWAY, M.D., 1892. Barons of the Potomack and the Rappahanock. New York, The Grolier Club.

COOPER, R.A., 1967. Ideas and their execution: English prison reform. *Eighteenth-Century Studies*, vol. 10, No. 1.

CRITTENDEN, Victor, 1982. A bibliography of the First Fleet. Canberra, ANU Press.

CROWLEY, F.K. (Ed.), 1974. A new history of Australia. Melbourne, Heinemann.

DALLAS, K.M., 1969. Trading posts or penal colonies: the commercial significance of Cook's New Holland route to the Pacific. Hobart, Fuller's Bookshop Publ. Div.

DINWIDDIE, J.R. (Ed.), 1984. The correspondence of Jeremy Bentham, vol. 6: Jan 1798 to Dec 1801. Oxford, Clarendon Press.

DUNBABIN, T., 1960. William Raven R.N. and his *Britannia*, 1792-95. *The Mariner's Mirror*, vol. 46. No. 4.

DUNN, Richard S., 1977. A tale of two plantations - slave life at Mesopotamia in Jamaica, and Mount Airy in Virginia, 1799 to 1828. *William and Mary Quarterly*, Series III, vol. XXXIV, No. 1.

EKIRCH, A. Roger, 1984. Great Britain's secret convict trade to America 1783-1784. *American Historical Review*, vol. 89, No. 5.

EKIRCH, A. Roger, 1985. Bound for America: a profile of British convicts transported to the colonies 1718-1775. *William and Mary Quarterly*, 3rd Series, vol. 42, No. 2.

EKIRCH, A. Roger, 1987. Bound for America: the transportation of British convicts to the colonies 1718-1775. Oxford, Clarendon Press.

FREDMAN, L.E., 1972. Where was Australian history first taught? Item, Royal Australian Historical Society, *Newsletter*, Feb. 1972.

FROST, Alan, 1980. Convicts and empire — a naval question 1776-1811. Oxford, University Press.

FROST, Alan, 1981. New South Wales as *terra nullius* — the British denial of Aboriginal land rights. *Historical Studies*, vol. 19, No. 77, pp. 513-23.

FROST, Alan, 1987. Arthur Phillip, 1738-1814, his voyaging. Melbourne, Oxford University Press.

GAILEY, H.A., 1964. A history of the Gambia. London, Routledge & Keegan.

GILLEN, Mollie, 1982. The Botany Bay decision, 1786 — convicts, not empire. *English Historical Review*, vol. XCVII, No. CCCLXXXV.

GILLEN, Mollie, 1989. The founders of Australia: a biographical dictionary of the First Fleet. Sydney, Library of Australian History.

GRAY, J.M., 1966. History of the Gambia. London, Frank Cass.

263

HANCOCK, W.K., 1954. Country and calling. London, Faber & Faber.

HARDY, John & FROST, Alan (Eds.), 1988. Studies from Terra Australis to Australia. Canberra, Australian Academy of the Humanities, Occasional Paper No. 6.

HENEY, Helen, 1978. Australia's founding mothers. Melbourne, Thomas Nelson.

HIBBERT, Christopher, 1963. The roots of evil: a social history of crime and punishment. London, Weidenfeld & Nicholson. See pp. 139 et seq. on Transportation.

HUGHES, Robert, 1987. The fatal shore, a history of the transportation of convicts to Australia 1787-1868. London, Collins Harvill.

HUME, L.J., 1971-73. Bentham's Panopticon, an administrative history, Part 1. *Historical studies*, vol. 15, pp. 707-721.

JONES, A.G.E., 1981. The British southern whale and seal fisheries [in 2 parts]. *Great Circle*, vol. 3, No. 1.

JONES, A.G.E., 1986. Ships employed in the South Seas trade, 1775-1861, and General Register of shipping and seamen. Transcripts of register of shipping, 1787-1862. Canberra, Roebuck.

KING, Robert J., 1952. Terra Australis — *terra nullius aut terra Aboriginum? Journal of the Royal Australian Historical Society*, vol. 72, part II, pp. 75-91.

KLINGELHOFER, Herbert E., 1963. Matthew Ridley's diary during the peace negotiations of 1782. *William and Mary Quarterly*, Jan. 1963, pp. 95 et seq.

KNIGHT, Roger, 1988. The First Fleet, its state and preparation, 1786-1787. pp. 121-136 *in* HARDY & FROST, 1988.

LLOYD, A., 1971. The wickedest age — the life and times of George III. Newton Abbot, Devon; David & Charles.

MACKANESS, George, 1931. The life of Vice-Admiral William Bligh, R.N., F.R.S. [2 vols.] Sydney, Angus & Robertson.

MACKANESS, George, (Ed.), 1976. Fresh light on Bligh: some unpublished correspondence. Australian Historical Monographs, vol. V (new series). 1949, reprinted 1976 by Review Publications, Dubbo, New South Wales.

MACKAY, David L., 1985. A place of exile : The European settlement of New South Wales. Melbourne, Oxford University Press.

MARSHALL, Dorothy, 1973. Industrial England 1776-1851. London, Routledge & Kegan Paul.

MARTIN, Ged (Ed.), 1978. The founding of Australia: the argument about Australia's origins. Sydney, Hale & Iremonger.

MARTINEZ-SHAW, Carlos, 1988. Terra Australis and the Spanish. pp. 57-69 *in* HARDY & FROST, 1988.

MILNE, Alexander Taylor, 1981. The correspondence of Jeremy Bentham, vol. 4, Oct 1788 to Dec 1793. London, Athlone Press.

MITCHELL, Ann M., 1982. Frederick Watson and Historical Records of Aust-ralia. *Historical Studies*, vol. 20, No. 79, pp. 171-197.

MORGAN, Kenneth, 1985. The organisation of the convict trade to Maryland — Stevenson, Randolph and Cheston 1768-1775. *William and Mary Quarterly*, XLII, pp. 201-27.

MORGAN, Kenneth, 1987. English and American attitudes towards convict transportation 1718-1775. *History*, 72, pp. 416-31.

O'BRIEN, Eridsford Michael (Eris), 1937. The foundation of Australia 1786-1800, a study in English criminal practice and penal colonization in the Eighteenth Century. Sydney, Angus & Robertson.

O'BRIEN, Eris, 1950. The foundation of Australia 1786-1800, a study in English criminal practice and penal colonization in the Eighteenth Century; 2nd Edn. Sydney, Angus & Robertson. [first printed 1937]

PLAYFAIR, Giles, 1971. The punitive obsession: an unvarnished history of the English penal system. London, Victor Gollancz.

PLUMB, H.J., 1976. The first four Georges. Fontana/Collins.

ROBINSON, Portia, 1985. The hatch and brood of time: a study of the first generation of native-born white Australians 1788-1828, vol. 1. Melbourne, Melbourne University Press.

ROBINSON, Portia, 1988. The women of Botany Bay: a reinterpretation of the role of women in the origins of Australian society. Macquarie Monograph. Sydney, Macquarie Library Pty Ltd.

SANDERSON, Ivan T., 1956. Follow the whale. London, Cassell and Co. Acts expanding waters available to the whalers are detailed from p. xix.

SCHMIDT, F.H., 1986. Sold and driven: assignment of convicts in Eighteenth-Century Virginia. *The Push from the Bush*, No. 23. History Department, University of New England. [this is a chapter from a Ph.D. thesis].

SHAW, A.G.L., 1966. Convicts and the colonies: a study of penal transportation from Great Britain and Ireland to Australia and other parts of the British Empire. London, Faber.

SMITH, A.E., 1934. Transportation of criminals to the American colonies in the Seventeenth Century. *American History Review*, vol. XXXIX.

SMITH, A.E., 1947. Colonists in bondage: White servitude and convict labour in America 1607-1776. University of Carolina Press.

SMITH, A.E., 1965. Colonists in bondage: White servitude and convict labour in America 1607-1776. Gloucester, Mass., Peter Smith [reprint of SMITH, A.E., 1947]

STACKPOLE, Edouard A., 1972. Whales and destiny: the rivalry between America, France, and Britain for control of the southern whale fishery 1785-1825. University of Massachusetts Press.

STEVEN, Margaret, 1983. Trade, tactics and territory — Britain in the Pacific 1783-1823. Melbourne, Melbourne University Press.

STURMA, Michael, 1978. Eye of the beholder: the stereotype of women convicts, 1788-1852. *Labour History*, No. 34.

SUMMERS, Anne, 1975. Damned whores and God's police: the colonization of women in Australia. Ringwood, Victoria; Penguin Books.

THOMAS, Leila, 1925. The establishment of New South Wales in 1788. *Journal of the Royal Australian Historical Society*, vol. XI, Part II, pp. 63-83.

WOOD, F.L.W., 1933. Jeremy Bentham versus New South Wales. *Journal of the Royal Australian Historical Society*, vol. XIX, Part VI, pp. 329-51.

Index

INDEX